LORD OF ALL

LORD OF ALL

Developing a Christian World-and-Life View

D. JAMES KENNEDY

JERRY NEWCOMBE

CROSSWAY BOOKS

A MINISTRY OF
GOOD NEWS PUBLISHERS
WHEATON, ILLINOIS

Lord of All

Published by Crossway Books
        a ministry of Good News Publishers
        1300 Crescent Street
        Wheaton, Illinois 60187

Cover design: Josh Dennis

Cover photo: Photonica

First printing, 2005

Printed in the United States of America

Library of Congress Cataloging-in-Publication Data
Kennedy, D. James (Dennis James), 1930-
Lord of all : developing a Christian world-and-life view / D. James Kennedy and Jerry Newcombe.
    p. cm.
Includes bibliographical references and indexes.
ISBN 1-58134-677-8 (tpb)
1. Christianity—Philosophy. 2. Christianity and culture—United States. 3. Church and state—United States. 4. Ideology—Religious aspects—Christianity. I. Newcombe, Jerry. II. Title.
BR100.K465   2005
230'.01—dc22   2004026607

Q		15	14	13	12	11	10	09	08	07	06	05
15	14	13	12	11	10	9	8	7	6	5	4	3	2	1

CONTENTS

ACKNOWLEDGMENTS

Special thanks are due to a handful of people who helped make this book possible. This includes:

Chip MacGregor of Alive Communications.

Lane Dennis and Marvin Padgett of Crossway Books.

Kirsti Newcombe, who helped edit several early versions of the manuscript.

Nancy Britt, who helped edit a later version.

Mary Anne Bunker, my ever-efficient secretary.

INTRODUCTION
THE CHRISTIAN WORLD-AND-LIFE VIEW

For from him and through him and to him are all things. To him be glory forever. Amen.

ROMANS 11:36

The Christian world-and-life view. That is not a phrase, probably, that is intimately familiar to you. Perhaps you know it by the German term, *Weltanschauung*. No? That is no more familiar, is it? In fact, less? What is a world-and-life view—a *Weltanschauung*? Well, let me tell you first of all, you have one. Everybody has one. Many people just sort of absorb it as they go through life. They have not critically examined it; it has just become what they believe in.

A world-and-life view is a set of assumptions or presuppositions that determine the way we look at the world and our place in the world. These then largely determine how we consider everything that comes down the path.

What is your world-and-life view like? Is it a Christian world-and-life view, or is it a non-Christian/anti-Christian view? There is a Christian world-and-life view, and there are a number of other world-and-life views that are all arrayed against the Christian view. Chuck Colson and Nancy Pearcey ask, "What is the major challenge today? In the broadest categories, the conflict of our day is theism and naturalism."[1]

In an editorial for *The American Prospect*, Clinton's Secretary of State Robert B. Reich also wrote about the importance of worldview.

Note who he lumps in with whom (namely, believers of all kinds are lumped in). Suddenly the Salvation Army becomes the equivalent of the Taliban.

> The great conflict of the 21st century may be between the West and terrorism. But terrorism is a tactic, not a belief. The underlying battle will be between modern civilization and anti-modernist fanatics; between those who believe in the primacy of the individual and those who believe that human beings owe blind allegiance to a higher authority; between those who give priority to life in this world and those who believe that human life is no more than preparation for an existence beyond life; between those who believe that truth is revealed solely through scripture and religious dogma, and those who rely primarily on science, reason, and logic. Terrorism will disrupt and destroy lives. But terrorism is not the only danger we face.[2]

Reich is so wrong on many fronts. But consider this: Who has proven to be the great killer of all time? Atheistic states.[3] The Fascists and the Communists killed tens of millions of human beings, and they claimed to believe in science and not religion. Reich is correct about one thing though—the root of the conflict concerns which worldview will prevail.

NATURALISM

Naturalism has nothing to do with wildlife or vitamins. It has to do with the idea that nature is all there is—that there is nothing in the universe except matter (materialism). That is one worldview. The fact is, Colson says, that this, indeed, is what we use to explain most everything else. What is the most fundamental question? What does the universe consist of? Is it only matter? Is ultimate reality God or the cosmos?

You remember Carl Sagan, a very rabid evolutionist and naturalist, and his famous ten-part series *Cosmos* that aired on educational TV a number of times. In his first sentence he made this clear statement: "The cosmos is all that is or ever was or ever will be."[4] That is a worldview—a purely naturalistic, materialistic, evolutionary, atheistic worldview.

I say it is a worldview because it is an assumption. It is not the result of any scientific test. Sagan never saw that there was never anything besides the cosmos. He did not know that there was nothing beyond it. He most certainly did not know that there was no God, no supernatural element. What is the ultimate reality? Is it matter and the cosmos, or is it God and His revelation?

Those two views have been in direct conflict for the last several centuries and are in our own time.

Chuck Colson and Nancy Pearcey in their book *How Now Shall We Live?* state:

> A debilitating weakness in modern evangelicalism is that we've been fighting cultural skirmishes on all sides without knowing what the war itself is about. We have not identified the worldviews that lie at the root of cultural conflict—and this ignorance dooms our best efforts. The culture war is not just about abortion, homosexual rights, or the decline of public education. These are only skirmishes. The real war is a cosmic struggle between worldviews—between the Christian worldview and the various secular and spiritual worldviews arrayed against it. This is what we must understand if we are going to be effective in evangelizing our world today and in transforming it to reflect the wisdom of the Creator.[5]

A worldview, said Colson and Pearcey, "is simply the sum total of our beliefs about the world, the 'big picture' that directs our daily decisions and actions."[6] A worldview needs to be carefully considered and decided upon. Otherwise we will be subconsciously directed into making decisions and may not know why we are making them.

May I point out that every worldview is based upon faith. It is based upon some kind of assumptions or presuppositions that we probably have never proved. Many of them *cannot* even be proved. As one writer said, "Every human being has faith in something which affects his understanding of everything." Scientists operate by faith. Some have had the candor to admit it; others would deny it vehemently.

We have seen in the last several centuries, since the French Enlightenment in the 1780s, the rise of rationalism. That is not to say anything about reason. We should be rational and reasonable, but rationalism is the idea that reason is the *only* source of knowledge and understanding, and it rules out entirely faith in God or in His Word. Rationalism, naturalism, materialism, and atheism are all based upon evolutionism.

Though the Enlightenment existed fifty years before Darwin, philosophers had struggled to get some kind of worldview together, but not with great success, until Darwin's *The Origin of Species* provided for them a comprehensive worldview that made atheism palatable for the first time and something that could be talked about in public. This view has been promulgated in Western society for the last 150 years like few things have ever been.

SECULARISM

At its core this worldview is atheistic, evolutionary, relativistic, materialistic, and secularistic (in that it is only of this world). The word *secularism* comes from the Latin word *secularis*, which means "the present world" or in other words, "life as conceived without any relationship to eternity or to God." That is secularism. The Western world has become almost 99 percent secular. Listen to any talk show on television. This smoked plastic dome that has settled down upon the city of man does not allow him to see past death into the future. Is there a heaven? Is there a hell? He cannot know. Is there a God? "The dome is too smoky. I cannot see up to God. I cannot see out into the future." That is secularism, and this nation and the Western world have been overwhelmingly secularized in a Darwinian, atheistic, materialistic life.

This view is being promulgated in virtually all of the public schools in this nation, from kindergarten through graduate school. John Dunphy, in *The Humanist*, said some time ago:

> The classroom must and will become an arena of conflict between the old and the new—the rotting corpse of Christianity, together with all its adjacent evils and misery, and the new faith of humanism, resplendent in its promise of a world in which the never-realized Christian ideal of "love thy neighbor" will be finally achieved.[7]

He says that a teacher must become as zealous as the most fundamental evangelist in propagating this faith to every student. Oh, they may learn about God and heaven in Sunday school, "but five days a week we have them right here in our schools." That is the idea.

HUMANISM

Maybe you didn't know you had a fundamentalist-evangelist-teacher propagating atheistic humanism in your schools. What is this never-realized ideal of Christian love? What has it produced? It has produced not only the Enlightenment worldview that spawned the French Revolution, but in the twentieth century it also produced World War I, World War II, and Communism, which, according to the U.S. Congress killed 135 million people during peacetime—more than all of the wars of history. It has also produced behaviorism, Nazism, and Fascism. All of these are squarely based upon the evolutionary, atheistic view of humanism. That is the marvelous goal they supposedly are bringing to the world. It is not pretty, to say the least.

Someone like Robert B. Reich, quoted above, may disavow this, but the facts speak for themselves. Ideas have consequences.

Humanism is just another way of talking about atheism. There was a time, years ago, when it was not politically expedient to be an atheist, and so, instead of that, they switched to humanism. Atheism says, "down with God"; humanism says, "up with man." But in the end it is the same. Man is up there in the place of God, and God is down here, abased.

This worldview probably got its initial impetus from the pre-Socratic philosopher Protagoras, who made one statement that has been reverberating for over two millennia. He said, very simply, "Man is the measure of all things." That seems to be very innocuous, but millions of people have died because of it, because ideas have consequences. That last statement seems more true with every passing year.

Christians have always believed that God is the measure of all things, that God tells us what is good and what is bad and what is right and what is wrong. God tells us where to go and how to get there. But that is rejected by humanism, in which man becomes the judge of all things. Man decides what is moral and what is immoral, what is virtuous and what is not, what is evil and what is good, what is right and what is wrong. That has led to catastrophic consequences in our world.

The Enlightenment period began with two ideas—great ideas, if they were true. The first one was the inherent goodness of man, and the second was the inevitability of moral progress—progress of every sort in the world. That was to lead to the Golden Age. At the beginning of the twentieth century, many were saying, "The Golden Age is upon us. It is coming. Every day in every way we are getting better and better." Then came World War I, and the blood flowed in the trenches of France; then World War II—with Iwo Jima, Bataan, Corregidor, and all the rest. Then came the Cold War, and Communism spread across the world like a blight, killing millions.

THE DEATH OF HUMANISM

Among the deaths was the death of the idea of the inherent goodness of man. How could such inhumanity to man possibly be true in a world where there is no bad boy and no bad man? If the torture chambers of the Nazis and the Gulag weren't enough, in our day and age we can go to the Near East and visit one of Saddam Hussein's torture chambers. Consider how people who displeased him were tossed into shredders and vats of acid. Man's inhumanity to man.

The inevitable progress ended in a fiery crash, and the Golden Age turned into a bloody age, and the marvelous, romantic picture of humanism died. In his book *Thinking Straight in a Crooked World*, Gary DeMar describes well the humanistic mentality of Western man since the Renaissance—this belief in the inherent goodness of man and the inevitability of his progress.[8]

But the shocking revelations of the twentieth century pretty well burst that bubble. That was especially true in the latter half of the twentieth century, when it was apparent that the once proud dogmas of optimistic humanism were dead and buried and had been replaced by a mood of cynicism and despair. H. G. Wells, just before his death in 1946, wrote a book, *The Mind at the End of Its Tether*, in which he stated: "The end of everything we call life is close at hand and cannot be evaded."[9] Things looked very, very bleak, to say the least.

Why is this? Because "modern man has simply come to realize the logical implications of his foolish autonomy," said Gary DeMar, "and is beginning to pay the price."[10] Jean-Paul Sartre, the French existential philosopher, was right. This fact of the logical consequences of man's foolish flight from God ought, indeed, to make man happy, gay, and joyous. That was the promise. But what was the reality? Even the unbeliever Sartre observed, "[It] ought to give him nausea."[11]

REAPING WHAT IS SOWED

Do you remember the Death of God Movement? That too is part of this. It is interesting that man didn't realize that when he was throwing things at God, he was throwing boomerangs that would come back and hit him in the head. God is very much alive, but non-Christian man is in a state of morbid decay and despair. He comes closer and closer to nihilism and despair as he becomes more self-conscious of the logical consequences of his view. Author Gary DeMar put it this way:

> There is at the present time then, a radical disintegration of the non-Christian man as he reaps the harvest produced by the seed he has sown. After many years the crop is approaching full maturity, and the ingathering is proving a most unpleasant time. He has laid up treasures on the earth, and the sphere of his ultimate values, the place of his only reward and enjoyment. His values are dead on the vine, being merely the dictates of social and personal convenience. The ethic of evolution, the survival of the fittest, has yet to take its full toll. The world has still to see the full maturing of Marquis de Sade's "natural behaviour" based on the principle of

"what is" is right. The simple equation—matter plus time plus chance—has yet to reveal and yield its full horror.[12]

The Bible says, "All who hate me love death" (Proverbs 8:36). In a non-Christian world today, a culture of death has been developing. It is not God who has died; He is very much alive. Rather, it is man who is dying. The facts of history are very discouraging, and the logic of materialism is crushing him.

THE DEATH OF HOPE

Modern man longs for death. We have in many of our schools in America today classes on suicide. The French philosopher Albert Camus said that the only philosophical idea worth consideration today is suicide.[13] Ernest Hemingway embraced it, Camus endorsed it, and thousands have followed in their train. Preoccupation with death is a distinguishing mark of our time. Indeed, when you have the death of hope—and materialism and humanism are hopeless views of life—that leads directly to the hope for death. Many people have discovered that life in the humanistic world, the atheistic world, is not worth living.

Samuel Beckett, the playwright, said:

> How am I, an a-temporal being imprisoned in time and space, to escape from my imprisonment, when I know that outside space and time lies Nothing, and that I, in the ultimate depths of my reality, am Nothing also?[14]

How far removed this is from the Christian view that we have been made in the image of God, that God has placed eternity in our hearts, that God has given His own Son to redeem us from our sin and has prepared for us a place in paradise forever and ever. We have a glorious calling in this life: "to glorify God and to enjoy Him forever" and to be coworkers of Christ in the redemption of the world. Life has meaning, and life has purpose. Life has a glorious future, while none of the godless worldviews offer anything but despair at the end.

The director of the British Humanist Association (note well—this is not some Christian minister's opinion. This is the opinion of one of the world's leaders of the humanist movement), H. J. Blackham, said that "the most drastic objection to humanism . . ." is what? I would love to ask a bunch of college students that question, wouldn't you? Remember the glorious picture of what humanism was going to produce over against the "rotting corpse of

Christianity"—the new, the glorious, the vibrant picture of humanism was to captivate the minds of people. Well, here's what one of the world's leading humanist says: "The most drastic objection to humanism is that it is too bad to be true."[15] Wow!

Bertrand Russell summed that up very eloquently when he said:

> That man is the product of causes which had no prevision of the end they were achieving [evolution]; that his origin, his growth, his hopes and fears, his loves and his beliefs, are but the outcome of accidental collocations of atoms; that no fire, no heroism, no intensity of thought and feeling, can preserve an individual life beyond the grave; that all of the labour of the ages, all of the devotion, all of the inspiration, all the noonday brightness of human genius, are destined to extinction in the vast death of the solar system, and that whole temple of Man's achievement must inevitably be buried beneath the debris of a universe in ruins—all these things, if not quite beyond dispute, are yet so nearly certain, that no philosophy which rejects them can hope to stand. Only within the scaffolding of these truths, and on the firm foundation of unyielding despair, can the soul's habitation henceforth be safely built.[16]

There is the humanist's world-and-life view of the world. It's not a pretty sight, to say the least. The most powerful objection against humanism, says the humanist, is that it is just too bad to be true.

THE TRUTH OF GOD

I have heard a particular objection many times when I have proclaimed the gospel; people have said to me, "Oh, that's just too good to be true." What a marvelous contrast that is to "too bad to be true." But *mirable dictu*, marvelous to tell, the gospel, as glorious and wonderful as it is, is true. It is truth itself. It is the truth of God. It has been established by all manner of empirical evidences, and it stands against all of the onslaughts of unbelievers.

SIX GREAT SPHERES

Theologian Hermann Dooyeweerd once talked about God's sovereignty in terms of different spheres of existence. God is sovereign over different aspects or spheres of life. With thanks to Mr. Dooyeweerd for this concept, we want to look at different spheres of life.

We want to explore in this book a Christian world-and-life view by considering six great spheres that every Christian should be vitally interested in and should be working to Christianize. They are:

- the world,
- humanity,
- the nation,
- the school,
- the church,
- the family.

Every Christian church should be endeavoring to do what it can to strengthen each of these great spheres.

JESUS IS NOT TO BE EXCLUDED FROM ANYTHING

Listen to what the great Dutch theologian Abraham Kuyper had to say about Christ's sovereignty over all the spheres of life—not just spiritual things. He believed in the sovereignty of the Triune God over the whole of the cosmos in all of its spheres and kingdoms; the Triune God is sovereign over everything—not merely over the church but over every sphere of life. Here are Kuyper's own words about the second person of the Trinity:

> The Son is not to be excluded from anything. You cannot point to any natural realm or star or comet or even descend into the depth of the earth, but it is related to Christ, not in some unimportant tangential way, but directly. There is no force in nature, no laws that control those forces that do not have their origin in that eternal Word. For this reason, it is totally false to restrict Christ to spiritual affairs and to assert that there is no point of contact between him and the natural sciences.[17]

Thus it all belongs to Him. This is my Father's world. He is Lord of all.

CONCLUSION

What is your worldview? Have you embraced Christ? Have you invited Him into your heart as Lord and Savior of your life? Do you know why you are here and what you are to do and where you are going? Do you have an everlasting certainty and hope in your heart of paradise, or are you looking at nothing but the darkness of the grave? The Christian world-and-life view is glorious beyond our full understanding. I hope it is yours.

PART I

THE SPHERE
OF THE
WORLD

INTRODUCTION TO THE SPHERE OF THE WORLD

In British Columbia, 500 miles northeast of Vancouver, the Fraser River divides into two streams. One flows eastward to the Atlantic Ocean; the other flows westward to the Pacific Ocean. The fork in the river is known as The Great Divide. Six inches after the division takes place, the river's future course is unchangeably fixed.

The evolution-creation controversy is just such a juncture in human thought, and it has tremendous impact on the value of human life. Is evolution just some sort of theory taught in high school biology classes with no further ramifications? No. It has influenced every part of our life. I am sometimes saddened that so few Christians seem to be able to grasp the significance of that.

We need to Christianize the world. That is not a small task. In the next several chapters we want to explore two foundational issues—both of which are related.

- What is our origin? Why are we here? Are we just the product of time and slime, or are we specially designed creatures, set here on this planet for a purpose?
- Do we have value as human beings? This question flows out of the first one, because our opinion of who we are flows out of our understanding of where we came from and why we are here.

1

THE ROOT OF THE PROBLEM

Where is the one who is wise? Where is the scribe? Where is the debater of this age? Has not God made foolish the wisdom of the world?

1 CORINTHIANS 1:20

✠

Recently I preached a sermon called "The Root of the Problem," and my wife asked me the day before, after hearing the message title, "So, what is it?"

I replied, "What do you think it is?"

She said, "Why, sin, of course."

My wife is a very perceptive lady, and I said, "Honey, that's right. If you go to the etiology of mankind's whole problem, eventually you get back to sin."

But I was also thinking of something more recent, a more modern human construct that is indeed the root of nearly all of the problems we face today, in fact for the last century and a half. It would be interesting to have all of you readers guess your answer. I'm sure some of you would get it right. I fear others of you would not.

I also think that when I tell you what I think it is, many of you will not believe me. I trust that before we finish this chapter, you will see why I say what I do. The root of the problem of most of the great ills that have afflicted society and do afflict it today are caused by the teaching of evolution. It has been called "The Big Lie." It has deceived hundreds of millions of people and has probably brought about more deaths than any other view in the history of the world.

EVOLUTION

Evolution simply says that the whole universe is made up of nothing but matter; that matter, time, and chance—the trinity of materialism—have brought all things into existence that exist. Therefore, there is no God. One scientist (John Lenczowski) said he was confident that if you interviewed social scientists at our elite universities across the country, and if they were willing to be honest about the matter, you would find out something surprising. He said you would find that perhaps 99 percent of them would not be willing to sign the Declaration of Independence.[1]

Why? They do not believe in a Creator; they do not believe we have been created equal or any other way. They do not believe that we have been endowed with certain inalienable rights by this Creator. They believe none of that, and if they were honest, they would not sign the document that made us Americans.

He says, "Parents can work hard to educate their children to be patriots and morally upright citizens. But four years of college of the kind I experienced—where I was surrounded by a culture of drugs, sexual libertinism, political radicalism and little homework—can destroy the efforts of the best parents in America."

If that doesn't do it, he says, a couple of years of graduate school are almost certain to destroy any vestige of belief in God, moral absolutes, morality, Americanism, patriotism, or any other of our values. That is due to evolution. Evolution has made our public schools and universities and colleges like the one he attended a mortal danger to the lives and souls of young people—with tragic consequences.

Dr. Ernest Gordon, dean emeritus of the Princeton University Chapel, also the hero and author of the book *Bridge Over the River Kwai*, is a fascinating and godly man. (Unfortunately, the movie totally ignored the Christian aspects of the story.) Anyway, Dr. Gordon said:

> During the late [1950s] I was invited to address the senior class of an English department in a city high school. When I arrived at the school, I introduced myself to the assistant headmaster, whose office was at the entrance. He guided me to the appropriate lecture hall.
>
> Twenty years later, I was invited to the same school for the same purpose. I again presented myself to the same office, but it was no longer the habitat of an educator. It was the command post of a police inspector. Corridors and classrooms were monitored by police officers who reported regularly to the inspector. The reasons for the change were obvious: violence, assault, rape, drug-induced madness.

I interpret this scene as evidence of the end times of a civilization that had once benefited from the Christian worldview, one that exalted creation and people and provided ideals essential for an authentic education. I recognize that civilization does not create Christians. However, the community of faith created and still creates the civility that is evidence of civilization. The demoralized school is the tragic consequence of society's rejection of the biblical worldview that provided the intellectual dynamic of Western education.[2]

At the heart of all that is the doctrine of evolution that, first of all, got rid of God—since there is no Creator, there is no God. Since evolutionists believe that all life arose spontaneously from matter, there was no need for a God to create anyone.

Another of the fruits of evolution has been the proliferation of atheists. Do you realize that before Darwin, an atheist was as scarce as a hen's tooth? Oh, there were a few around, but very, very few. Do you know why? Because if you said you were an atheist, all I had to say to you was, "Look around, buddy. Where did all of this come from?"

And the atheist would say, "Ah . . . bu . . . da . . . I don't know."

Then came Charles Darwin. One evolutionist said, "The greatest contribution of Charles Darwin was that he made atheism respectable." For that, this atheistic evolutionist was forever grateful—or at least for whatever few years he had left in this world, until the day of the Great Judgment, which will come for all of us.

So evolution got rid of God, or at least thought it did. Does this make any difference in our current society? Yes, it does. I was talking to an expert in legal affairs who has often appeared before the Supreme Court, and he told me that the main problem in the Supreme Court is very simple: Six of the judges are evolutionists, and three are not. Have you wondered why they vote the way they do when it comes time to decide:

• whether or not God should be taught in the classrooms? No.

• whether or not prayer should be directed to God? Nope.

• whether or not the Bible should be taught? No way.

• whether or not the Ten Commandments can be posted in a public classroom? We cannot have that.

• whether or not it is legal to abort a child? Of course.

• whether or not it is legal for a man to marry a man and a woman a woman? Some of the courts of this land have accepted same-sex marriage.

If there is no God, there are no moral absolutes. As an evil, atheistic character in Fyodor Dostoyevsky's *The Brothers Karamazov* says, "everything is permitted . . . since there is no infinite God, there's no such thing as virtue either and there's no need for it at all."³ Think about it. That statement is true.

Because of evolution, man has lost his significance. In Western civilization, it has always been held that man is a creature with a great purpose, He has been created in the image of God to fulfill His purposes in this world, and he has an everlasting life ahead of him. But now . . .

THE IMPACT OF DECISIONS

Indeed, we have seen in the courts in the past four decades four very significant decisions that have ushered us into this secular apocalypse. First of all, the Supreme Court ruled prayer out of our schools. Then they ruled the Bible out of schools. Next they ruled the Ten Commandments out of the schools. Now they have voted against the balanced treatment of creation along with evolution in the schools. So we have seen banished from the thought of our young people the idea that they have been created by anyone or that there are any laws or moral absolutes they should obey. By the way, the Supreme Court's decision against allowing the Ten Commandments to be posted on the walls of the schools in Kentucky, said, ". . . lest looking upon them from day to day, the students should be moved to obey them."⁴

If there is no Judge, then there is no one to whom we are accountable or responsible. Therefore, if God is dead or absent from both ends of the process of life, then it is true that, as the Dostoevsky character said, "Anything is permissible." And that is one of the basic motivations that lies behind the belief in evolutionism.

NO PURPOSE

Today students are taught that man has no purpose, because teleology, the science of purposes, is the *bête noire*, the black beast, of evolution. Evolutionists cannot stand for anything to have purpose. Teleology must go. Therefore, everything is not preplanned by a divine intelligence and a beneficent God who providentially provides for His creatures. It all happens purely by chance, with no forethought of what the end might be. Therefore man has no purpose; consequently he has no significance.

"ACCIDENTAL TWIG"

Stephen J. Gould was the most influential evolutionist in America, a professor at Harvard University for twenty years—and then he had a great awakening: He died recently, and he met the Creator face-to-face. That must have been a horribly shocking event, to say the least. Overnight he became a creationist.

However, in one article by him he said: "Man—or even woman—as the crowning achievement of some grand cosmic plan? What mortal conceit." To Gould the idea of the creation of man was merely a mortal conceit. "We are but an afterthought," said Gould. "We are a little accidental twig"[5]—the kind you would pick up off the lawn of your backyard and throw into the garbage. That is what our students are learning in our colleges: They are nothing but dried-up, little accidental twigs of no significance and no purpose.

So man lost all of his divinely bestowed significance and importance with the onslaught of evolution. The results of that have been staggering. Among them is the fact that suicide is the second largest cause of death among college students in America. As of this writing, there has been a rash of suicides at the very place I earned my Ph.D., New York University. When life has no meaning or purpose and no future, then why not? Tune out. Tune in. Live a life of drugs, alcohol, sex. Life really doesn't have any meaning after all, because it has been "demonstrated scientifically" that evolution is a "fact," and you have to get used to it. Students are told it is a fact that is believed by all scientists. How many times have we heard that?

WHY WAS EVOLUTION ACCEPTED SO READILY?

I remember listening a few years ago to a television broadcast on public television in which a young lady was interviewing Sir Julian Huxley. He was the grandson of Thomas Huxley, who popularized evolution during Darwin's day. Darwin was too meek and mild to get out and defend his own theory, but he had a bulldog, Thomas Huxley. His grandson was Sir Julian, and he was, a few years ago, the most important evolutionist in the world—even knighted by the king. He was also the president and founder of UNESCO (United Nations Educational, Scientific and Cultural Organization). He was a world ambassador for evolution. If Sir Julian spoke, that was the law, the last word. The lady interviewing him asked, "Why do you think evolution caught on so quickly? Why do you think the scientists leaped at *The Origin of Species*?"

I remember exactly where I was sitting while watching this public broadcasting television station and Huxley's response, verbatim. The greatest living evolutionist in all of the world, Sir Julian Huxley, said, "We all jumped at the *Origin* because . . ." I would love to ask a college class of seniors in the science department that question: "Why did scientists leap at the *Origin*?"

They would say that Charles Darwin presented such unimpeachable evidence that proved the fact of evolution that we, in our scientific integrity, could not help but accept his conclusions. That is what virtually every student in our public schools is taught. But what did the greatest evolutionist on earth, Sir Julian Huxley, say? He said this: "[I suppose the reason] we all jumped at the *Origin* was because the idea of God interfered with our sexual mores." Remember: If there is no God, everything is permissible.

By the way, that is not a lone opinion. Aldous Huxley, author of *Brave New World* and the brother of Julian, was one of the great agnostic evolutionists of the twentieth century, also following in the footsteps of his grandfather, Thomas Huxley. He said the same thing. He believed in the meaninglessness of the world, which Darwin taught, because, he said, "We objected to the morality, because it interfered with our sexual freedom."

Such statements from various highly placed evolutionists could be quoted. What was evolution really all about? Science? Evidence? . . . No. Sex. It unleashed *The Kinsey Report*, the sexual revolution, feminism, divorce, homosexuality, and all of the rest of those ills. Does evolution really make a difference in our world? Believe me, it does. The people I am quoting to you are not merely evolutionists—they are the world's greatest evolutionists, and what they often say to each other, they don't say to the public.

I further will say that 95 percent of what you read here, you have never read in the newspaper. They will say, "But evolution is a fact, and therefore we must live with it, adjust to it." That is what many people have tried to do because they have been told it is a fact. It's not a theory, we are told—it is a fact.

NOT A FACT

But in truth, evolution is *not* a fact; it isn't even a scientific theory. Evolutionists say, "Evolution is not a theory; it's a fact." However, the greatest authority in the world says it's not a theory, it's not even a hypothesis, it's metaphysics. It's basically theology. We will focus in a later chapter on how evolution is crumbling in our time.

Others will say, "All scientists believe in evolution, and therefore we must believe it." I would say the most persuasive argument used in our colleges and high schools as to why students ought to believe in evolution is that all scientists believe it. You have probably heard that statement made. There's just one problem . . .

IT'S NONSENSE

In actuality, evolution has failed at every point. All of the major pillars of evolution have collapsed in the last twenty years. For example, the idea that the amazing and almost unbelievable complexity of a cell could have risen by chance. Sir Fred Hoyle, of Cambridge University and Oxford, one of the greatest living astronomers, developer of the Steady-State theory of creation, said that the idea that a cell could have risen by chance "is evidently nonsense of a high order."[6]

What children are being taught in every public school as scientific fact in America is "nonsense of a high order." Yes, outstanding scientists have said there is no basis and no real evidence for evolution at all. It is not even a theory, much less a fact.

Hitler was a devout evolutionist and a follower of Nietzsche and Haeckel, and he taught evolution to his troops. He gave them a copy of Darwin's book and Nietzsche's book, which talked about evolution of the god-man, of our becoming God. He was absolutely determined to create a super race by getting rid of the inferior races.

For example, Hitler said, "At this point someone or other may laugh, but this planet once moved through the ether for millions of years without human beings and it can do so again some day if men forget that they owe their higher existence, not to the ideas of a few crazy ideologists, but to the knowledge and ruthless application of Nature's stern and rigid laws. Everything we admire on this earth today—science and art, technology and inventions—is only the creative product of a few people and originally perhaps of one race. On them depends the existence of this culture. . . . All the human culture, all the results of art, science, and technology that we see before us today, are almost exclusively the creative product of the Aryan. This very fact admits of the not unfounded inference that he alone was the founder of all higher humanity, and therefore representing the prototype of all that we understand by the word 'man.'"[7] And so, because of his view of evolution, he believed the Aryan was superior to other races (including the Jews, the Gypsies, the Slavs, and so on).

Because of this, Hitler was adamant that Aryans should not breed with non-Aryans: "The stronger must dominate and not mate with the weaker, which would signify the sacrifice of its own higher nature. Only the born weakling can look upon this principle as cruel, and if he does so, it is merely because he is of a feebler nature and narrower mind; for if such a law did not direct the process of evolution then the higher development of organic life would not be conceivable at all."[8] So who are you, asks Hitler, to question the marvels of evolution? Hitler tried to speed up evolution, to help it along. And millions suffered and died in unspeakable ways because of it.

RACISM—AN EVOLUTIONARY CONCEPT

Racism is basically an evolutionary concept. The word *race* is never even used in the Bible, except for a foot race. But all of the nineteenth-century evolutionists were strong racists, including Darwin, who said that the inferior races at some time in the future would all be destroyed by the superior races. Hitler and others set out to do so. We also know that Margaret Sanger, the founder of Planned Parenthood, set out to get rid of "the human weeds," as she called them, so that the superior stock might prevail.

Also, you may know that Karl Marx, the founder of Communism, felt that evolution was exactly what he needed as a pseudo-scientific foundation for that Godless worldview. He even wanted to dedicate *Das Kapital* to Charles Darwin. Darwin's wife had a fit, and Marx said he wouldn't do it because he didn't want to cause unhappiness in his family. Darwin also hoped his wife would let go of his nose. She was much more conservative than her husband, to say the least.

Communism is based upon evolution, as are Nazism and Fascism. The Communists have killed more people in peacetime than all those killed in all religious wars combined. According to *The Black Book of Communism*, "rough approximation, based on unofficial estimates" finds that the "total [killed by the Communists] approaches 100 million people killed."[9] The Communists killed, according to the Senate Committee of the United States of America, 135 million people in peacetime. They are the greatest mass murderers of all time—Stalin and Mao and Pol Pot and all the rest—and all of that compliments of evolution. As a Dutch Marxist said in 1912, "If we turn to Marxism we immediately see a great conformity with Darwinism."[10]

Author Ian Taylor says that Fascism and Communism were two sides of the same coin in that evolution provided the basis for both—therefore human life was cheap. "Fascism or Marxism, right wing or left—all these are only ideological roads that lead to Aldous Huxley's brave new world, while the foundation for each of these is Darwin's theory of evolution. . . . The result is that both Fascism and Marxism finish at the same destiny—totalitarian rule by the elite."[11]

Therefore, we can conclude with a statement made by a very famous evolutionist, Sir Arthur Keith, at one time the number-one evolutionist in Great

Britain. At the end of World War II Keith said that what we had just seen for the first time in history was a modern secular technological state that had based itself entirely upon the principles of evolution. He was horrified. He had written twenty books defending evolution, and then he saw it in Nazi Germany and the Holocaust—and he was appalled. Keith also said this:

> Meantime, let me say in conclusion, I have come to this: The law of Christ is incompatible with the law of evolution . . . as far as the law of evolution has worked hitherto. Nay, the two laws are at war with each other; the law of Christ can never prevail until the law of evolution is destroyed.[12]

Again, this comes from Sir Arthur Keith, at one time a leading evolutionist in Great Britain.

CONCLUSION

Some are predicting that by the middle of this century, evolution will be known simply as a small religious sect of the twentieth century. Paul Lemoine, director of the National Museum of Natural History, was an atheist, but a critic of evolution nonetheless. He said, "Evolution is a kind of dogma which its own priests no longer believe, but which they uphold for the people."[13] Another Frenchman, Jean Rostand, a biologist and member of the Academy of Sciences of the French Academy, once wrote, "Evolution ["Transformism"] is a fairy tale for adults."[14]

I pray that the Lord will topple this whole monstrous edifice, which has brought more death, more evil, more vice, more vileness into the world than any other human theory ever promulgated. I pray that the law of Christ will prevail and that this One who came and commanded us to care for the weak, not destroy them, to help those who are sick and the poor and not let them die, that His views will prevail, though they are the very antithesis of evolution. I pray that His love and mercy and grace will cover the world. I also pray that the collapse of this horrible edifice may come soon and may come completely and totally. I pray that the wondrous effects of Christ's ethical, moral, and spiritual teaching will once more prevail in our nation and in the world.

2

"THIS IS MY AMOEBA'S WORLD"

O Timothy, guard the deposit entrusted to you. Avoid the irreverent babble and contradictions of what is falsely called "knowledge," for by professing it some have swerved from the faith. Grace be with you.

1 TIMOTHY 6:20-21

O ver the centuries the attacks upon the Christian church have changed, and they have increased both in intensity and in comprehension. For example, there was a time when the attacks focused upon the literal or allegorical interpretation of Scripture—a time when critics or skeptics fixed their attacks on some of the miracles of the Bible. Then they progressed to attacks upon the Virgin Birth or the bodily resurrection or the Second Coming of Christ. Following those were attacks upon the deity of Christ and His atonement.

But today the basic assault upon Christianity is total and all-encompassing. The basic attack is upon the very existence of God Himself—the foundation for all religion and all spiritual life.

This attack, of course, is coming to us in the form of a scientific dogma—the dogma of evolution. If it had its way, this dogma would rid the world of the last vestiges of any belief in God.

We are told today that we have not been wonderfully and marvelously fashioned by the hand of God, but rather we are the product of a clever and cunning amoeba. I'm sure that some of us will be moved to a spirit of adoration when we think of such a thing. "This is my amoeba's world. I rest me in the thought, that he has produced all things." I think it would be only appropriate that every morning all of us would get down on our knees and give thanks and praise to the amoeba that has created us. Well, in case you think that's not what some believe, let me read you a poem by Arthur Guiterman, an evolutionist. Though this is somewhat tongue-in-cheek, nevertheless it contains the real element of what they believe. This "Ode to the Amoeba" is a hymn or paean of praise to our creator—the great god, Amoeba.

Recall from Time's abysmal chasm
That piece of primal protoplasm,
The First Amoeba, strangely splendid,
From whom we're all of us descended.
That First Amoeba, weirdly clever,
Exists today and shall forever,
Because he reproduced by fission;
He split himself, and each division
And subdivision deemed it fitting
To keep on splitting, splitting, splitting;
So whatsoe'er their billions be,
All, all amoebas still are he.
Zoologists discern his features
In every sort of breathing creatures,
Since all of every living species,
No matter how their breed increases
Or how their ranks have been recruited,
From him alone were evoluted.
King Solomon, the Queen of Sheba
And Hoover sprang from that amoeba;
Columbus, Shakespeare, Darwin, Shelley
Derived from that same bit of jelly.
So famed he is and well-connected,
His statue ought to be erected,
For you and I and William Beebe
Are undeniably amoebe.[1]

That essentially is the religion of many modern people today. The idea is that we have naturally arisen out of some concatenation of amino acids and some primordial slime and have crawled and slithered onto the banks of some muddy edge of some ancient pond, and from there, into the trees and back down again. We have shed our tails and most of our fur, and here we are, worshiping the living myth we've created—called God.

Martin Luther said that we need to fight where the battle is the hottest.

Though we may be ever-so faithful to fight somewhere else, if we're not there where the battle is most fierce, we are indeed traitors to the cause of the King.

Well, here is the battle, and here is the most all-encompassing attack that Christianity has ever faced. Today we live in a time when a number of things have been happening simultaneously. There has been a tremendous renaissance and revival of the teaching of creationism. Simultaneous to that has been a collapse of many of the basic pillars upon which evolution has stood—attacks that are multiplying. These attacks are made not merely by creationists but by evolutionists themselves, and more and more of the basic pillars of evolution are crumbling. We will see that point by point in the next chapter.

"EVOLUTION IS SCIENTIFIC—CREATIONISM IS RELIGIOUS"

Several laws requiring equal time have been passed by various states. In 1981 Arkansas passed a law requiring a fair and balanced treatment. That law was struck down by a higher court in 1982. Louisiana then passed a "balanced treatment act" that was struck down by the U.S. Supreme Court in 1987.

Let's look at the matter. U.S. District Court Judge William R. Overton, when he threw out the law in Arkansas, did it on this basis: he said in effect, "Evolution is scientific. Creationism is religious. Therefore, religion cannot be taught in the schools; e.g., creationism must go." Very interesting. Do you remember the Scopes Trial in 1925? At that time, the only thing that was allowed to be taught was creationism, and the evolutionists, led by atheist Clarence Darrow and the ACLU—which could be called the *Anti*-Christian Liberty Union—went to court to overthrow that law. Darrow said, "[I]t is bigotry for public schools to teach only one theory of origins."[2]

Well, well, now isn't that interesting?

The same ACLU today is doing its very best, sending their lawyers to Arkansas, to keep only one theory of origins (now that it's evolution) taught in our schools. It seems like the bigotry is now on the other foot. They do that wherever evolution is even slightly challenged. In recent years in Ohio, the ACLU and their allies tried to prevent a measure that mandated that if Darwinian evolution were to be taught, the schools should also teach the scientific problems with Darwinism. (Nothing about creationism or divine design.) This is only science vs. science. Yet the ACLU even tried to stop that. Thankfully, they have been unsuccessful in that particular case.

Evolution is scientific; creationism is religious, it is claimed. We hear that said over and over again, *ad nauseum*. But how true is that? The fact of the matter is, neither evolution nor creationism fully meet the rigorous demands of science. The basic tenets of science are: It must be observable, testable, repeatable, and falsifiable. The fact is, neither evolution nor creation is any of those. Therefore, the issue of origins does not really fall into the realm of strict science.

We can set up two models. We can look at all of the evidence and see whether it points to one or the other, see what predictions they make, and then conclude which belief is true.

METAPHYSICS

Dr. Karl Popper is the greatest living philosopher of science in the world today. He has been described by a Nobel prize winner as the greatest philosopher of science who ever lived. Dr. Karl Popper said not only that evolution is not a fact—it is not even a theory. And not only is it not a theory, it is not even a scientific hypothesis, because it cannot be falsified. Every scientific hypothesis must be able to be proved wrong. Evolution cannot. There is no way anyone has ever conceived of being able to prove evolution wrong. When they prove one part of it wrong, evolutionists simply change the theory to make it fit another part.

It is, he said, at best a metaphysical research program. Now, metaphysics is a lot closer to religion than it is to science, which is to say that evolution really isn't scientific. In fact, most of the evidence points away from the evolutionary model and points to the creationist model.

EVOLUTION IS RELIGIOUS

We are told that evolution is scientific and not religious. Is that true? Or is evolution religious? Well, I believe that evolution is not only religious, it is more religious than creationism. That may startle some people. On what do I base that statement? First, more religions in this world are based upon evolution than on creation, including Hinduism, Buddhism, Taoism, Confucianism, Unitarianism, Scientology, and Science of Mind. Liberal Christianity was born with the publication of Darwin's *Origin of Species*. Neo-orthodoxy is rampant in virtually every mainline Protestant seminary in America. Much of Roman Catholicism, especially the followers of Teilhard de Chardin in many of the Catholic parochial schools, teaches evolution. These and many more facts show that vast numbers of religions are based upon evolution, including the religion of secular humanism, which declares itself to be a religion and has been declared by the Supreme Court to be a religion.[3] It is founded upon evolution.

Therefore, to say that evolution is not religious is utterly inconceivable. It is incredible that any intelligent person could make such a statement as that.

Furthermore, evolution is not only the basis of numerous religions, it, in itself, is based upon faith. Hundreds of statements by evolutionary scientists could be called forth to indicate that. The head of the Department of Anatomy at an Australian university said that evolution is a time-honored tenet of faith. He said that evolution is therefore a matter of faith on the part of biologists, and it takes faith to believe that biogenesis did occur—that cells came into existence in that way. Evolution is based upon faith, and it's the same kind of faith that is seen in religion.

Dr. Arthur Field points out that evolution is based upon belief in the reality of the unseen—belief in fossils that cannot be produced, belief in embryological evidence that does not exist, and belief in breeding experiments that refuse to come off.

H. S. Lipson pointed out: "In fact, evolution became in a sense a scientific religion; almost all scientists have accepted it, and many are prepared to 'bend' their observation to fit in with it."[4]

Further, Dr. John Howett of London said that evolution is based and accepted on faith alone, for three quarters of the record is nonexistent, and there are gaps that cannot be covered.

Did you know that we can find statements from scientists who actually declare that evolution is their god? Not merely a tenet of their religion or the pillar of their religion, but their god itself. May I quote you one? Charles Darwin referred to natural selection as deity: "I speak of natural selection as an active power or Deity."[5] And numbers of other scientists have also said that evolution is virtually their god.

So we see that evolution is not merely scientific, it is not even good science, and it is certainly religious.

IS CREATIONISM RELIGIOUS?

Well, what about creationism? Let's make one thing clear: You can teach either biblical creationism, or you can teach scientific creationism. They are quite different. Biblical creationism is certainly religious. The first several chapters of Genesis teach it. That portion of Scripture talks about God creating the heavens and the earth in six days—creating all that there is, creating man, and woman out of man, then resting on the seventh day. It talks about the great deluge of Noah and of other major events.

That is precisely what the scientific creationists do not want taught in our schools. What they want taught is scientific creationism, which never mentions Genesis, which never mentions the Bible, which doesn't even mention God, though, of course, there is nothing basically wrong with mentioning God or the Creator in school. If there were, it would be unconstitutional to read the Declaration of Independence, which says that Americans have been "endowed by their Creator with certain unalienable rights." It has a number of other references to God and to the Creator. And the Supreme Court has said there is nothing unconstitutional in mentioning God in our schools. But some overzealous teachers have gone too far in censoring any mention of God—like the public schools in Maryland at Thanksgiving time 2004, encouraging their students to give thanks to anyone—anyone but God.

But scientific creationism does not deal with Genesis or the Bible. It deals with things like biology, cytology (the origin of the cell), anthropology, chemistry, and physics. It deals with embryology and with astrophysics and all sorts of subjects like this that are not found in the Bible at all. It deals with merely scientific evidence that points to one of the two models. Did life arise, as evolutionists say, gradually? Or did it arise abruptly? If you look at the fossil records, you will see that there is a record of an abrupt rise. Every single phylum of invertebrate fossils are found in the oldest rocks, the Cambrian rocks. They suddenly appear. It has been observed that 75 percent of the record is gone, from the very beginning. Evolution is already 75 percent completed before we find the first fossil, and here we have all of these extraordinarily complex fossils found in the very earliest rocks. We will see this more clearly in the next chapter when we talk more about the fossil record and the Cambrian Explosion.

CHRISTIANITY AND SCIENTISTS

We had a debate at our church many years ago, and an evolutionist-scientist made the incredible claim that not only is creationism not scientific, but, he went on to say, creationists are therefore not scientists. Can you imagine the unmitigated gall of any person making a statement like that? The truth is that creationists gave the world science. Creationists invented science. Without creationists, there wouldn't be any science, and for that man to stand up and say that creationists aren't scientists is utterly astounding.

Let us take a little deeper look. First of all, who invented science? It was Sir Francis Bacon, who is credited with having been the inventor of the scientific method—that combination of induction and deduction, of hypothesis and proof (empirical proof). Bacon was a devout Christian. He believed in

God, he believed in Christ, he believed in the Bible, and he believed in creation. Here is what he said: "There are two books laid before us to study, to prevent our falling into error; first, the volume of the Scriptures, which reveal the will of God; then the volume of the Creatures, which express His power."[6] This from the founder of science. He wasn't a Christian? Think again.

Who was the greatest scientist who ever lived? A poll taken of scientists just a few years ago concluded that the greatest scientist who ever lived was Sir Isaac Newton. If you read a list of the things he discovered, it is awesome. The mathematical laws of gravity are just one piece of that huge puzzle from this gigantic intellect. He was also, among other things, the co-discoverer of calculus. Sir Isaac Newton believed in God, he believed in Christ, he believed in the Bible, and he believed in creation. To the utter chagrin of modern evolutionary scientists, he wrote more books on theology (not all of which were necessarily orthodox) than he did on science. And yet he became the greatest scientist who has ever lived, according to modern scientists themselves.

CHRISTIAN SCIENTISTS

If the scientific method was invented by a Christian, and the greatest scientist who ever lived was a Christian, what about the people who gave us all of the various branches of science? Who were they? Let me tell you about them. They were all men who believed in God, believed in Christ, believed in the Bible, and believed in creation. There was not an evolutionist among them. Who were they?

The inventor of antiseptic surgery was Joseph Lister (1827-1912), who was all of the above. (It is from his name we get the name of the germ-killing mouthwash Listerine.) Lord Lister said, "I am a believer in the fundamental doctrines of Christianity."[7]

The pioneer of bacteriology was Louis Pasteur (1822-1895). His biographer, Rene Vallery-Radot, writes about Pasteur's religious views: "Absolute faith in God and in eternity, and a conviction that the power for good given to us in this world will be continued beyond it, were feelings which pervaded his whole life; the virtues of the Gospel had ever been present to him."[8]

Sir Isaac Newton (1642-1727) developed the disciplines of calculus and dynamics. He said, "I have a foundational belief in the Bible as the Word of God, written by men who were inspired. I study the Bible daily."[9] Newton also said, "Atheism is so senseless. When I look at the solar system, I see the earth at the right distance from the sun to receive the proper amounts of heat and light. This did not happen by chance."[10]

Celestial mechanics and physical astronomy were developed by Johannes Kepler (1571-1630), who said that science was "thinking God's thoughts after Him." He observed, "we astronomers are priests of the highest God in regard to the book of nature," doing all this study to "the glory of God."[11]

Oxford professor Robert Boyle (1627-1691) is the father of chemistry and gas dynamics. He left a large sum of money in his will so that a series of lectures would be taught in his university in England defending the Christian faith. These were called the Boyle Lectures. An unbeliever? Hardly.

Comparative anatomy and vertebrate paleontology were founded as scientific disciplines by the Frenchman Georges Cuvier (1769-1832). He was a devout Lutheran. Author Ian Taylor says of Cuvier: "His theory of creation withstood the theory of evolution in France for almost the entire nineteenth century."[12]

Computer science was developed by Charles Babbage (1791-1871) (with input from another Christian scientist, Blaise Pascal). According to biographer H. W. Buxton, "Mr. Babbage regarded the phenomena of the Cosmos as the immediate and direct consequence of an eternal decree of the Divine intelligence. . . ."[13] The whole world was like a giant machine, and God was the Programmer.

Electromagnetics and field theory were developed by Michael Faraday (1791-1867), who had about twenty-two honorary doctorates. He was once given a huge award by the king at a banquet on a Wednesday night. After the banquet, the people talked awhile, and then he was called up to receive his award. But he had slipped out to go to a prayer meeting.

Energetics and thermodynamics were developed by Lord Kelvin (1824-1907), a great Christian who once said, "With regard to the origin of life, science . . . positively affirms creative power."[14]

Gregor Mendel (1822-1884) pioneered studies of genetics. He was a humble Catholic monk in Czechoslovakia. Ian Taylor, author of *In the Minds of Men*, notes that if Mendel had known about Darwin's theory before he did his genetic experiments with peas, he might never have conducted his research. Furthermore, because Darwin's theory began to gain influence in academic circles, there was a reluctance to initially accept Mendel's pro-creation conclusions. Taylor writes, "Since Mendel's genetics challenged the Darwinian idea of natural selection, it is just possible that any interest shown in his work was actively discouraged."[15]

Glacial geology and ichthyology were studied by Louis Agassiz (1807-1873) of Harvard, a great Christian man. Ian Taylor notes that Agassiz was among those scientists who "were convinced of the historicity and universality of the Noachian Flood."[16] This is no minor point, because those days were filled with skepticism about the Flood in academic circles.

James Simpson (1811-1870) of Edinburgh, Scotland, developed gynecology. He also pioneered the use of anesthesiology for childbirth. He defended his practice before his critics by appealing to Genesis 2 in the Bible, when God put Adam to sleep for the "surgery" in which He removed his rib.

Leonardo da Vinci (1452-1519) is the father of hydraulics. Humanistic in some respects, nonetheless da Vinci created some great Christian works of art, including the definitive version of Christ's Last Supper.

Matthew Fontaine Maury (1806-1873) is the father of both hydrography and oceanography. He derived some of his scientific ideas from the Scriptures. How could a man of science do that? Maury defended his actions thus in a public address he once gave: "I have been blamed by men of science, both in this country [the U.S.] and in England, for quoting the Bible in confirmation of the doctrines of physical geography. The Bible, they say, was not written for scientific purposes, and is therefore of no authority in matters of science. I beg your pardon: the Bible is authority for everything it touches."[17]

Hydrostatics was developed by Blaise Pascal (1623-1662). Scientists are very concerned about proof. Note what he says about proof and God: "Jesus Christ is the only proof of the living God. We only know God through Jesus Christ."[18]

Systematic biology was pioneered by Carl von Linnaeus (1707-1778). He created a labeling system for natural science—a labeling system he ultimately got from the Bible. Each organism was given a Latin name in two parts: the genus and the species. This method is known to us as the binomial nomenclature system. Examples include *"homo erectus," "Homo sapiens,"* and so on. These classifications are so commonplace that we don't even realize how revolutionary and how important the innovation was. He gave the world a mechanism by which we could name new species. His mechanism—again based on the Bible—is still at work today.

Historians Will and Ariel Durant wrote that Linnaeus "mapped the teeming world of life with the care and devotion of a scientific saint."[19] Even the late atheistic Harvard professor of science Stephen Jay Gould acknowledged that Linnaeus's contribution to biology came about because of his Christian faith. Gould explained that Linnaeus "proclaimed that species are the natural entities that God placed on earth at the creation. They are His, not ours—and they exist as they are, independent of our whims."[20] On the campus of Oxford University there is a pro-evolution museum; this was the same place where the infamous debate was held between Thomas Huxley and Bishop Samuel Wilberforce, a debate that was a turning point in favor of evolution. Throughout the building are life-size statues of various scientists throughout the ages. Many of them are mentioned in this book. The statue of Linnaeus shows him holding a large book with a cross on it—a Bible, no doubt.

In addition to all these scientists are numerous other Christians who were scientists who pioneered specific studies. These include:

• Dimensional analysis and model analysis were developed by Lord Rayleigh (1842-1919).

• James Clerk Maxwell (1831-1879) was the father of electrodynamics and statistical thermodynamics.

• Ambrose Fleming (1848-1945) was the father of electronics.

• Entomology of living insects was developed by Jean-Henri Fabre (1823-1915).

• The study of fluid mechanics was created by George Stokes (1819-1903).

• William Herschel (1738-1822) was the father of galactic astronomy.

• Studies in isotopic chemistry were pioneered by William Ramsay (1852-1916).

• The study of non-Euclidean geometry was pioneered by Bernhard Riemann (1826-1866).

• David Brewster (1781-1868) was the father of optical mineralogy.

And other scientific studies were also pioneered by Bible-believing Christians, including:

• Paleontology—John Woodward (1665-1728).

• Pathology—Rudolph Virchow (1821-1902).

• Reversible thermodynamics—James Joule (1818-1889).

• Stratigraphy—Nicholas Steno (1638-1686).

• Thermokinetics—Humphrey Davy (1778-1829).[21]

And on and on it goes. These men were all Christians, all believers in creation. The evolutionist who declared that anyone who believes in creation is not a scientist had better go back and read a little of his own history to find out if that is true. He will find what we have just shared.

WHO ARE THE REAL CENSORS?

The attempt to suppress all of the scientific evidence for creationism and the scientific problems with evolution is a form of censorship. It is exceedingly ironic that the ACLU, People for the American Way, and others like that who cry constantly against censorship are in the forefront of this attempt to censor out scientific information.

Keep in mind that creationists are not trying to get rid of evolution. They are trying to have a balanced statement, even as Darwin said there must be if there would be fairness.

Of course, when all of the evidence on one side is presented and all the evidence on the other side is repressed, this is not education. It is no less than brainwashing. Scientific pedagogical studies have shown that students learn better under testing, and it has been shown that they learn better when both models are presented—when the evidence for each side is given, and they are able to make up their own mind.

ANTI-CHRISTIAN BIGOTRY

Finally, may I say that at its base what this amounts to is anti-Christian bigotry. Now call again to mind the words of Clarence Darrow, who said it is the height of bigotry to teach only one view of origins. Furthermore, when you read the statements of leading evolutionists you see, as has been documented in a number of books and writings on the subject, that these men, nearly all of the leading evolutionists, were motivated by a tremendous antipathy and hostility toward the Christian message, God, and the Bible.

For example, Jean-Baptiste Lamarck (1744-1829) predated Darwin by a few decades and was one of the earliest evolutionists. It has been pointed out that Lamarck's philosophy amounted to a hatred for the tradition of the Flood and biblical creation. Indeed, in reaction to everything that recalled the Christian theory of nature, Darwin himself was very subtly undermining Christianity. He had come to reject Christianity, he said. He came to reject the Bible as no more valuable than the writings of the Hindus or the most barbaric pagans. He was undermining the Christian view, but he was doing it very, very subtly. In a letter that Darwin wrote to one of his friends, he said that Charles Lyell (another early evolutionist, 1797-1875) had shown that it was much more successful to undermine Christianity without attacking it directly, and that the attacks of people like Voltaire, in spite of the fact that Voltaire's writings were filled with wit and tremendous genius, had produced little lasting good: Real good seems only to follow the slow and silent side attacks. The real good, as Darwin says, is the undermining of Christianity, and it must be done insidiously. That is nothing other than anti-Christian bias and bigotry.

The same thing is true for all of the leading evolutionists of that time. Of Thomas Huxley, who was Darwin's bulldog, it is written that he had a life-long war with Christianity. He said we need a regiment of ironsides, men with unusual bravery, to fight against Christianity. Furthermore, consider Ernst Haeckel, the Huxley of Germany and the early leader of the evolutionary movement there. He was the founder of the idea that ontogeny recapitulates phylogeny—that the fetus in the womb goes through all of the states of the evolutionary process, which was accepted for many years but is totally repu-diated today, and yet still appears in textbooks in high schools and colleges. But Haeckel described himself at first as an evangelical and a believer in orthodox Christianity, until he became involved with evolution. Then he came to have a strong hatred for Christianity and for everything for which it stood.

In our day, too, many of the leading evolutionists are on an anti-Christian crusade—men like George Gaylord Simpson or the late Steven J. Gould and Niles Eldridge, atheists and Marxists. The leaders of the evolutionary move-ment today and down through the years have been atheists, though many of the followers try to straddle the fence. Huxley said he looked with contempt upon those who tried to have one foot in each camp and tried to reconcile that which was unreconcilable. You cannot have a world governed by ran-dom chance and at the same time a world governed by Divine Providence. They just will not fit together. You have to make a choice.

Note what *Time* magazine once observed: "Charles Darwin didn't want to murder God, as he once put it. But he did."[22]

CONCLUSION

There is a great, great deal involved in this struggle. Christians need to become informed, and Christians need to pray about this.

There is a God who has created you, a God before whom one day you must stand and answer for your life. You cannot evade or avoid that. You will come before Him with whom we each and all have to do. There is a God who has loved us enough to send His Son to die for our sins. You can do what Huxley did and what Darwin did—you can reject the offer of salvation that is offered to you in the Scriptures. But I assure you that one day you will stand before the great Judge of heaven and earth and give an account of that, and that account will be that you have believed a fable. You have believed a myth—a cunningly devised fable—a science falsely so-called, which many have followed and have erred concerning the faith. I would urge you not to so err, but rather to seek the truth and embrace Christ by faith—to place your trust in Him as the living divine Savior and to know that God has given you purpose. He has created you with meaning and significance for your life, and that life is going to go on forever and ever. We do not have the hopeless, miasmic emptiness that the evolutionist offers to mankind—a meaninglessness and emptiness to life that has made suicide the second greatest cause of death among young people in our country today because in their view life has no purpose or meaning.

Christ gives us that purpose. But the redemption of Christ is based upon the creation of God. He both made us and offers to remake us in His own image. May we, by His grace, accept that gracious offer.

3

THE COLLAPSE OF EVOLUTION

Claiming to be wise, they became fools, and exchanged the glory of the immortal God for images resembling mortal man and birds and animals and reptiles.

ROMANS 1:22-23

✠

In 1912 scientists discovered a human skull with a jaw like an ape. They named him Piltdown man. He was in the textbooks, encyclopedias, museums, and even the dictionaries. For example, a 1941 *Webster's Collegiate Dictionary* has an entry on Piltdown: "A prehistoric station in Sussex, England, yielding remains of an extinct species of man, Piltdown man (*Eaonthropos dawsoni*) characterized by a retreating, apelike chin and thick cranial bones, but a human-like cranium."[1] He was the answer to the Darwinists' prayer, if they pray ("To whom it may concern . . ."). Ah, here at last was the missing link. Well, I'm sure most of you know the rest of the story. In 1953 this was discovered to be a deliberate hoax. The mystery of who created it remains unsolved. The fact that men accepted it so readily—and allowed it to shape acceptance of human evolution for more than three crucial decades—points to their bias in favor of any shred of evidence they can find in favor of macro-evolution. I say crucial decades because Piltdown man helped evolution become more widely accepted. But Darwin's missing links are still missing.

The purpose of this chapter is to consider the fact that much of what we find in the scientific evidence today works against evolution, not for it. Many of the key pillars of evolution are collapsing, but because of the politically correct zeitgeist of our age, most people are not exposed to these facts.

TO BE FAIR, PRESENT BOTH SIDES

Evolutionists today have absolutely a conniption at the very thought of both sides of the origins debate being presented in school. They want evolution alone taught—and that dogmatically. They think it is terrible that anyone would suggest such a thing as presenting both sides. But as one writer said, "A fair result can be obtained only by fully stating and balancing the facts and arguments on both sides of each question."[2] To present both sides of this argument is the only way, said he, to come to a "fair result"—presenting the facts for evolution and the facts for creation and letting people make up their minds. Obviously that was some sort of fanatical Christian making that statement, right? No. As a matter of fact that is found in the writings of Charles Darwin. He said it in his *The Origin of the Species*. But that has been conveniently forgotten in our time.

ICONS OF EVOLUTION

Recently Jerry Newcombe, coauthor of this book, interviewed Dr. Jonathan Wells for the television program, *The Coral Ridge Hour*. Dr. Wells has more than one earned Ph.D., including a Ph.D. in biology from the University of California at Berkeley. Dr. Wells has written a book that is devastating to the "evolutionist faith," if we could call it that. It's entitled *Icons of Evolution*. He points out that the major showpieces that evolutionists tout to prove evolution are fraudulent. But even though they are bogus, or there is sleight of hand involved, somehow these "icons of evolution" still make it into some of our science textbooks. Thankfully, because of Wells and others testifying at textbook hearings, some of these icons have been removed. Wells is a senior fellow with the Discovery Institute, based in Seattle, Washington, which has taken an active role in this fight. This is quite an uphill battle.

As we interviewed Jonathan Wells, he grabbed a modern volume and said, "I have here a typical example of a widely-used biology textbook. This book is used in thousands of schools around the country. By and large, it's not bad, but when it comes to evolution, it distorts, exaggerates, or even fakes the evidence."[3]

How so? By presenting as fact—
- Darwin's "Tree of Life"
- Haeckel's embryos
- the peppered moth
- Darwin's finches—

and by omitting the Cambrian explosion. Let's look at each of these.

DARWIN'S "TREE OF LIFE"

One of the most fundamental icons of evolution is Darwin's "Tree of Life." Wells notes, "[Darwin] called it that himself, 'the great tree of life"—and by that he meant the branching pattern you would get if all living things are descended from a common ancestor. So, this common ancestry claim is right at the heart of Darwin's theory. Things were not separately created. They all descended through ordinary biological processes from a common ancestor."[4] All that was required was time and "descent with modification" for one common ancestor to gradually branch off into many different species. Wells continues, "You would expect, as Darwin himself said, thousands of intermediate forms—thousands—and yet *we have none*. Every one of these lines [pointing from one creature to another] are just his theory, but it's presented as though it were a fact."[5]

Instead of what is presented by the textbooks, what do we find in the actual fossil record? We find creatures at all levels, fully formed. We find no transitional forms. We find no evolution in progress. Christian attorney Wendell Bird has even proposed changing the name of creationism to "abrupt appearances" because 1) the courts rule against anything with a Creator, and 2) we find in the fossil record organisms appearing abruptly at every level of the strata.

Wells summarizes, "Almost all of the evidence that we would expect to see there is missing. Darwin himself acknowledged this. He called it a serious problem for his theory."[6] Darwin said, "If it could be demonstrated that any complex organ existed which could not possibly have been formed by numerous, successive slight modifications, my theory would absolutely break down. But I can find out no such case."[7] But nearly 150 years after Darwin wrote *The Origin of the Species*, after the cataloging of more than 100,000,000 fossils in museums around the world, the findings have worked against Darwin's theory, not for it. The fossil record is so important that it's worth examining a bit further before we continue with the "icons of evolution."

In the 1980s a noncreationist, Michael Denton, wrote a book that was devastating to evolution. It was called *Evolution: A Theory in Crisis*. Note what he said in that book about the fossil record as it relates to Darwin:

> . . . the universal experience of paleontology . . . while the rocks have continually yielded new and exciting and even bizarre forms of life . . . what they have never yielded is any of Darwin's myriads of transitional forms. Despite the tremendous increase in geological activity in every corner of the globe and despite the discovery of many strange and hitherto unknown

forms, the infinitude of connecting links has still not been discovered and the fossil record is about as discontinuous as it was when Darwin was writing *Origins*. The intermediates have remained as elusive as ever and their absence remains, a century later, one of the most striking characteristics of the fossil record.[8]

A Fancy Way to Explain the Fossil Record

If you are an evolutionist, how do you explain the inadequate fossil record— this lack of transitional forms? In 1940 Dr. Richard Goldschmidt, professor at the University of California at Berkeley, after spending years and years seeking the missing links in the zoological record of the fossils, came up with a theory. Now, not believing in God, which to him was unthinkable, he devised a new concept of evolution. What was it? He called it the "Hopeful Monster Theory." Essentially it meant that one type of animal would lay an egg and another type of animal—a completely different species—would pop out. Since there appeared to be no evidence for gradual evolution in the fossil record, perhaps it happened quickly. Goldschmidt did not receive a warm reception for his proposal. But about thirty years later his idea was given new life.

A Makeover of the Hopeful Monster Theory

What happened in the succeeding decades since 1940 is that the evidence that had forced Goldschmidt to this conclusion pressed even more heavily upon the evolutionists. Enter two leading scientists—the late Dr. Stephen Jay Gould of Harvard University, who had been one of the most outspoken and prestigious evolutionists of recent times, and Dr. Niles Eldredge, who is the Curator-in-Chief of the permanent exhibition Hall of Biodiversity at the American Museum of Natural History in New York. These have been two extraordinarily prestigious gentlemen. They have come up with a new view (so they have called it) that they began to develop a couple of decades ago and presented at a world meeting of top biological evolutionists at the Field Museum of Natural History in Chicago. What did they call this makeover of the Hopeful Monster theory? "Punctuated Equilibria." Now, I think it is very obvious that "Hopeful Monster Theory" is not the language of science, is it? Not at all. I mean, a view with a name like that is certainly not going to play in Peoria, and it is certainly not going to fly at Dartmouth or Harvard. Therefore it was foreordained to fail. But Gould and Eldredge have certainly given it a Madison Avenue redress and has come up with a title that has scientific pizzazz: "Punctuated Equilibria." You see, that is scientific. And by scientific, it means that nobody knows what they are talking about—it's one of the inside secrets of the scientists.

Well, "Equilibria" means that in the species, the separate species, there is a stasis, or equilibrium, or steadiness—they do not change. Gould said they may add a few more bumps or get a little bigger, but they stay just the same. "Punctuated" means that between the separate species there is a punctuation—a dash, a colon, a semicolon, a period—that separates these separate species, which remain fixed and separate. So what we need is this huge jump, the same type of thing that Goldschmidt was talking about in the Hopeful Monster Theory, now dressed up in new garb and scientific terminology. Still, at its most rudimentary level, an example of what this fancy theory means—in layman's terms—is this: A reptile lays an egg, and out of the egg a bird pops out.

Again, Punctuated Equilibria was expressed at the Field Museum of Natural History to a world meeting of top evolutionists, the majority of evolutionists there accepted this theory. Furthermore, Gould, at that time and in his other writings, had very clearly demolished the concept that there ever have been any intermediate forms, transitional forms, missing links, between the species. Furthermore, Gould said that this new view is spreading throughout the whole world, and that virtually every evolutionist in the last decade or two of the former Soviet Union came to accept some form of punctuated equilibria.

Now, the point I want you to note is that hundreds of millions of students, for the last hundred years and more, have been taught that evolution was an absolute fact. The old textbooks stated that the best established proof and evidence of evolution was the gradual accumulation of micromutations, transitions from one species to the other. This has been the foundation of the whole evolutionary theory.

Now in light of that, hear what Dr. Stephen Jay Gould of Harvard University said in a speech at Hobart College, where he admitted that the fossil record offers no support for gradual change: "Everybody knows the fossil record doesn't provide much evidence for gradualism; it is full of gaps and discontinuities. These gaps are all attributed to the notorious imperfection of the record, but this is not an adequate explanation. The fossil record shows one thing which cannot be attributed to its imperfection; most species don't change. They may get a little bigger or bumpier, but they remain the same species. This remarkable stasis has generally been ignored. It if doesn't agree with your ideas, you don't talk about it . . . the fossil record doesn't show gradual change, and every paleontologist has known that ever since Cuvier."[9]

Gould said elsewhere, "New species almost always appeared suddenly in the fossil record with no intermediate link to ancestors in older rocks of the same region."[10] Thus the fossil record offers no support for gradual change, and yet we have been told that the best evidence for evolution is to be found in the gradual change indicated in the fossil record, that evolution is based upon the intermediate forms that link the various species together. But Gould said these intermediate links do not exist. Nonetheless, Gould was the first to point out that even though this pillar of evolution had crumbled, evolution was still true. Said Gould, "But evolution, like gravitation, is a fact. I don't mean to be dogmatic about it, but it's as much a fact as anything in science."[11] The issue at stake is not whether evolution occurred, but rather how it took place. Let me translate: There is no evidence for evolution, but it is a fact nonetheless, or so he said.

"Punctuated Equilibria" has been catching on worldwide. Thus, to explain away the realities of the fossil record—the missing links are still missing—evolutionists have to resort to a theory along the lines that, for example, a lizard gave birth to a bird.

THE CAMBRIAN EXPLOSION

Have you ever heard of the "Cambrian explosion"? This is more evidence that the fossil record works against Darwin's theory and for creation.

According to evolutionists, the earth supposedly came into existence 4.6 billion years ago. Hundreds of million of years later, life just came to be. Some sort of spark in the primordial slime supposedly began the whole process. Then one form morphed into another form, etc. Again, what do we actually find? According to evolutionists themselves, life actually began during the Cambrian period. Supposedly, this era dates back to about 500,000,000 years ago. Suspend for one moment your opinion about the date of the earth. (I do not accept such old ages—4.6 billion years ago, 500,000,000 years ago, etc. The dating of the earth is always based on certain assumptions—none of which can be proven, all of which would have been thrown completely out of whack by a universal flood.) But again, withhold judgment on that date for the time being. Scientists say that during this Cambrian period, life exploded into being on Planet Earth at every level of the fossil record. There is no progression. There aren't the simple forms on the bottom, slowly evolving to the more complex forms on top. You find organisms and animals fully formed and not transitioning from one type to another. The Cambrian explosion is sometimes called "Biology's Big Bang." It is a trade secret of the evolutionists.

A brilliant young geophysicist, another fellow with the Discovery Institute, Dr. Stephen Meyer, comments on this Cambrian explosion: "At that time, there was a sudden appearance of the majority of what are called the animal body plans, the new animal designs, the ways of organizing body parts, and you get all these brand new kinds of animals that come into the fossil record, very suddenly, without any discernable connection to the much simpler animal forms that existed before."[12] This is why evolutionists have had to resort to unproven positions like the Hopeful Monster Theory or Punctuated Equilibria.

HAECKEL'S EMBRYOS

Returning to the theme of "icons of evolution," Jonathan Wells alerts us to the drawings of embryos by the late-nineteenth to early-twentieth-century German evolutionist Ernst Haeckel. Says Dr. Wells: "Haeckel's embryos are a set of famous drawings that are still found in many biology textbooks. They illustrate a point that Darwin himself considered to be . . . by far the strongest single class of facts in favor of his theory—namely, that vertebrate embryos, that is, the embryos of animals with backbones—look very similar in their early stages. . . . So, Haeckel made some drawings in the 1860s to illustrate this point. Unfortunately, he faked them."[13]

In his book *Icons of Evolution*, Dr. Wells writes, "Haeckel faked his drawings; vertebrate embryos never look as similar as he made them out to be. Furthermore, the stage Haeckel labeled the 'first' is actually midway through development; the similarities he exaggerated are preceded by striking differences in earlier stages of development."[14]

So the reality is that embryos in the early stages look quite different. We now have sonograms and pictures to prove it. Nonetheless, Haeckel's false drawings make their way into textbook after textbook. Wells notes, "Typically, they tell students that these embryos look most similar in their early stages and that this provides good evidence for Darwinian evolution. And it's simply false."[15]

Even an evolutionist has been honest enough to admit this. The late Stephen Jay Gould admitted that Haeckel's drawings were fake: "To cut to the quick of this drama . . . Haeckel had exaggerated the similarities by idealizations and omissions. He also, in some cases—in a procedure that can only be called fraudulent—simply copies the same figure over and over again."[16] He also added, "We do, I think, have the right . . . to be both astonished and ashamed by the century of mindless recycling that has led to the persistence of these drawings in a large number, if not a majority, of modern textbooks."[17]

THE PEPPERED MOTH

Another icon of evolution that Jonathan Wells addresses is that of the peppered moth. This famous little insect is trumpeted in textbook after textbook as a "textbook case" of evolution. Lo and behold, like just about everything else to do with evolution, it turns out to be a fraud. Bernard Kettlewell, a British naturalist, first proclaimed to the world how these peppered moths provided evidence for Darwinian natural selection. The moths allegedly changed color and adapted to their environment in order for their species to survive.

It's interesting to note that even if the peppered moth case were true, it's still an example of micro-evolution—small change within its own kind. You begin with a moth. You have a moth in the middle. You end with a moth. What's the big deal? You don't have a moth becoming some other species or on its way to becoming some other kind.

But even this example of so-called micro-evolution had to be deliberately manufactured—by human design. Like the skull of Piltdown man, somebody had to falsify the facts to try and prove some facet of evolution.

Dr. Wells elaborates: "The theory was that as pollution, soot, darkened the tree trunks, the dark moths were better camouflaged, and the light moths got picked off by birds. It's a very plausible idea. If it were true, it wouldn't bother me in the least."[18] What researchers later discovered, however, was that peppered moths do not normally rest on tree trunks at all.

Apparently, Kettlewell actually staged the photographs by pinning the moths on tree trunks of similar color. So Wells says, "These photos were faked, and they're still there in the textbooks in the 1990s. They're still there now in some textbooks in 2004. And I think this is an outrage. This is not what science is supposed to be, and this is with taxpayer money."[19]

DARWIN'S FINCHES

Another icon of evolution is Darwin's finches. In fact, the way the beaks of these little birds seemed to change and adapt to their natural circumstances was the germ of the idea of Darwinism in the first place. He visited the Galapagos Islands (off the shores of Ecuador, South America) aboard the

H.M.S. Beagle. He noticed that a particular species of finches survived drought because their beaks grew tougher, making them strong enough to eat tough seeds, the only food available. Because of this, Darwin's finches became a prime example of natural selection.

But what do the facts show? Dr. Stephen Meyer notes, "Darwin's finches actually show that the evolutionary change that we can observe is very limited, very modest, and it's cyclical."[20] Dr. Jonathan Wells says, "What the books normally don't tell students is that after the drought, when the rains came back, the average beak size went back to normal. So, there was no net change."[21]

The changes in the finches are another example of micro-evolution, small changes within species. If we can call it that, micro-evolution poses no threat to the Bible. It appears to be documented in different ways. What evolutionists essentially do is extrapolate from these small changes, which can be observed, to larger, broader changes, which can't be observed and haven't been preserved in the fossil record. Why have they not? Because they never happened. Evolution is a giant shell game.

APE TO MEN

A colossal example of an icon of evolution is the idea that man evolved from the ape—or really that man and ape evolved from the same ancestor, some sort of ancient hominid. We see this sequence all the time in different textbooks, showing apelike creatures walking in a sequence until the final one is modern man, *Homo sapiens.* Does this jibe with the facts? Jonathan Wells observes, "When we see pictures like this, a nice neat progression from some apelike creature to a modern human, these pictures are largely imaginary. The fossils, which are very fragmentary, don't give us the data, the information we would need to reconstruct these creatures and the data that we do have from the fossils don't justify this kind of nice, neat progression here. This is just a story. It's a story into which certain pieces of certain fossils are put to make the story sound scientific."[22] The skulls and skeletons found are either ape or man. The missing links are perpetually missing. Dr. Wells has made a significant contribution to the debate through his wonderful book, *Icons of Evolution.*

The late Dr. Gould even admitted the lack of evidence for human evolution. He observed, "Look at human evolution. There is no evidence that the increase in size of the human brain is one of these slow and steady accumulative adaptive sequential advantageous changes, although I'm sure most of you believe it."[23] Again, this doesn't mean he didn't think that evolution happened; he was just honest enough to admit there was no evidence for it having happened. And we're the ones accused of "blind faith."

"DARWIN'S BLACK BOX"

The amount of scientific information Darwin had at his beck and call pales in comparison to what we know. Darwin wrote about the simple cell, assuming that it wasn't too complex. We now know that the "simple cell" is anything but simple. Microbiologists such as Dr. Michael Behe, professor at LeHigh University in Pennsylvania and author of the book *Darwin's Black Box*, have said that even the simplest cell that exists is so complex that it contains a great deal of information.

When Behe's book first came out, the coauthor of this book, Jerry Newcombe, interviewed him for our radio station (WAFG, Ft. Lauderdale). Newcombe asked him to explain things in terms of how much information would exist if it were translated into volumes of the *Encyclopedia Britannica*. How much information do we find not in the simplest cell of the human body, but in the simplest cell of the simplest organism? Dr. Behe said that even the simplest organism, a certain type of amoeba, contains at least one volume's worth of information (again, using the *Encyclopedia Britannica* as the model). But how about the simplest cell of the human body? How much information do we find there? Behe said that the average cell of the human body has at least two to three dozen volumes worth of information. We are "fearfully and wonderfully made" (Psalm 139:14). We are not "accidental twigs."

Michael Behe says, "It turns out that to Darwin and to nineteenth century scientists, the cell was a black box. They knew it was there; they knew it did wonderful things, like grow and metabolize and replicate, but they hadn't the foggiest idea how it worked."[24] Behe says the living cell is a masterpiece of design. It could not possibly have originated by chance: "In Darwin's day, scientists were vaguely aware that there were things such as cells, but most of them thought that they were like little pieces of Jell-O, little microscopic pieces of protoplasm. And in the middle of the nineteenth century, some scientists even thought that cells and life could kind of ooze up from the ocean bottom, just spontaneously, because they thought the cell was simple, so they thought that simple processes could process life."[25]

Behe shows in his book how each cell contains such incredible complexity that it is like a mini-factory with microscopic machines, interactive and interdependent parts, and assembly instructions. Each cell's nucleus contains lines of code or information we call DNA.

Stephen Meyer notes, "One approach is to try to explain the origin of information by chance, by the random shuffling of the parts of the DNA molecule. But that would be kind of like throwing Scrabble letters onto a table and hoping that they spelled out the Declaration of Independence. There's so much information in DNA that it's simply too improbable to think that purely random processes would produce the information that you need."[26]

God has spoken to us through the complexity of the universe. The more scientists study it with an open mind, the more likely they are to come to believe in Him. We close this chapter with the story of a science professor who abandoned evolution when confronted with the evidence.

THE LATE, GREAT DICK LUMSDEN[27]

To the late Dr. Richard Lumsden, former professor of biology at Tulane University and Medical School and the former dean of the graduate school, evolution was science, whereas creation was merely religion. He taught as much to his students.

Dr. Richard Lumsden stated, "What I would try to get across is that science is science. Science deals with the real world, with real phenomena. We don't bring into such discussions inferences of supernatural phenomena. Phenomena that would be above the natural—that would not subscribe to natural laws and so forth."

Dr. Lumsden, who studied at Tulane, Harvard, and Rice, couldn't believe it when the Louisiana state legislature passed a law (in the early 1980s) that if evolution were taught in the public school classroom, equal time had to be made for creation science. "My reaction to that was just total consternation. How in the world, first of all, could rational scientists seriously entertain this, again in my view then, supernaturalistic mythology, which had really no place in a science curriculum? Then, again, another point was: Who are these people telling us, Ph.D.-level scientists, how to teach and what to teach regarding science? So I just thought the whole thing was absolutely absurd and that it was an infringement of academic freedom. I was prompted at that point to give a lecture on the origin of life. The idea was to present an argument for the origin of cells, ergo life, and the evolutionist view is that chemicals were spontaneously generated in a primordial soup, if you will. And in the meantime, giving creation its due with as much mockery as I could summon."

So one day he gave a dogmatic lecture, waxing eloquent on behalf of the dogma of evolution. One of his remarks was, "Truly, in the beginning was the word, but the word was hydrogen." After that class, one of his graduate students came up to him and said that was a great lecture, as always. Lumsden points out, "Well, that got my attention. Flattery always did. And she said, 'but I have some questions.' And indeed she did. She had a legal pad, and I could see line after line after line."

So they made an appointment, which ended up lasting longer than anticipated. It was supposed to last twenty minutes, but it stretched out to three hours, with neither of them thinking about the time. The appointment also ended up changing Dr. Lumsden's life.

She said to him at the outset, "Now I'm not here to challenge anything. I just want to get my science straight."

"That's fair enough."

She said, "Last month you taught how mutations were genetic disasters. How, by natural selection, could they randomly produce new and better structures?"

He responded, "You've got a good point there. That's a good question. Good question. I'll probably have to think more about that."

She asked, "Aren't the odds of the random assembly of genes mathematically impossible?"

He said, "You've had your share of mathematics. Let's see if we can't figure that out. We wouldn't predict it to happen, but that doesn't mean it didn't happen." After calculating the odds, he paused, realizing that the probability of life just happening by chance was not merely unlikely but impossible. He regained his composure and said, "These are impossible numbers, but the fact remains: we're here. And in reality, the only way we could have gotten here is through the evolutionary process. So the fact that we're here really proves evolution, doesn't it?" (Note the circular logic he used to make his point.)

She moved on to the next question, constantly probing, making him think through the logical implications of what he had been dogmatically teaching as fact. She asked, "Where exactly in the fossil record is the evidence for progressive evolution—the transitional forms between the major groups?"

Dr. Lumsden said, "You know, most of them, come to think of it, are fully formed kinds in their own right. They're not really transitional. Well, Darwin said we'd find them or his theory is kaput."

She continued with the pleasant grilling. "The law of thermodynamics has things continually becoming more disorganized. So how does evolution go the other way?"

Puffing on his pipe, he tried to finagle his way out of that one too.

She probed, "How does evolution fit with the fundamentals of information theory?"

He said, "Hmmmm. You know, I've had a problem with that myself."

Looking back on this pleasant but embarrassing confrontation, Dr. Lumsden said, "I could buffalo a student when I felt myself getting a little bit in trouble. I had had a few years experience at this. It's a trade secret, but for the first time maybe in my life in explaining various facets of evolution theory, I began to listen to what I was saying, and what I was saying wasn't making very good scientific sense. Not only were we talking about a mathematical impossibility, we were talking about a physical and chemical impossibility, which gave me pause. This conversation with the young lady went on for approximately three hours, during which time I'm answering, I'm listening to my own responses (and trying not to betray this to the student), I was rapidly concluding that this is not making good scientific sense. What I'm telling this young lady, and what I told the students this morning is not good science.

"It dawned on me right then and there that evolution was bankrupt as a scientific theory. Well, if that were so, if life did not originate by naturalistic, materialistic, spontaneous process, what was the alternative explanation? 'Oh, my God.' And I said it then, not in blasphemy, but in awe. What happened that afternoon was first of all a mortal embarrassment to me as a professor. Professing to be wise, the professor was made a fool. And then, secondly, with the realization that, 'Hey, God exists and God created' was that experience of fear. Now, that's enough to turn a corner in anyone's life. I conversed with many of my colleagues in biology and chemistry and played the devil's advocate to them, just as this young lady had stuck it to me, as it were. And they were no better at explaining these observations than I had been to the young lady."

After much study and soul-searching, Dr. Lumsden became a creationist first and then a Christian. "One event led to the other, and the culmination was finding myself before a saving altar on my knees, that stiff-neck broken in obedience, asking Jesus to come into my life to be my Lord and personal savior." And so Dr. Richard Lumsden, former evolutionary professor, became a committed creationist—because of the scientific evidence. He has since openly debated evolutionists. He feels that in light of the great advances of science in the twentieth century, evolution is no longer tenable: "The evidence of science—the best in paleontology, the best in biochemistry, the best in genetics, and so on—is all compelling for creation. Creation theory does not rest on some purely metaphysical principles. It rests on the same science that evolution theory would rest on, except that the better explanation is creation, not naturalistic, materialistic, stochastic (or random) evolutionary process."

CONCLUSION

Where is the evidence for evolution, the scientific evidence? Ask people to marshal it, and chances are, they will bring forth an example of micro-evolution—some small insignificant change that is meaningless. Chances are also good that they will bring forth some sort of example that has already been disproved—they will bring forth what Jonathan Wells calls an "icon of evolution." A truly Christian world-and-life view can see through bogus science, which is what evolution is.

4

A NOBLE ORIGIN, A NOBLE DESTINY

When I look at your heavens, the work of your fingers, the moon and the stars, which you have set in place, what is man that you are mindful of him, and the son of man that you care for him?

PSALM 8:3-4

Think about it: "Either we are accidental byproducts of a purposeless process, or we are created in the image of God, deliberately, by design."[1] So says scientist Dr. Jonathan Wells. What are we? Your starting point determines your concluding point. If man is ultimately the by-product of time and chance and random forces, then no matter how some fancy talkers may sugarcoat the picture, we are worthless. But if humankind is some unique creation, designed by a loving Creator for a specific purpose, then we are special. What are we—man or ape?

THE WAR ON TELEOLOGY

Evolution from the beginning has been at all-out war with teleology. ("Teleology" means "the study of purpose"—the view that anything has an end for which it was made or created.)

Keep in mind what our Declaration of Independence says: God has created us equally, and our Creator has endowed us with inalienable rights. Without a Creator, there are no inalienable rights. We would have only those rights that are bestowed by the state. And the state that bestows them with one hand can withdraw them with the other, as every tyrannical state down through history has demonstrated.

The Western Christian view of man has always held that man is here for a purpose. The Christian view has been summed up in the first question of the Shorter Catechism of the Westminster Confession of Faith: "What is the chief end of man?" The answer is: "Man's chief end is to glorify God and to enjoy Him forever." The evolutionist would not question whether that is the chief end of man or some other end, but would say there is no end or purpose in any man's life at all, which is precisely what the evolutionary view of life has produced.

If life has no purpose, it has no meaning, and consequently it has no significance. Many in our culture are choosing to be perpetually entertained—lest they think through the implications of a meaningless life. When life has lost its purpose, meaning, and significance, be prepared for an epidemic of suicide, drugs, alcoholism, and maybe even a plunge into some form of Eastern mysticism, where a person might find some sort of irrational significance for life, or at least a feeling that will make the drabness of a meaningless existence bearable for a time.

As we continue to explore a Christian world-and-life view, we come next to the question of origins as it relates to the value of human life. Do we have a noble origin and therefore a noble destiny? Or an ignoble origin with an ignoble destiny?

THE COLLEGE QUESTIONS

Do you remember the old college questions: Where did I come from? Why am I here? How should I live? Where am I going? Who am I? Those are some of the most important questions any person is ever going to have to answer—in or out of college. If you have never wrestled with them, then God apparently wasted a brain on you, because if a person doesn't examine such tremendous questions as those, what is he living for at all?

There are today basically two different sets of answers to those questions—diametrically antithetical one to the other. Consider the answers given by the person who believes in creation—the creationist.

• *Where did I come from?* I came from the heart and mind of the almighty and omnipotent and omniscient God. I have been made a little lower than the angels.

• *Who am I?* I am a child of the King, a prince of the royal realm.

• *Why am I here?* I am here to serve and glorify the Almighty and to enjoy Him forever.

• *How should I live?* I should live according to the commandments He has given to me in His Word, which are designed for my good and my advancement.

• *Where am I going?* I am going to Paradise, which is beyond my comprehension. "What no eye has seen, nor ear heard, nor the heart of man imagined . . . God has prepared for those who love him" (1 Corinthians 2:9).

The Christian—the creationist—has a noble origin and a noble destiny. And in between, his life is crammed full of meaning, value, significance, and purpose.

But the other set of answers are those given by the adherents to evolution—those who trust in the system that is taught in almost every public school in this country, or practically in the world today—a set of answers that are being learned by nearly all of our students from kindergarten through graduate school.

I talked recently to a student who attends a college in Minnesota. He told how his biology teacher, from the very beginning, said that his purpose in the class was to show students that evolution was the way things are and the way things should be and that he was going to do his very best to persuade Christians to abandon their faith and to adopt the "faith" of evolution. Evolution is faith, not science, as many of the best-known evolutionists have admitted many times.

Dr. L. Harrison Matthews (a noted evolutionist), who wrote the "Introduction" in the 1971 edition of Darwin's *Origin of the Species*, said: "The fact of evolution is the backbone of biology, and biology is thus in the peculiar position of being a science founded on an unproved theory—is it then a science or faith? Belief in the theory of evolution is thus exactly parallel to belief in special creation—both are concepts which believers know to be true but neither, up to the present, has been capable of proof."[2]

Evolutionists have a very different set of answers to the questions, Where did I come from? Why am I here? Where am I going? Bertrand Russell, one of the twentieth century's leading philosophers, was an atheist, an unbeliever, and an evolutionist. He wrote a book entitled *Why I Am Not a Christian*. (He failed to mention in his book his multiple adulteries, his repeated fornications, his seduction of the daughters of his hosts, and many other sins too numerous to mention, which are the real reason he wasn't a Christian.) Russell gave these answers to the college questions: "We started somewhere, we don't know where; we are here, we don't know why; we are going to some great oblivion, we know not whither."[3]

Those are the answers to the basic questions of life that Russell has given to us. And yet, in spite of the fact that evolutionists have nothing to offer, they have completely dominated our world today.

IS THE ISSUE SIGNIFICANT?

Is the doctrine of creation, as opposed to evolution, important? Well, the very first phrase in the first sentence of the first chapter of the first book of the Bible says that it is: "In the beginning, God created the heavens and the earth" (Genesis 1:1). That is where God began, and that is where all of life and theology and action ultimately have their beginning. Ernst Mayr, professor at Harvard and one of our country's leading evolutionists, has written: "Man's worldview today is dominated by the knowledge that the universe, the stars, the earth, and all living things have evolved through a long history that was not foreordained or programmed." What is evolution, according to Mayr? It is "man's worldview today."[4]

Rene Dubos, in *American Scientist* magazine, says: "Most enlightened persons now accept as fact that everything in the cosmos—from heavenly bodies to human beings—has developed and continues to develop through evolutionary processes."[5]

Another scientist said that evolution is the totality of reality. The totality of reality is God, and for such adherents as these, evolution is their God—as Darwin himself, one time, candidly admitted.

What kind of a view of man is given to us by evolutionists? Is man a noble creature with a noble origin and a noble destiny? Here is what the evolutionists say:

• "Man Is A Machine" (French philosopher Julien Offray de la Mettrie).[6]

• ". . . the outcome of accidental collocations of atoms" (British atheist Bertrand Russell).[7]

• Man is no more significant than "a baboon or a grain of sand" (Oliver Wendell Holmes, Jr.).[8]

This is what man is to them. Next to nothing at all. Yet this is what students are being indoctrinated with from kindergarten all the way through graduate school.

A man by the name of Charles Potter started a Humanist church. Where one might expect to find a cross or crucifix, he erected a statue entitled "The Chrysalis." A chrysalis is that from which the butterfly emerges, but here the statue consisted of a naked man emerging chrysalis-like from an ape-skin.

As evolution continues to be taught as fact, it is no wonder students today are plagued with so many problems and doubts. It is no wonder self-worth has gone right down the tube, and millions of students are trying to discover some sort of worthwhile self-image. Believing you are nothing but an accidental happening in the slime doesn't create much self-worth. Yet this is what our students are being told over and over. Thus the honorable place that had been given to man is quickly aborted, and man is dragged down into the slime.

Author Erwin Lutzer said, "an evolutionary view of man leads to frightening conclusions."[9] If you think this is just a theory in a biology classroom, let me say that it applies not only to every academic discipline but to everything else, including international relations.

For example, all the tyrannical dictators of the twentieth century were ardent evolutionists. Every one of them! This includes Mao Tse-tung, who was responsible for the killing of at least 55,000,000 Chinese. Some estimates put the number at 72,000,000. Either statistic gives Mao the dubious honor of being the greatest mass-murderer in history. He outdoes Stalin and Hitler too.

In his classic novel 1984, George Orwell said of the future of man if then-present totalitarian trends continued (namely, Stalinism): "If you want a picture of the future, imagine a boot stamping on a human face—forever." Not a very pretty picture. But when God is removed, and man follows only an evolutionary view of man, we lose our freedom.[10]

What we believe about man has very real consequences and will generally affect how we treat our fellowman. May I say that the view of evolution was directly responsible for about 200,000,000 deaths in the twentieth century alone. This is an issue of tremendous significance.

THE PERFECT MURDER

Two young men were born with silver spoons in their mouths—both the sons of millionaires. They were students at the University of Chicago and thoroughly Nietzschean, which means they were evolutionary as well. They believed in Friedrich Nietzsche's concepts of the superman. In fact, they believed they were it—at least one of them thought the other was the superman. They decided to do the type of thing students in universities do to show their intellectual superiority. Did they decide to make A pluses? No; they decided to commit the perfect murder—to find a fourteen-year-old boy and kill him . . . because, after all, what is life? Nathan Leopold was very disappointed to discover that his friend Richard Loeb was not Nietzsche's superman, as he had thought him to be. The two were caught, tried, and sentenced to life in prison. Loeb was even murdered in prison about a decade later. Following Nietzsche was a disaster for them.

Here is how author Hal Higdon put it in his suspenseful book on the case, *The Crime of the Century*: "Maremont [a fellow student] frequently argued philosophy with Leopold, particularly with ideas of the German philosopher Friedrich Wilhelm Nietzsche, who died in 1900, but whose ideas had become faddish on college campuses in the twenties. In Nietzsche's philosophy, the goal of the evolutionary struggle for survival would be the emergence of an idealized superior, dominating man. Leopold thought his friend Richard Loeb came as close to being that man as anyone he had met. 'Leopold believed Nietzsche literally,' Maremont would recall. 'He was convinced Loeb was a superman.'"[11]

What is human life worth to an evolutionist? It is nothing but junk. As Wolf Larsen, an evolutionist, said, "Life? Bah. It has no value. Of the cheap things, it is the cheapest."[12] It is disposable.

BELIEFS DETERMINE ACTIONS

How we believe and what we believe about our fellowmen will determine how we act toward them. We wonder about many decisions of the Supreme Court of the United States in the twentieth century. One of our Supreme Court Justices (and by no means the only one), Oliver Wendell Holmes, Jr., highly regarded, said, "I see no reason for attributing to man a significant difference in kind from that which he belongs to."[13]

You are just not worth anything at all, folks . . . no more than a grain of sand, which can be taken up by the handfuls and thrown away. That is what evolutionists have been doing throughout the twentieth and twenty-first centuries—just taking human life by the handfuls and throwing it away because it has no real value. Our mighty brain, which Zig Ziglar has pointed out is capable of containing more information than the millions of volumes in the Library of Congress, if it were built by human beings would be larger than the Empire State Building and would require more electricity to run than would power a city of thousands and cost billions of dollars; and yet this man-made brain would not be able to originate one single thought—which we can do in the blink of an eye.[14]

But the evolutionist view disagrees. As the late Harvard behavioral psychologist B. F. Skinner, one of the leading movers and shakers of human thought in the last century, said, "Thought is, so to speak, a 'secretion of the brain,' as bile is a secretion of the liver."[15] You see, it is not nearly as significant as you thought it was. Skinner's book is titled *Beyond Freedom and Dignity* because, you see, you have no freedom and you surely have no dignity.

"Life, bah. . . . Of the cheap things, it is the cheapest." Do you wonder how people can do the kinds of things they do to other people? It is because of what they have been taught and what they have come to believe. "For as [a man] thinks in his heart, so is he" (Proverbs 23:7, NKJV).

Dr. Francis Schaeffer summed up the evolutionary view of life when he said, "The concept of man's dignity is gone. We are in the post-Christian world. Man is junk. If the embryo is in the way, ditch it. If the old person is in the way, ditch him. If you're in the way . . ."[16]

Evolution can only create an environment of meaninglessness for life and worthlessness for man. Life has no purpose. It is just an accident that took place in the slime or in the clay. You are just not worth much of anything at all. How different that is from what God offers.

Fortunately, some have been honest enough to admit how they feel about all of that. Skeptic W. O. Saunders, an evolutionist and unbeliever, said this about the materialist or unbeliever:

> For him there is only the grave and the persistence of matter. All he can see beyond the grave is the disintegration of the protoplasm and psychoplasm of which his body and its personality are come. . . . But in this material view I find no ecstasy or happiness. Is this the end and all of human life and endeavor? . . . Therefore, would I try to convey to your mind and heart something of the wistfulness and loneliness of the man who does not believe in God.[17]

That is what unbelievers have to offer. And we wonder why so many young people are killing themselves?

In the first chapter, we alluded to a remark from Albert Camus, a famous French author. He said, "There is but one truly serious philosophical problem [in the twentieth century]." Only one? There's only one philosophical problem, only one question that you should be directing your mind toward? Would you like to understand what is at the pinnacle of the whole evolutionary-atheistic view of life? It is not merely the most important—it is the only significant question of our time, said Camus. "It is," he said, "suicide."

Have you been studying "the only significant question" as you should? Let me assure you that students in school are. In our public schools, students are being taught how to write suicide notes. They are being shown a variety of methods of committing suicide and given recommendations about which ones are preferable. They are told about and taught and indeed build models of their coffins. The Bible says that those who hate God love death, and that is what all of this is: just death and more death—the death of human aspirations, the death of human dignity, the death of human meaning, the death of significance, and the death of all future hopes. As Dante warned those entering hell: "Abandon all hope, ye who enter here."[18] The fruit of evolution is hopelessness, which is a characteristic of hell.

Probably this has never been more eloquently expressed than by one of the great unbelievers of the early part of the twentieth century, Robert Ingersoll, the leading atheistic evolutionist and skeptic of his day. His brother, whom he loved probably more than anything in this world, suddenly died, and his brother was an unbeliever, so no clergyman could be called. How does an atheist have a funeral? Well, extraordinarily eloquent Robert, standing beside his brother's grave, preached the funeral sermon himself. His words are probably some of the most poignant and saddest I have ever heard:

> Whether in mid-sea or among the breakers of the farther shore, a wreck must mark at last the end of each and all. And every life, no matter if its every hour is rich with love and every moment jeweled with joy, will, at its close, become a tragedy, as sad, and deep, and dark as can be woven of the warp and woof of mystery and death. . . . Life is a narrow vale between the cold and barren peaks of two eternities. We strive in vain to look beyond the heights. We cry aloud, and the only answer is the echo of our wailing cry.[19]

CONCLUSION

This is what unbelief offers to man. I thank God that in His Word we read: "[W]hat is man that you are mindful of him? . . . Yet you have made him a little lower than the heavenly beings. . . . You have given him dominion over the works of your hands; you have put all things under his feet" (Psalm 8:4-6). What is man? He is a prince in a royal realm. His origin is from the heart and mind of God, and his destiny is in paradise forever. ". . . nor [has] the heart of man imagined, what God has prepared for those who love him" (1 Corinthians 2:9). This is the glorious origin and destiny of all who trust in Christ. When you consider the choice, it seems as if there is only one logical option. When you consider further that the evidence for evolution, as we have seen in the previous chapter, has been collapsing of late, it seems like an easier choice still.

Because of the widespread acceptance of evolution, we see how life has become cheap. For the next several chapters, we want to explore life and death issues from a Christian perspective. As we attempt to Christianize the sphere of the world, we need to not only reclaim a biblical understanding of origins and the sciences, but we also need a biblical understanding of the value of human life itself.

PART II

THE SPHERE

OF

HUMANITY

Introduction to Christianizing the Sphere of Humanity

The Christian worldview of life is simply that God is the giver and taker of life. He decides.

Jesus said, "Truly, I say to you, as you did it to one of the least of these my brothers, you did it to me" (Matthew 25:40). These words of Jesus Christ in His parable of the sheep and the goats changed the view of human life for the last 2,000 years. The Christian view of life is not only that God has made and planned and given meaning to each human life, but that Christ takes every act of kindness as a personal service to Himself. Because of this, Christians have helped their fellowman from the beginning.

As the godless view of man gains more and more acceptance, we see human life cheapened at every level of society—from the killing of the unborn to the killing of the elderly. Why? Because if God didn't make us, and we're nothing, then who cares what we do to each other?

Many of the conflicts we see played out in the streets of America and on battlefields in the desert boil down to this: a clash of worldviews.

THE BIBLE AND LIFE

I call heaven and earth to witness against you today, that I have set before you life and death, blessing and curse. Therefore choose life, that you and your offspring may live.

DEUTERONOMY 30:19

✦

Is human life cheap? It depends on which worldview prevails—the Christian one that sees man made in God's image, or the pagan one that sees us as the product of time plus chance plus impersonal forces of nature.

Read the papers today and you're liable to come across some new, grisly story. I remember hearing about a vicious crime a few years ago—and there have been many—when a group of young teenagers in America stabbed an immigrant ice-cream truck driver. The poor man was just trying to make a living in his newly-adopted country. Instead, he was stabbed by inner-city toughs, who danced around him as he writhed on the ground, slowly dying, while the teens helped themselves to ice cream bars and other goodies from his truck. How cheap human life has become!

Life has indeed become cheap in modern America.

This has had many manifestations: abortion, infanticide, the push for cloning and destroying embryonic stem cells for their body parts, homicide, suicide, euthanasia.

Think about all the gratuitous violence that Hollywood pumps out or that rappers celebrate. Inner-city life in many places in this country approximates a war zone. Why has life been so cheapened? We believe there are several factors to this, but one of them is abortion. As Mother Teresa so pointedly asked years ago, "And if we accept that a *mother* can kill *her own child*, how can we tell others not to kill?" (emphasis ours).[1] That's a great question.

Consider the example of modern rappers. Usher became the number one rapper of 2004. Rapper Joe Budden did a remix of Usher's song "Confessions." This remix includes a scenario in which one guy tells his girlfriend that if she's pregnant, she better abort the baby. Otherwise he'd deliver a powerful blow to her stomach to make sure it's "leakin'."[2] This is how cheap human life has become in some parts of our culture—assault and abortion are celebrated in song.

Also in 2004, Planned Parenthood came out with a T-shirt for sale. Emblazoned on the shirt was a proclamation that I'm sure girls and ladies were proud to tell the world: "I had an abortion."[3] As we get further and further from God, life becomes cheaper and cheaper.

As we look at a Christian worldview in various spheres of human existence, we come now to the sphere of life and death. Even many professing Christians have a sub-Christian view of human life.

In the next several chapters we want to explore some of these life-related issues. In this chapter we will look at an overview of the Bible on life and death. We will consider the sanctity-of-life ethic derived from the Bible vs. the quality-of-life ethic of today. Next we will look at what can happen when a previously Christian culture chooses death over life. Namely, we will glean a few lessons from Nazi Germany. We will also look at cloning and embryonic stem cell research. Finally, we will also consider the Bible and suicide.

Today the word *choice* has been distorted to mean death. In the Old Testament, God spoke to His people through Moses about choice. He said, "Choose life." What this really meant was that by choosing Him, they were choosing life. This is something we believe God would say to America today: *Choose life*. That includes how we view abortion.

In the Image of God

The starting point of all discussions about the value of human life from a biblical perspective can be found in the book of Genesis. (That's the way many starting points can be found.)

> *So God created man in his own image,*
> *in the image of God he created him;*
> *male and female he created them. (Genesis 1:27)*

That we are made in God's own image has become a cliché. Therefore it has lost some of its punch. But this is a radical concept. The implications that flow from this starting point—how we view the value of man—are immense and immeasurable.

Consider the issue of abortion in the light of this well-known passage from the Psalms:

> *For you formed my inward parts; you knitted me together in my mother's womb. I praise you, for I am fearfully and wonderfully made. (Psalm 139:13-14a)*

If this isn't a strong declaration for the unborn child, for the rights of the fetus (which is simply Latin meaning "unborn child"), I don't know what is.

Jeremiah also reiterates the theme of God doing something for him while he was yet in the womb. "Before I formed you in the womb I knew you, and before you were born I consecrated you" (Jeremiah 1:5). God consecrates people, not blobs of tissue.

In the Gospel of Luke we read about Elizabeth being pregnant with John the Baptist and also about her cousin, Mary, who was carrying Jesus. The baby in Elizabeth's womb leaped for joy when Mary came to see her with Jesus in her womb. Things don't have joy!

You never hear a woman say that the fetus inside her leaped for joy. It is always the babe or baby. The Greek word for *baby* in Luke is *brephos*. What does that mean? The same term was used to describe Jesus, the babe lying in a manger, clothed in swaddling clothes. That was a baby, not a tumor.

SANCTITY OF LIFE VS. THE QUALITY OF LIFE

At the heart of the conflict over abortion is a battle between worldviews. Is human life just the product of time plus chance, or are we uniquely made in the image of God? I would like for you to grasp, if you can, a little bit more of the overall context, significance, and undoubted consequences of the direction and course being taken today. There is a great clash in our country between the concept of sanctity of life and the concept of quality of life. People have heard and read many such discussions, but I am afraid that most do not grasp the full implication of what that means.

SANCTITY OF LIFE

The concept of sanctity of life is a spiritual concept; it is a religious concept. The word *sanctity*, which comes from the Latin word *sanctitas*, from *sanctus*, means "holy" or "sacred unto God," inviolable, that which God has declared is of great value. It is, therefore, a spiritual concept.

However, for a humanist or an atheist or an unbeliever of almost any kind, there is no such thing as sanctity of life. Unless there is a God who has given us a spirit and who sanctifies us, there cannot be a sanctity-of-life ethic.

Carl Sagan said there is not and never has been anything in the universe but matter. If one has that kind of a totally non-spiritual view, we have in the quality of life simply a physical understanding of life. Now, we may indeed say that one person has come closer to the perfect ideal of human life than another person, or that one is somewhere in between; but if every soul has been created by God and has infinite value, then there is no degree of qualification between the two.

Consider again—in this light—the Declaration of Independence: "We hold these truths to be self-evident, that all men are created equal, that they are endowed by their Creator with certain unalienable rights, that among these are Life . . ." In contrast, it is only from a purely atheistic, humanistic, secularistic view that one can determine that a life is to be valued solely upon the physical characteristics of that life.

THE SLIPPERY SLOPE

Outside Atlanta is the famous Stone Mountain. Perhaps you have been there and even have climbed it. If you go there, you will notice a long, slow incline to the top of the mountain. From there it begins to gradually decline for about a hundred feet and then falls off precipitously hundreds of feet to the ground below. Back at the top is a fence barrier to keep people from going down that very long and very gradual decline. Those who ignore this warning tend to go just a little bit farther to get a better look over the edge. Before they realize it, their feet are slipping and sliding. Then they plunge into the air and land hundreds of feet below. Many people have fallen off that mountain and died as a result. That slippery slope leads to the precipice and to death. Today our society is right now a good way down such a slope.

Dr. C. Everett Koop, former U.S. Surgeon General, said there is something that the abortionists, the infanticide promoters, and the euthanasia proponents always do: They take a few extreme examples and use them to gain sympathy for ideas and practices that later are not limited to extreme cases. For example, what have we heard about abortion? The poor girl who is the victim of rape or is the victim of incest—surely, you're going to allow her to have an abortion. Using such examples over and over again, they have succeeded in making abortion legal. Now over 40,000,000 American babies have been killed, less than 2 percent of which had anything to do with rape or incest. The same thing is now happening with euthanasia and infanticide.

DELIBERATE STARVATION

Some of our modern courts have rendered decisions on life and death. They have taken us another step down a slippery slope, the courts having already decided that it is legal to let a person die. There is a great difference between letting a person die naturally and causing him to die by starvation. I would agree that we need not go to heroic mechanical means of keeping a person alive for many, many years when he simply has machines breathing for him and making his heart beat, and he really is not "alive." The person may or may not die in the near future if he is allowed to do so naturally, but he will most certainly die if food and water are removed. He is then made to die slowly.

Let me say, it is a very short step between making a person die by starvation and making him (or her) die by a legal and lethal injection of poison. More than a decade ago philosopher Dr. Helga Kuhse, speaking to 500 participants in a euthanasia conference, said that once you show people how painful it is to starve to death, they will gladly accept lethal injections "in the patient's best interest."[4] That is a small step down that hill.

QUALITY OF LIFE

Quality of life is a physical concept. No one can look at another and determine the quality of that person's soul. If life is merely molecules in motion, then we can have a quality-of-life ethic. But if we believe there is an infinite, eternal, and unchangeable God who is a Spirit and has given us everlasting spirits, and if we have an inalienable right to life, we cannot buy into that kind of an ethic.

Here is the conflict in its brutal simplicity: the Judeo-Christian concept of life vs. the humanistic, evolutionary view. The humanists may pride themselves on their creation of a new man, but make no mistake—take their perspective to the nth degree and you have one group of people deciding whether others should be able to live or die.

Perhaps the battleground where this clash of worldviews is the hottest today is in the abortion chambers across the land.

"FORMER FETUSES, UNITE"

You certainly can find all types at a public protest. You can also find all sorts of strange signs. Coauthor Jerry Newcombe went to a massive pro-life rally in Washington, D.C. many years ago and will never forget one of those signs at that rally. A young man held high a handmade poster proclaiming,

"Former Fetuses, Unite!" It may seem comical, it may seem so obvious, but it's true: We're all former fetuses.

This reminds me of a quip from Ronald Reagan. During one of the 1980 presidential debates between him and Jimmy Carter, he was asked by a reporter why he did not support the pro-choice position. In his characteristic folksy manner, the future President declared, "Well, I happen to notice that everyone who is pro-choice has already been born." Good point.

HARDENED HEARTS

Father John Powell, long-time professor at Loyola University (Chicago), once said that when a woman has an abortion, she either becomes guilty or hard—as in hardhearted. That's a great insight. While millions of women who are "post-abortive" suffer in silence, millions of others celebrate abortion as if it's a good thing.

Even the most determined pro-abortion-rights person will admit that having an abortion is difficult and gut-wrenching. Have we become so callused about such a sensitive issue? Indeed, some people try to make it accepted by trivializing it. This reminds me of the poem by Theo Kogan on the web site PunkVoter.com (reproduced here verbatim):

> As a person and as a WOMAN I value my freedom, whether its the free-
> dom to speak out,
>> to look the way I want,
>> live the way I want, create art and music,
>> choosing what I want to do with my body,
>> whether it's my hair color,
>> tattoos, piercing,
>> squeezing a zit,
>> plucking a hair or having an abortion.[5]

In other words, aborting your unborn child is no more consequential than pulling out an unwanted hair. How sad this is.

A MOST VOLATILE ISSUE

As we examine a Christian world-and-life view, we cannot gloss over the divisive issue of abortion. Cal Thomas says, "Abortion is the most volatile issue that has faced America since the civil war."[6] The abortion decision has changed how Americans look at human life. It substituted the pagan-humanistic view—the quality-of-life ethic—for the Judeo-Christian view—the sanctity of life.

Part of what made the abortion decision so bad is that it converts physicians from healers to killers. Dr. William J. Brennan, professor at St. Louis University, points out just how scary this shift is:

> The perversion of medicine in the service of killing is accompanied by a redefinition of barbaric acts as valid medical procedures. An astounding bit of alchemy sets in whereby the physician healer not only becomes a killer, but in the process of this most radical of transformations, destruction loses its most repulsive features and becomes incorporated into the fabric of respectable medical practice.[7]

"AN ACT OF RAW JUDICIAL POWER"

We should never forget that when the decision came down, not all the Supreme Court justices agreed with *Roe v. Wade*. Justice Byron White, who was appointed by President John F. Kennedy, dissented on the decision and called it "an act of raw judicial power."[8] Justice William Rehnquist (who was promoted to be the Chief Justice in the mid-1980s) also dissented.

An interesting fact of the *Roe v. Wade* decision is that it purports to be based on the Constitution. What provisions of the Constitution were cited to make the case? Where do we find the right for a woman to "terminate a pregnancy"? Where do we find the "right to privacy"? We don't.

Here are the two portions of the Constitution that are cited as the "constitutional basis" for *Roe v. Wade*:

> Amendment #9: "The enumeration in the Constitution, of certain rights, shall not be construed to deny or disparage others retained by the people."
>
> Amendment #14: "SECTION 1. All persons born or naturalized in the United States, and subject to the jurisdiction thereof, are citizens of the United States and of the State wherein they reside. No state shall make or enforce any law which shall abridge the privileges or immunities of citizens of the United States; nor shall any State deprive any person of life, liberty, or property, without due process of law; nor deny to any person within its jurisdiction the equal protection of the laws."

So where exactly is the provision in the Constitution that gives women the right to kill the unborn? Michael Farris is a constitutional attorney, homeschool specialist, and president of Patrick Henry College. He has this to say about the "constitutional" basis of decisions like *Roe v. Wade*: "They're just making this stuff up! Show me the amendment. Show me the language. Show me the textual provision, and then maybe I'll agree with you. But until then, it's just thin air. It's smoke and mirrors. It's a shell game with our Constitution."[9]

Interestingly, today even Roe herself (Norma McCorvey) disagrees with *Roe v. Wade*. Norma McCorvey has become a Christian, is thoroughly pro-life, and has even attempted to correct the terrible legal precedent her case caused more than thirty years ago. Norma has documented her story in her book *Won by Love*.[10]

PARTIAL-BIRTH ABORTION

Every abortion, no matter how old the fetus is, ends up with a dead body. I believe abortion is wrong, but partial-birth abortion is monstrous. Yet many still do not even grasp what it actually is. We must warn you that the following contains some graphic descriptions. Reader discretion is advised.

In the last few years there's been a battle over partial-birth abortion. In fact, three times now Congress has voted to ban it. But former President Clinton vetoed the ban twice. Finally, in 2003, Congress passed a ban again, and this time President Bush signed it into law. Tragically, within hours the ACLU and their ilk filed suit, effectively blocking the law, tying it up in court. So far various courts have ruled the ban "unconstitutional," even though they have acknowledged the barbarity of the procedure we're about to describe.

In 1995 former U. S. Congressman Charles Canady of Florida introduced the original bill to ban this grisly procedure on a national level. He said, "Abortion methods are the dirty little secrets of the abortion industry. We have exposed one of those methods in the debate over partial-birth abortion."[11]

THE ACTUAL PROCEDURE

What actually happens in a partial-birth abortion is so grisly that it has actually caused some who are pro-choice to switch sides after viewing one. This happened with Brenda Shafer, a nurse for eighteen years. She notes that a partial-birth abortion starts at twenty weeks and goes all the way to forty. A forty-week unborn baby is "full term." She adds, "In California, they will do a partial-birth abortion procedure at 40 weeks for any reason."[12]

She explains what actually happens in a partial-birth abortion, which is a three-day procedure. On days 1 and 2, a laminaria is applied to force the cervix to dilate. We pick up with what the abortionist does on Day 3:

He turns the baby in utero to bring the baby's feet out first and brings them down with the forceps through the cervical canal. He then has both of the baby's feet on the outside of the mother. He begins to pull out the baby completely until he has everything except the head on the outside of the mother.

If that baby's head slips out at that point—as the doctor's holding it back and it comes out—if the doctor would kill it, once the head is delivered, then that doctor goes to prison for murder because at that point, it's considered a person in this country. But as long as he keeps that head in, by three inches, and then kills it, it doesn't matter how he kills it, it doesn't matter how inhumane or anything. It's abortion and it's legal in this country.

He then takes a pair of scissors and stabs the baby in the back of the neck and opens them up to make a hole in the back of the neck and into this hole, he puts a suction catheter; and he turns the suction machine on and literally suctions out the baby's brains. At this point the baby goes limp, and it's dead.

And he brings the head out and cuts the cord and literally throws the baby into a pan. That's how they do a partial birth abortion procedure.[13]

WHY PARTIAL-BIRTH ABORTION?

"It's a terrible procedure," says Tom Coburn, a medical doctor of obstetrics and former U.S. Congressman from Oklahoma. "It's the worst kind of murder. Even if abortion were justified, this would not be justified, because it is a method of cruelly killing an infant only for the convenience of the abortionist, so he can do it quicker, and so he can do it more."[14] Coburn will be in the Senate (thank the Lord) by the time this book is published.

This is an important point worth underscoring. This procedure is done *so the abortionist can do more abortions.*

Democratic Congressman Bart Stupak of Michigan, who cosponsored the original act against partial-birth abortion, asks: "Is there any difference between this and infanticide? No. I don't believe so. When they snap the back of the neck, when they cut it, the brain stem, the baby's hands will clutch, so there's pain, there's misery, there's everything in this."[15]

FROM PRO-CHOICE TO PRO-LIFE

An interesting irony, already alluded to, is that one of the key witnesses against partial-birth abortion—again, nurse Brenda Shafer—used to favor abortion rights. The turning point came in 1993 when her nursing agency asked her if she would be willing to take on a new job.

Says Brenda, "They called me up one day and asked me if I would work at the abortion clinic, and I told them I would, because I didn't think I had a problem with abortion. I'd always told my two girls that if they got pregnant at an early age, I would make them have an abortion."[16] But she wasn't prepared for what she saw as she witnessed a partial-birth abortion. "I stood there and watched this baby kicking his feet, moving his little hands and fingers, hanging from his mom. One of the things that really sticks out in my mind is actually when I saw the baby go limp, and the life drained out of it, and his brain was suctioned out. I can't even began to tell you how much that affected me—knowing that that baby was dead, and there wasn't anything we could do. At that point, I was even almost irrational. I was thinking maybe if I put his brains back in him, he would be okay and, of course, I was trying to hold it together to keep from throwing up and just keep from losing it. That's one of the visions in my mind, I just keep seeing that baby—just the life drained out of him—and then it was over. His whole life was over before it even got to begin too much, and it really affected me, and that's one of the things I'll never forget."[17]

What did she do next? "After I left the clinic that day and after seeing three of these partial-birth abortion procedures, I quit. As a matter of fact, I went to the agency that sent me there, and I quit that agency. I told them what had happened, and, of course, they were in shock, and they were very upset that this could happen. They even offered to pay for psychiatric help if I needed it. I remember going home that night and telling my family what happened, and I just can't believe that they do this in this country. Those are babies, and people lose babies every day, and they're so upset. But women choose to kill a child like this, and it just upset me so much and, obviously, it changed my mind about abortion. I no longer believe in abortion and speak out against it. As a matter of fact, my 17-year-old-daughter got pregnant, and I now have an almost three-year-old granddaughter. The first thing we said to each other when she found out she was pregnant was 'you're having an abortion.' But I just don't believe in it anymore."[18]

Although she witnessed the partial-birth abortions many years ago, she is still haunted by what she saw. Here is something she said about five years after seeing them: "When it first happened to me, I couldn't sleep for days; I just wanted to forget about it; I just wanted to get it out of there. I just couldn't believe that it happened to me, and I didn't want to remember it, and I didn't want to think about it, because it hurt so much."[19] She is now troubled by nightmares in which she hears a baby crying. She even feels that she was essentially an accessory to murder. "And it still bothers me."[20]

Being a nurse for nearly two decades has prepared her for many tragic scenes. But nothing prepared her for partial-birth abortion. "I've seen just about every kind of death you can imagine. I've had people die in my arms. I've seen young people. I've seen old people die, and death is very, very hard. It doesn't mean that you're not a professional. It doesn't mean that you don't care, but you try to hold it together. You try to be a professional, and I've seen all kind of things happen. But I have to say that of all the things I've ever seen, [seeing a partial-birth abortion] affected me the most, because it was just so tragic. To know that we are allowing this to happen in the United States, and we say it's okay in the name of choice—I think that's one of the biggest things that bothers me."[21]

One of the important points to highlight about partial-birth abortion is that it blows the lid off regular abortion. Even though we don't see the baby in the womb in non-partial-birth abortions, he or she is still torn apart in an abortion in one grisly form or another. In fact, someone in the clinic has to piece the parts together after each abortion to make sure the womb is completely empty.

CHRISTIAN RESPONSES TO ABORTION

A Christian world-and-life view is opposed to abortion. This is why Christians go out of their way to help provide an alternative for unwed mothers so they don't go that route. That is why Christians provide counseling and healing for those—including professing Christians—who have had abortions. There is forgiveness for all sins when we repent and call on Jesus Christ. Since the 1980s, thousands of pregnant women have received all manner of help by calling 1-800-BETHANY.

CONCLUSION

We're all former fetuses. Isn't it time we unite to protect the most vulnerable among us? I believe a Christian world-and-life view will always honor and cherish life. That is why from the beginning of the church to the very present day, Christians have worked hard to provide for the orphans (and the widows too) and to protect the life of the unborn. It goes back to the simple Christian worldview: God is the giver and taker of life. It is not up to us to take life, only to care for it.

What happens when men follow the exact opposite? What happens when men carry to the full extreme the opposite worldview—in stark contrast with the Christian view? We have certainly gotten a taste in partial-birth abortion. Most of us are not like Brenda Shafer—we have never witnessed such a horrible thing. But what happens when a whole society slides down the slippery slope of devaluing human life by first removing the Christian protections for the most vulnerable among us? Let's take a closer look.

6

LESSONS FROM THE NAZIS REGARDING HUMAN LIFE

The good person out of his good treasure brings forth good,
and the evil person out of his evil treasure brings forth evil.
MATTHEW 12:35

Adolf Hitler is the great villain of the twentieth century. There may have been others responsible for more monstrous evil than even he—e.g., Stalin or Mao. But in poll after poll of the most evil men ever, Hitler wins hands down.

We can learn all sorts of lessons from the Nazis about the devaluation of human life. Hence we devote an entire chapter to this. In a book on the Christian worldview, here is a chapter on the anti-Christian worldview.

DIFFUSING A MYTH

Every once in a while you hear people talking about Hitler as if he were a Christian. He certainly grew up as a Catholic, but he became rabidly anti-Christian as a young man. Hitler was a disciple, intellectually, of the philosopher Nietzsche, a rabid anti-Christian.

Hitler said, "The heaviest blow that ever struck humanity was the coming of Christianity. Bolshevism is Christianity's illegitimate child. Both are inventions of the Jew."[1] Heinrich Himmler, the ruthless head of the Gestapo, said, "We shall not rest until we have rooted out Christianity."[2] William Shirer, a journalist who covered the Nazi regime and wrote *The Rise and Fall of the Third Reich*, said, "the Nazi regime intended eventually to destroy Christianity in Germany, if it could, and substitute the old paganism of the early Germanic gods and the new paganism of the Nazi extremists."[3] So in the German churches, the Bible at the altar was replaced with *Mein Kampf* and the crosses atop steeples were replaced by the swastika. Hitler himself said that he and the Nazi Party were fighting against "the God of the deserts, that crazed, stupid, vengeful Asiatic despot with his powers to make laws! . . . that poison with which both Jews and Christians have spoiled and soiled the free, wonderful instincts of man and lowered them to the level of doglike fright."[4]

Bertrand Russell was no friend of Christianity. He lived during World War II, and he fully recognized that Hitler was thoroughly anti-Christian. He said: "Nazis and Communists dismissed Christianity and did things which we deplore. It is easy to conclude that the repudiation of Christianity by Hitler and the Soviet Government is at least in part the cause of our troubles and that if the world returned to Christianity, our international problems would be solved."[5] But he obviously did not agree with that conclusion. Regardless, contrary to what some liberals say today, what the Nazis did was the antithesis of Christian belief and action.

IT BEGAN WITH EUTHANASIA

We should never forget that before Adolf Hitler ever killed a single Jew, he murdered about 275,000 handicapped people. First, there was the abortion that had been prevalent in Germany for over twenty years; then there was infanticide, the killing of babies; then there was the destruction of 275,000 adult handicapped people. This point cannot be emphasized enough and will be made with slight nuances repeatedly in the following pages.

LESSONS FROM NAZI GERMANY

Perhaps the Nazi Holocaust is the worst case in history of a society going down the slippery slope. The Holocaust killed some 6,000,000 Jews and 6,000,000 to 11,000,000 others, many of whom were Christians. The Nazis decided who should live and who should die, and the world was bathed in blood as a result. As our Jewish friends remind us, we must never forget the lessons learned by the Holocaust. It occurred because of the fatal mix of a pagan view of man with a quality-of-life ethic and an abuse of modern technology. We must learn from the past and not go down that road, although we have already begun, somewhat, by accepting abortion-on-demand, some infanticide, and now some euthanasia.

THE PRE-HOLOCAUST HOLOCAUST

To elaborate further on what we call the pre-Holocaust holocaust—the killings in Nazi Germany prior to the systematic killing of Jews, Gypsies, Slavs,

Christian nonconformists, etc.—we will consider the remarks of Dr. C. Everett Koop, Surgeon General under Reagan. While President, Ronald Reagan wrote a short book on the killing of the unborn, entitled *Abortion and the Conscience of the Nation*. The book includes some powerful essays, including one from the Reagan administration's top physician, C. Everett Koop. For years Koop had served as the surgeon-in-chief of the Children's Hospital of Philadelphia. Here's what Koop wrote about the pre-Holocaust killing:

> Medical science in Nazi Germany collaborated with this Hegelian trend, particularly in the following enterprises: the mass extermination of the chronically sick in the interest of saving "useless" expenses to the community as a whole; the mass extermination of those considered socially disturbing or racially and ideologically unwanted; the individual, the inconspicuous extermination of those considered disloyal to the ruling group; and the ruthless use of human experimental material in medical military research. Remember, physicians took part in this planning.
>
> Adults were propagandized; one outstanding example being a motion picture called "I Accuse," which dealt with euthanasia. This film depicted the life history of a woman suffering from multiple sclerosis and eventually showed her husband, a doctor, killing her to accompaniment of soft piano music played by a sympathetic colleague in an adjacent room. The ideology was implanted even in high school children when their mathematics texts included problems stated in distorted terms of the cost of caring for and rehabilitating the chronically sick and crippled. For example, one problem asked how many new housing units could be built and how many marriage-allowance loans could be given to newlyweds for the amount of money it cost the state to care for "the crippled, the criminal, and the insane." This was all before Hitler. And it was all in the hands of the medical profession.
>
> The first direct order for euthanasia came from Hitler in 1939. All state institutions were required to report on patients who had been ill for five years or more or who were unable to work.[6]

"WHAT IS USEFUL IS RIGHT"

One American who helped with the prosecution of Nazis at the Nuremburg trials was Leo Alexander. He was disturbed by emerging parallels he could see as early as 1949 between the Nazi medical mentality that led to the Holocaust and some philosophical assumptions found on the part of some doctors even in America. Thus he warned us in 1949 in words even more relevant to today:

The case therefore that I should like to make is that American medicine must realize where it stands in its fundamental premises. There can be no doubt that in a subtle way, the Hegelian premise of "what is useful is right" has infected society, including the medical portion of society. Physicians must return to their older premises, which were the emotional foundation and driving force of an amazingly successful quest to increase powers of healing and which are bound to carry them still farther, if they are not held down to earth by the pernicious attitudes of an overdone practical realism.[7]

Koop points out one of the great evils of this pre-Holocaust holocaust—the deafening silence it was met with among the medical establishment: ". . . when the first 273,000 German aged, infirm, and retarded were killed in gas chambers, there was no outcry from that medical profession either, and it was not far from there to Auschwitz."[8]

THE SANCTITY-OF-LIFE VS. THE QUALITY-OF-LIFE ETHIC

As we saw in the last chapter, so we pound away again. At heart this is a conflict of worldviews. In Ronald Reagan's powerful little book is also to be found an essay by a British wit and philosopher who converted to Christ late in life, Malcolm Muggeridge. He wrote:

The sanctity of life is, of course, a religious or transcendental concept, and has no meaning otherwise; if there is no God, life cannot have sanctity. By the same token, the quality of life is an earthly or worldly concept and can only be expressed legalistically, and in materialistic terms; the soul does not come into it.[9]

Like Koop, Muggeridge also quotes Dr. Leo Alexander, "who worked with the chief American counsel at the Nuremberg tribunal":

Whatever proportion these crimes finally assumed, it became evident to all who investigated them that they had started from small beginnings. The beginnings at first were merely a subtle shift in emphasis in the basic attitudes of the physicians. It started with the acceptance of the attitude, basic in the euthanasia movement, that there is such a thing as life not worthy to be lived. This attitude in its early stages concerned itself merely with the severely and chronically sick. Gradually the sphere of those to be included in this category was enlarged to encompass the socially unproductive, the ideologically unwanted, the racially unwanted, and finally, all non-Germans. *But it is important to realize that the infinitely small wedged-in lever from which the entire trend of mind received its impetus was the attitude towards the non-rehabilitable sick.*[10]

Muggeridge brings home again the point that the Holocaust began long before the Jews were systematically killed:

> Initially, the holocaust was aimed, not against Jews or Slavs, but against handicapped Aryan Germans, and was justified, not by racial theories, but by Hegelian utilitarianism, whereby what is useful is per se good, without any consideration being given to Judeo-Christian values, or, indeed to any concept whatsoever of good and evil. Subsequently, of course, the numbers of the killed rose to astronomical figures, and the medical basis for their slaughter grew ever flimsier; but it should never be forgotten that it was the euthanasia program first organized under the Wiemar Republic by the medical profession, which led to and merged into the genocide program of 1941-45. "Technical experience gained first with killing psychiatric patents," Wertham writes, "was utilized later for the destruction of millions. The psychiatric murders came first."[11]

STRIKING PARALLELS

"There are striking parallels between what happened to the unwanted in the Third Reich and what's happening to the unwanted both before and after birth today."[12] So writes Dr. William J. Brennan, professor at St. Louis University, the author of the carefully researched books *Dehumanizing the Vulnerable: When Word Games Take Lives*[13] and *The Abortion Holocaust: Today's Final Solution*[14]—books about these striking parallels. (Dr. Brennan is not to be confused with the former Associate Justice of the Supreme Court with the same name—but with a pro-abortion philosophy.)

While there are distinct and major differences between the Nazi Holocaust and what's happening in America today, some emerging trends disturb Dr. Brennan. "It's the same kind of mentality that we don't respect human life, and we have to dehumanize it and then we find the technology to get rid of it."[15] He adds, "The Nazis dehumanized their victims extensively. They called them subhuman, non-human, parasites, animals, objects, non-persons. The same terminology dominates the lexicon of today's abortion semanticists."[16]

Do you realize that the Nazis technically did not break the law in the Holocaust? Brennan points out: "The Nazis did not commit a crime at Auschwitz when they exterminated the Jews. There were over 400 laws, ordinances, and decrees passed leading up to the final solution, and each defendant at Nuremberg invoked the law to justify their involvement in the Holocaust. They said, 'Well, I'm not responsible.' What is legal is moral is a frightening slogan used to justify all types of atrocities down through history. Legality was used to justify the ownership of slaves, slave trade, the extermination of Indians on the American frontier, the killing of the Jews, and the destruction of the unwanted unborn and born dead babies today."[17] Brennan goes on to say, "One of the major terms, if not the major term used by the pro-abortion propagandist, is the term 'choice'—the right to choose. I found a very similar term used by the Nazis to cover up their killing. They called it selection. They had the right to select. It was doctors who were making selections in the death camps, just as doctors today, in conjunction with women, are making choices in the abortion chambers. The right to select in the past, the right to choose today, I believe, represents an arrogant assumption of the awesome power to destroy those who cannot defend themselves."[18]

"Is there a point where a life has no value?"[19] asks one man. "No. Never." Hugh Gallagher is a paraplegic and author of *By Trust Betrayed*, which documents the fact that the first victims of the Holocaust were not the Jews but the handicapped, and that the initiators were physicians. He says of the Nazi Holocaust:

> Disabled German citizens, more than 200 to 300,000 of them were killed by their physicians as part of a so-called euthanasia program. This was an idea, this was a proposal brought to the German government by the physicians of Germany, by the medical establishment. The proposition was that disabled people who were severely physically disabled or chronically mentally ill, had lives not worth living. They were useless eaters, and they deserved final medical assistance. Thus, the German government gave the physicians authority to provide this final medical assistance—a humane death—when in the judgment of the doctors, the patient had a life not worth living. There was heavy monitoring of this program at first, with many forms and strict guidelines. When they started the program, they killed patients on a one-by-one basis, and then it began to accelerate, until at the end, they were clearing out whole wards of hospitals. They developed killing techniques that later were used in the concentration camps. This is where the showers, the use of gas, that sort of thing was developed.[20]

Thus the Holocaust began with the extermination of the handicapped. The idea of killing off those who were less than perfect and quote-unquote "tidying up the gene pool" did not actually begin with the Nazis. It was discussed by doctors and philosophers all over the Western world the previous half century. Gallagher adds, "it was only when the Nazis took power in 1933 that the physicians were able to convince the government to institute a real program."

William Brennan points out: "The whole reason that Nazi Germany came to be is that some took it upon themselves to choose who would live and who would die. Unless we are aware of the grievous mistakes of the past and how they were performed and the rationalizations and language used to justify them, we will not be attuned to what is happening today. We must get in touch with the past in order for us not to continue to repeat the atrocities of the past."[21]

It is within man's fallen nature to take advantage of others and to exploit the weak and maybe even kill them. What the Nazis did was atrocious, but we must never forget that these atrocities can happen again. Statistically the atrocities of the Communists were even worse than those of the Nazis. Both the Nazis and the Communists had a sub-Christian view of humanity. Humanists point to the evil things done in the name of Christ, but their eyes are closed to the far worse things done in the name of humanism.

CONCLUSION

William Brennan describes the influential book that helped cheapen human life in Germany before the Nazis took power and put into practice the thoughts and ideas already circulating:

> In *Permitting the Destruction of Unworthy Life* (1920), jurist Karl Binding and psychiatrist Alfred Hoche invoked a litany of dehumanizing phrases to disparage the physically and mentally ill as well as those with handicaps and deformities. Binding saw *"no grounds—legally, socially, ethically or religiously"* for not allowing the destruction of "incurable idiots" who are *"the fearsome counter image of true humanity."* He supported extending "the same act of kindness [euthanasia]" to "monstrous births" (pp. 248-49). Hoche's linguistic attacks on the "mentally dead" and the "incurably insane" are laced with demeaning expressions—"complete idiots," "empty human shells," "dead weight existences," "defective people," "wholly worthless," "valueless lives," and "lives not worth living" (pp. 258-63).[22]

Add to that the idea that Hitler and the Nazis wanted to speed evolution along and that they viewed such allegedly inferiors (as Jews) as nonpersons. In 1923 Hitler declared, "Jews are undoubtedly a race, but not human."[23] In 1936 the German Supreme Court refused "to recognize Jews . . . as 'persons' in the legal sense."[24] This was all an undoubtedly lethal mix, and it led to many in a formerly Christian country engaging in such unspeakable horrors. May we never forget the lessons regarding human life from this most monstrous regime.

7

CLONING AND THE STEM-CELL RESEARCH DEBATE

I call heaven and earth to witness against you today, that I have set before you life and death, blessing and curse. Therefore choose life, that you and your offspring may live, loving the LORD your God, obeying his voice and holding fast to him, for he is your life and length of days.

DEUTERONOMY 30:19-20

☩

God gave the ancient Israelites a choice: life or death. Frankly, it was a choice between Him or other gods (who are actually not gods). By choosing Him, they chose life. By choosing foreign gods, they were embracing death. That is the context of the passage quoted above.

But take it to the broader issue. As we consider a Christian world-and-life view in the realm of human life, there is a real choice between life and death. God's way is the way of life. The humanistic way is the way of death.

The church faces a number of bioethical issues today. Exactly what the Christian position is on some of these things can seem tricky. For example, if "therapeutic cloning" reaps all sorts of benefits for patients with Alzheimer's or Parkinson's or other debilitating diseases, shouldn't we embrace it—isn't that choosing life in that context? This chapter will explore human cloning and stem-cell research and will attempt to provide a Christian perspective on these difficult questions.

WHICH REAGAN SON SHOULD WE BELIEVE?

During the summer of 2004, one of the issues brought up in the presidential campaign was that of stem-cell research. The debate even divided the Reagan brothers. At the Democratic National Convention in Boston, Ronald Prescott Reagan weighed in on behalf of embryonic stem-cell research and implied that President Bush is cruel and anti-science for not allowing it, for, he said, it holds all sorts of cures in its power. The other Reagan son, albeit the adopted one, Michael, spoke at the Republican National Convention in New York City on behalf of adult stem-cell research but in opposition to the embryonic version.

Who's right?

What is a Christian view of cloning? What is a Christian view of stem-cell research? These new scientific breakthroughs that supposedly hold out promise for patients of Alzheimer's and Parkinson's disease and other ailments are often touted in the headlines.

The basic answer, in our opinion, is simple:

• adult stem-cell research—good.

• embryonic stem-cell research—bad.

With the one, no one is hurt. Cells from one part of one's own body are used to bring healing to another part of his or her body. With embryonic stem-cell cloning, a potential life is snuffed out for the sake of someone else.

Adult stem-cell research so far is the only one of these technologies that's actually providing benefit and against which no conservative has a problem. But embryonic stem-cell research is harmful and a further step down the slippery slope. The same is true for human cloning.

The goal is to create new human beings in order to harvest their organs for others. Welcome to the twenty-first century. Cloning is no longer a subject for a futuristic sci-fi flick. It is being discussed in medical labs, bioethics conferences, talk shows, and legislatures.

HUMAN CLONING

Perhaps no idea has stoked the fears and imaginations of modern Americans more than the possibility that human beings could be replicated by scientists in a lab. Hollywood producers have had a field day with the idea of human cloning.

In *The Boys from Brazil*, made in the 1970s (one of Gregory Peck's last movies), the remains of no less than Adolf Hitler have been cloned a multitude of times. Now it's up to the Nazi-hunting character played by Laurence

Olivier to stop them. When the Olivier character calls cloning "monstrous," one scientist (not necessarily in on the Hitler conspiracy) says to him, "Why? Wouldn't you want to live in a world full of Mozarts and Picassos?"

In Woody Allen's *Sleeper* (also from the 1970s), futuristic scientists attempt to clone their dead dictator, who died in a car accident. All that's left of their leader is his nose.

In the vulgar, second Austin Powers film, Dr. Evil, the mad scientist character played by Mike Myers, clones a dwarf image of himself: "Breathtaking. I shall call him: Mini-me."

This is just the tip of the iceberg as Hollywood deals with cloning. But are these ideas accurate? Most of our ideas about cloning have been formed exclusively by the movies and the media.

Wesley J. Smith is the author of the book *Culture of Death*. A frequent contributor to *National Review*, he writes and speaks on issues regarding the sanctity of human life. Smith is not easily dismissed as a conservative writer because he is liberal on other issues. For example, he has written four books with Ralph Nader, not exactly a card-carrying member of the Christian Coalition. Smith points out how Hollywood's view of cloning has muddied the waters:

> . . . the idea that cloning is like an Arnold Schwarzenegger movie, where you create an adult Arnold who becomes the bad Arnold who becomes the bad Arnold versus the good Arnold, isn't the way it is. . . . Cloning starts at the embryonic stage, and then you develop a whole new unique human being. Because someone has the DNA of Albert Schweitzer doesn't mean that Albert Schweitzer's clone would become Albert Schweitzer. Perhaps that person would become a custodian, or perhaps that person would become a deep-sea diver. You don't know.[1]

Dr. Smith even warns about those who want to use human cloning to create nearly perfect human beings with all the right traits. Then such cloned people will rule over and be served by those naturally born (you and I). As far-fetched as this sounds, Dr. Smith says you can find an advocate of such a position in no less a school than Princeton—Lee Silver, author of *Remaking Eden*.

Another critic of cloning is Alexander Morgan Capron, a professor of law and science at the University of Southern California. He was appointed by former President Clinton to the National Bioethics Advisory Commission. He examined more closely the claim of human cloning announced in

November 2001 and said that it came dramatically short of the results widely touted in the media: "The embryo only got to six cells before it stopped functioning. There were two others that got to four cells. My own sense about it is that the company [A.C.T. of Massachusetts] wanted to try to get attention to itself. It is in a very competitive business. It is trying to raise money for its work and to get itself all the attention that it got."[2]

WHAT EXACTLY IS CLONING ANYWAY?

Alexander Morgan Capron explains it this way: "The word 'clone' and the idea of 'cloning' simply today means, 'making a genetically identical or almost identical copy.'"[3] Author Dr. Scott Rae, professor at Biola University, serves as a bioethicist at six hospitals in the Los Angeles area. He says, "what most people mean by human cloning, when they use the term today, is taking an adult cell and producing an identical twin of that person. They'll take any one of your cells, taken from any part of your body, and they will take out the genetic material, take out the nucleus, and they will transfer that nucleus to a human egg that has had its nucleus removed."[4]

After that, a catalyst—such as an electrical charge—is applied to the now artificially fertilized egg in an effort to stimulate growth. Rae sums it up this way: "So you're just putting your genetic material into an egg and implanting that into a uterus, chemically treated, and if all goes according to plan, it starts growing and dividing like an embryo would that's produced sexually."[5]

The first real cloning of mammals became a reality in February 1997 with the well-publicized birth of Dolly the sheep. For the first time an organism was cloned from an adult of the same species. After this major success, it seemed inevitable that the technology would eventually be applied to humans. But what is often ignored in the talk of human cloning is the costly path of embryo experimentation that it took to get to Dolly—involving more than 270 attempts before Dolly was even conceived.

Alexander Morgan Capron notes: "It takes hundreds, at the very least scores, of eggs to create a single live birth. And many of those that get up to birth, or near birth, are deformed in various ways and have all sorts of problems."[6]

Furthermore, Dolly developed premature arthritis and has already died. If Dolly had been conceived in a normal way, she would likely still be alive today. Dr. Robert Evans, director of the Veritas Institute for the Study of Bioethics and Public Values in Auburn, California, has taught at Harvard and Oxford Universities, as well as at Knox Theological Seminary in Ft.

Lauderdale. Before Dolly's death, he said, "They're discovering that Dolly is developing a premature arthritic condition, which may prove to be disabling for Dolly. And so the long-term unforeseen consequences of cloning, even in animals, has yet to be traced through."[7]

Most in the scientific community believe that future advances in human cloning will prove to be even more costly in terms of human life. Capron points out, "The process of learning how to do it would require the use of hundreds, perhaps thousands or tens of thousands of eggs, that would be stimulated to create embryos, which would then have to be studied and sacrificed in the laboratory, and to anyone who believes that research on human embryos is wrong, this is a very troublesome thing."[8]

Though the popular conception of cloning means copying full-grown individuals, the primary interest that most scientists have in the technology is in producing embryos for the harvesting of stem cells. This means that the debate on cloning is inextricably linked with the debate on stem-cell research.

STEM-CELL RESEARCH

Robert Evans says, "Human embryonic stem cell research, by nature, requires the destruction of a human embryo in order to extract that stem cell line. And if we agree that an embryo, in and of its own nature, bears the image of God, then we are necessarily effacing the image of God in the process of cloning human embryonic stem cells or deriving them from cloned embryos."[9]

Wesley J. Smith states: "If we said that it is acceptable to clone a human being and strip mine it for its body parts, then what we are saying in the law is that life does not have value simply because it's human."[10] Nonetheless, experiments in human cloning are currently legal in the United States. Attempts to ban cloning have failed.

REAGAN VS. REAGAN REVISITED

President Ronald Reagan died in the summer of 2004. His son, Ron, and his widow, Nancy, shocked the world with their pronouncements in favor of stem-cell research because they were advocating *embryonic* stem-cell research. As Tony Perkins, president of the Family Research Council in Washington, D.C., noted, this was not in step with the former President's pro-life views:

> As President, Ronald Reagan never compromised his belief that life begins at conception and should be granted full protections under the law.

Michael Reagan, the other son of Ronald Reagan and a board member of the Alzheimer's Foundation, has defended his father's record passionately.

Yet the Democratic Party and almost all media outlets purposely refuse to make the simple distinction between embryonic and adult stem cells. Science has proven that embryonic stem cell research has not delivered one successful cure and deliberately kills human life in the process. Adult stem cell science, however, has thousands of cures and is completely ethical. Why is it that Ron Reagan assaults his father's memory and refuses to recognize the science of adult stem cell research? Hopefully the real voice of Ronald Reagan will make its way into this debate.[11]

Newsweek magazine had a cover story on stem-cell research. Unfortunately, they did not mention the success with adult stem cells; but at least they admitted that the other kind has not proven successful—yet (if it ever will). They write, "Not a single person has yet been cured by embryonic stem cells, but the early science is tantalizing."[12]

ATTEMPTS TO BAN CLONING

Capron tells of his attempts to ban cloning, at least for now: "I was a member of the national bioethics commission and in June of 1997 we recommended to President Clinton, and he recommended to Congress, that a moratorium be enacted—a ban of five to ten years in duration—against any attempt to create a baby through cloning."[13]

However, because many lawmakers want to leave open the possibility of harvesting stem cells from human embryos for therapeutic benefits, no such moratorium has ever been enacted. One was passed in the U.S. House of Representatives by an overwhelming margin, but as of this writing, the bill languished in the Senate for months.

Capron says, "Cloning right now would be like driving a baby carriage off a cliff. I mean, the risk to any child created in this way, the physical risk, is far beyond any kind of experiment that anyone would allow in any other context. I mean, if you were researching a drug, and you had the kind of horrible results we have had in animals, you would never take this drug into a clinic and use it with human beings. It would never be permitted. It's like saying, 'Well, it fails in animals, so we'll try it in humans.' You just don't do that."[14]

A POTENTIAL SCIENTIFIC NIGHTMARE

In the terrifying sci-fi novel *Coma*, the protagonist stumbles across a nightmare institution in South America where human beings are harvested for their parts. These adults are drugged, and they are hanging by strings in a lying down position, suspended in midair. They are comatose and unwitting victims, waiting for the doctors and nurses who work in the institution to slice them open to remove a body part needed for someone else.

This is science fiction. Imagine if you had the same scenario, only you couldn't see the victim because he or she (and it's always one or the other) was invisible to the naked eye. Dr. David Prentice of the Family Research Council says (if present trends continue), "We will make not only human beings, as cloned human beings, a commodity with embryo farms, kind of an embryo body shop—spare parts factory, but we'll make human eggs a commodity as well."[15]

KILLING OF THE EMBRYOS

An important point to grasp in this issue is that by definition, by conducting embryonic stem-cell research or therapy, an embryo will die. Again, even the humanists have to admit this is a potential life.

The embryo dies when its stem cells are extracted. Yet some portions of the scientific community hope to harness their power to someday help a paraplegic walk or to cure diseases like Alzheimer's or Parkinson's.

Sometimes we see a famous actor making a widely touted appearance before a congressional hearing, advocating stem-cell research, such as the late Christopher Reeve. Unfortunately, neither he nor the media carefully distinguish between embryonic stem-cell research and adult stem-cell research. Again, that distinction is critical. It's the difference between choosing life and choosing death.

An amazing and appalling remark during the 2004 presidential campaign came from John Edwards, the vice-presidential hopeful. He basically said that if his running mate John Kerry were to become President, then people like Christopher Reeve would be able to walk again. This was a very callous remark, holding out false hope for those suffering serious diseases. *Washington Post* columnist Dr. Charles Krauthammer, who is wheelchair-bound, said it was the most demagogic remark he's heard in Washington, D.C. in his twenty-five years of covering campaigns. In any event, embryonic stem-cell research is held up as the great hope of mankind, despite its dismal track record to produce anything but dead embryos.

A million and a half patients in America are suffering from Parkinson's disease. Jim Branham is one of them. He testifies, "Through the last couple of years before I was diagnosed I had reached a point where physically I could not brush my teeth. Had to get an electric toothbrush. Couldn't put my belt through my belt loops. My wife had to put them on that way. Couldn't tie my shoes. There was just a lot of physical difficulties at that time."[16]

In Parkinson's, the brain fails to produce a chemical called dopamine, which allows it to control the body movements. Patients with early forms of this disease—and Jim is one of them—suffer with tremors, stiffness, and difficulty with motor skills in general.

So what does Jim need? Embryonic stem-cells to come to the rescue? They have been loudly proclaimed as the solution in the secular media. What Jim needs is not embryonic but adult stem cells. Furthermore, even if research proved the embryonic stem cells more effective than adult (again, the exact opposite is the case), as a Christian, Jim would not want new human beings killed so that he might live. He comments, "I just don't think I ever want to benefit from someone else's life, especially a baby that's never even had a chance to live. We were all an embryo at one time. . . . God has created the process, and that's when life starts, and I think to destroy that, you're actually killing a human being."[17] He is articulating a Christian worldview on life and death issues. Christ gave His life that we might live. He didn't demand our lives from us so that He might live.

A decade ago Jim may have been resigned to suffer in silence with his disease. But today there is hope because each of us possesses our very own stem cells that can be used for therapy. This is a pro-life position and does not involve taking the life of an embryo.

UCLA professor Dr. Marc Hedrick says, "I would say to anyone who has a neurological disorder like Parkinson's or Alzheimer's, that there's absolutely hope in using stem cells to treat them. And I think adult stem cells have a lot of potential."[18] Dr. Hedrick is the president of StemSource, a revolutionary company that conducts research with adult stem cells taken from human fat.

Americans are obsessed with the issue of overweight. Perhaps this is finally the solution! We can have the unwanted fat cells of one person sucked out and given to needy patients. Dr. Hedrick explains how he came about this research:

> It was really a finding by accident, quite honestly, but since that accidental discovery several years ago, we've shown that you could actually take the cells that are hidden in fat tissue and make them become muscle, bone, cartilage. We're also very hopeful these cells will go beyond just the skeletal tissues, the muscle and the cartilage and bone, and actually can turn into cells called ectoderm, or nerve cells, for example. So if we

can prove some of the things that we're finding, these cells might have the potential to become nerve cells, then it might be a source of stem cells for problems such as Parkinson's, Alzheimer's disease, or even spinal cord injury.[19]

Interestingly, there's a great deal that those fat cells have to contribute. They are rich in life-giving elements. Dr. Hedrick points out: "The typical liposuction patient will donate about two liters of their fat tissue, and typically that tissue's just discarded or thrown away. What we've shown is that's a rich source of a lot of things, including stem cells. From a typical liter, for example, half of what you get normally from a cosmetic surgery patient, you can get several hundred million stem cells, and perhaps even more."[20]

And it's not just fat cells. Researchers have also discovered other adult stem cells to be helpful for patients. If our media wasn't so biased against the pro-life position, we would know more about these amazing discoveries.

For example, author, attorney, and human life advocate Wesley J. Smith points out another source of adult stem cells—bone marrow. "They've found a stem cell in human bone marrow that may be as good as embryonic stem cells are supposed to be; there needs to be research on that."[21]

The farce of the way the media couches the debate, says Smith, is that the embryonic stem cells have proven hitherto unmanageable for researchers: "It turns out that these embryonic cells are so energetic that they can't be controlled and often cause cancers or tumors. At the same time, we are already treating human diseases and maladies with stem cells derived from adult tissues or umbilical cord blood. There are four million babies born each year in this country. Every umbilical cord contains stem cells from each of those babies. What a tremendous resource."[22]

We should hasten to add that when people talk about *adult* stem cells, they are merely talking about stem cells from someone already born. Thus adult stem cells could come from a one-day-old or a one-hundred-year-old. The term is perhaps a misnomer, and the humanists perhaps take advantage by clouding the issue.

One of the great things about adult stem cells is that when a patient receives stem cells back from his own body, there is a built-in acceptance. Dr. Hedrick, professor at UCLA, states, "When you use your own stem cells, you don't have to worry about rejection, you don't have to worry about giving yourself a disease that you don't already have. You don't have to worry about any of the ethical or political issues with other kinds of stem cells."[23]

To recap our top story:
- adult stem cell research—good.
- embryonic stem cell research—bad.

It is that simple.

CONCLUSION

God is the source of all life. In Him is life (John 1:4). There is a strong theme throughout the Bible that God is the Lord of life. He is the Creator and the sustainer of life. He decides the hour of our birth and the hour of death. Jesus said that we can't even add a single hour to our life span (Matthew 6:27).

In Genesis, God prevents men from controlling life. Remember, Adam had eaten of "the tree of the knowledge of good and evil" and had to live with the consequences. But there was another tree in the garden, and that tree we do not see again until the end of the Bible, when all life is restored. That is "the tree of life" (Revelation 22:2). Only at the end of time are redeemed men and women finally allowed to enjoy its fruit. In Genesis, after man's sin, an angel with a flaming sword guarded the tree of life (Genesis 3:24), so that no man or woman could eat of it.

The angel of the Lord is still guarding that tree and will not give man access to its fruit, so that we may live eternally. In other words, power over life and death still rests with God. Only Jesus has the power to give eternal life (John 3:36). God has connected eternal life to belief in His Son. Because God is the source of life—both physical and spiritual life—there is great danger in messing with it. It is one thing to work to cure diseases and ease suffering. But it is quite another to manipulate life and death. Therefore, I do not believe God allows human cloning. We can only experiment with life and death to our own detriment and destruction.

8

SUICIDE IS NOT
A VIABLE OPTION

*But he who fails to find me injures himself; all who hate me
love death.*

PROVERBS 8:36

One of the modern myths that our culture has bought into is the idea that suicide is a viable option. When you're tired of this life or you are in too much pain, and it's time to "check out," then it's pointless to wait it out—just take your life into your own hands and call on one of Dr. Kevorkian's helpers.

As of this writing, Dr. Jack Kevorkian—Dr. Suicide—is in prison and has been for years. But people who have bought into his death-loving mentality freely roam our streets.

No one who has read the newspaper or listened to the news for the past several years could possibly have failed to have heard about Dr. Jack Kevorkian and his suicide machine, or the best-selling book *Final Exit* by Derek Humphry, co-founder of the Hemlock Society. Nor could they have failed to hear about the law that Oregon voters said yes to—the law that allows physician-assisted suicide.

Yes, indeed, there is something abroad in our land, and it is death. It is stalking our country like a ghastly giant, and this is a very, very serious matter. In fact, Dr. Arthur Caplan, the director of the University of Minnesota's Center for Biomedical Ethics, said the most significant bioethical event he has seen in America—in fact, in the history of our country—"is not artificial hearts, it's not grandmothers who give birth to their grandchildren." It is this matter of doctor-assisted suicide because, he said, "It is a break from a 2,000 year old tradition that says [in the words of the Hippocratic Oath] doctors cannot harm." As Dr. Charles Krauthammer puts it: "How then to draw the line? Easy. Doctors must not kill. The bright line must be drawn precisely between passive and active measures."[1]

WHAT CAN WE DO WITH THE CHRONICALLY ILL?

The seriousness of this matter could be further underlined by pointing out what we saw so clearly in a previous chapter, that the Nazi Holocaust, with all of its incredible atrocities, could finally be traced back to a very small beginning: the blurring of the line between healing and killing on the part of physicians. The issue of what to do about the chronically sick began the whole thing. What do you do about those who are not going to get well? That may seem like a very little thing, but it was the first step down a slippery slope that led to Auschwitz.

As serious as this is, it has also spawned its own class of humor, dark humor though it is. I was shown a cartoon that pictured a doctor's waiting room where elderly patients were gathered with their crutches and canes and wheelchairs. The nurse steps cheerily to the door and announces, "The doctor will kill you now."

Then there is the cartoon that shows an aged hag-like woman lying in bed in her own home. Above the bed it says, "Home sweet home." Standing next to the bed is her son Leon, a middle-aged man, and standing next to him is his rather debauched wife with a cigarette in one hand and a newspaper in the other whose headline reads, "British Doctor Predicts Death Pill for Aged." Leon, with a rather demonic smile on his face, is dropping a pill into a glass of water. Underneath, the mother is saying, "I knew I should have aborted you like all the rest, Leon."

Yes, what goes around comes around. Which reminds me of a story from ancient times when it was customary to take the aged father, put him in a basket, carry him onto a mountainside, and leave him there for the elements to dispose of or the wild beasts to devour. As one son was putting his old father in the basket, his father said, "Remember, son, to bring the basket back, because they're going to need it for you." The son changed his plans at that point.

THE SLIPPERY SLOPE

This is, indeed, a slippery slope. More than thirty years ago, when *Roe v. Wade* was passed, many of us were saying that it was indeed the first step down that slippery slope and that it would lead to infanticide, suicide, and euthanasia. Many mocked and said that was ridiculous—it would never happen. Yet, it *is* happening. In case you don't know, last year more than 5,000 babies, already born, were left to die NPO (nothing by mouth) in hospitals in America.

Infanticide is alive and well in our country today, and legalized suicide is just around the corner. It's already passed by ballot and by court decisions in the state of Oregon.

As to the idea that legalized abortion would open the door for euthanasia, please note what Francis Schaeffer wrote in 1978—just five years after the Supreme Court's infamous decision:

> The next candidate for arbitrary reclassification as nonpersons are the elderly. This will become increasingly so as the proportion of the old and weak in relation to the young and strong becomes abnormally large, due to the growing antifamily sentiment, the abortion rate, and medicine's contribution to the lengthening of the normal life span. The imbalance will cause many of the young to perceive the old as a cramping nuisance in the hedonistic life-style they claim as their right. As the demand for affluence continues and the economic crunch gets greater, the amount of compassion that the legislature and the courts will have for the old does not seem likely to be significant, considering the precedent of the nonprotection given to the unborn and newborn.[2]

There is a very small step between doctor-assisted voluntary suicide and doctor-assisted involuntary suicide. Some of you will say, "Well now, that is an exaggeration. Certainly we wouldn't have doctors doing anything like that." Is that a fact? There is one country where it is quasi-legal and therefore most definitely allowed, if not legalized, and that is the Netherlands, where doctor-assisted suicide has now become, in the last several years, a common practice. In fact, in the Netherlands 130,000 people die each year. Last year 2,300 of them were voluntary doctor-assisted suicides.

Here is how Charles Krauthammer puts it: "There is good reason why the categorical Hippocratic taboo is so ancient and so universal: A license to kill inevitably corrupts the doctor and endangers the patient. Euthanasia, once permitted, is not as easily contained as its promoters pretend."[3]

How do we know? Because in Holland, according to a Dutch government report, there were 1,000 doctor-assisted involuntary suicides last year.

We are used to calling that murder, and that is precisely what it is. But you see, we don't always call things what they are. Killing patients without their permission is becoming commonplace now in Holland. It is simply up to the doctors, the article says, to decide whether a person should be healed or put to death. Be careful about your next doctor's appointment if this ever comes here. It might be your last. "The doctor will kill you now" is no longer just a cartoon. It is a reality—at least in Holland.

AGAINST A CHRISTIAN'S WILL

Here is a first: A hospital in Minneapolis recently sought court permission to stop treatment of a comatose patient who had indicated she did not want to have treatment stopped because she was a Christian and believed life was sacred. Her family also told the hospital they did not want treatment discontinued, but the hospital is going to court to stop treatment—in spite of everybody's wishes to the contrary.

Bioethicist Leon Kass observes, "The line between voluntary and/or involuntary euthanasia cannot hold."[4] It never has, and it never will. Ask the survivors of Dachau.

A MATTER OF SEMANTICS

However, they don't call it killing any more than they call the baby in the womb a baby. A baby is, first of all, killed verbally, as it is transmuted into "products of conception" or maybe just "P.O.C." And so it is with this matter of murder of oneself. It is called other things, like "death with dignity." That has such a nice ring to it, people everywhere are flocking to its banner. May I remind you that some virtues in this world are more important than dignity.

A soldier is ordered by his commanding officer to watch at a certain post, maybe in the midst of a snowstorm. His feet are killing him because of the cold. He's trembling all over in a very undignified way. He decides he will be a soldier with dignity; so he goes into the pub to warm himself and have a cup of hot coffee or ale. I'm sure the court-martial will not consider dignity to be an all-surpassing virtue.

When Jesus Christ, naked, was lifted up on a cross, it was extraordinarily undignified. He was the object of ridicule and scorn and laughter and mockery. Indeed, He could have come down and reclothed Himself in His robes so He could reclaim His dignity; but He felt there were other virtues more important than dignity.

Final Exit is the title of the popular best-selling book I mentioned before.

There is an element of truth in that title, but it's never brought out. It is a final exit because the place to which they go—namely, hell—has no exit.

Charles Hodge of Princeton, perhaps the greatest theologian America ever produced and the most incredible scholar of the Bible, put it this way: "It is a very complicated crime; our life is not our own; we have no more right to destroy our life than we have to destroy the life of a fellow-man. Suicide is, therefore, self murder. . . . It is a crime which admits of no repentance and, consequently involves the loss of the soul."[5]

Let me make something very clear. Some who are reading this book have no doubt lost loved ones to suicide. I believe, and most theologians would agree, that it is possible even for a Christian to have temporary or even permanent insanity—loss of the rational faculties; and therefore even a believer could, in such a mental state as that, commit suicide without the forfeiture of his soul. But for the most part, as Hodge says, "Suicide is most common among those who have lost all faith in Christianity." They have lost any belief in God or in the future.

A SECULAR SOCIETY

I am reminded of the meaning of *secularism*. Again, the word comes from *saeculum*, a Latin word for "time" or "generation," meaning time only in this world, with no view of God or eternity. It is like a smoked dome being placed over the city of man, so that people are not able to see up to God or out to a future life. We live in a secular-saturated society.

Consider the talk shows on television. There is no reference to God unless it is blasphemy and no serious reference ever to a future and everlasting existence in another world. It is entirely under the smoked dome of the deceit of secularism. It is no wonder then that people who have been deceived into believing those lies would suppose that suicide is a natural way out when life becomes too burdensome.

Derek Humphry says on the cover of his book *Final Exit* that he is offering self-deliverance. We ought to keep in mind that we are not only delivered *out* of something, but we are delivered *into* something, but that is never discussed at all because such discussions are taboo under the smoked dome of secularism. No thought is given to the future life, and so many people, supposing themselves to have obtained their ease, have merely leaped out of the frying pan into the fire.

Shakespeare knew better, saying through Hamlet that indeed one might be tempted to "with a bare bodkin [or dagger] . . . his quietus make" and thus bring himself quiet and peace, to end it all:

To die: to sleep:
No more; and by a sleep to say we end
The heartache and the thousand natural shocks
That flesh is heir to, 'tis a consummation
Devoutly to be wish'd. . . .
[Ah yes, but what lies ahead in]
The undiscovered country from whose bourn
No traveller returns, puzzles the will
And makes us rather bear those ills we have
Than fly to others we know not of?
Thus conscience doth make cowards of us all.

Hamlet, Act III, Sec. 1

Today we are blinded to all such eternal and divine considerations. God has made it very clear: "You shall not murder" (Exodus 20:13). We must not murder our neighbor, brother, mother, father, or ourselves. We are not our own.

It is interesting that in *Roe v. Wade* the argument was given that the Supreme Court simply wanted women to have the autonomous control of their own bodies. Isn't it fascinating that Humphry, in *Final Exit*, posits his argument simply on the fact that a person needs to have the autonomous control of his or her own body?

But the problem is that your life is not your own. "You are not your own, for you were bought with a price" (1 Corinthians 6:19–20). Nor is your life simply some chemical or biological accident, a concatenation of amino acids in some ancient primordial slime. Rather, it is a divine gift given to you by God. It is sacred and inviolable, and it is not to be taken and flung back into the face of God thanklessly.

WE ARE NOT OUR OWN

We are doubly not our own: We did not create our life; it was created by God. And beyond that, God came into this world and died in great agony to redeem it. So it is twice His: by creation and by redemption. Our life is not our own autonomously to do with as we will. We are not to desert the post where our Captain in the well-fought fight has set us. That is not our decision to make.

The history of Western civilization and Christianity is replete with those who have suffered all sorts of persecution for the sake of Christ. Today we live in a world where materialistic and worldly thoughts are all there is, or so it is believed. Think of the millions of martyrs who died very undignified deaths: mauled by lions, tossed about by bulls in the Colosseum, eaten by dogs, bitten by snakes, or burned alive.

The Bible says that it is given unto us not only to believe in Christ but also to suffer for His sake. Through suffering, Christ learned obedience; and through suffering God indeed cleanses and perfects us. We are not to desert our God-given post. If we do, we are indeed deserters from the army of God.

We are not to murder ourselves. We are not to fling back the gift of life that is given to us, and we are not to desert our heavenly assignment. Why then do we have this specter of death everywhere in our country today? This is not God's doing. Robert Schuller, noted author, put it right: "God's in the life, not death business. He wants our full and enthusiastic participation."

If God is not in the death business, somebody else must be. We can say it is the humanists, the atheists, and the secularists—and surely they are. In the Bible God says, "All who hate me love death." Notice what all of these secularists and unbelievers love: They love abortion. They love the death of infants (infanticide). They love suicide. They love euthanasia. They love death because they are at enmity with God. They hate God. God said that, not I. That is their basic problem.

There is a dark presence behind all of the death business of this world. That great destroyer himself, Satan, is the power behind it. Satan is the arch-deceiver. Unbelievers have been deceived by Satan who, because of the malignant enmity that he holds against God, desires to destroy mankind, whom God loves. Worst of all, he succeeds because he is so beguiling and deceiving, and he blinds them. Then they do his work for him; they destroy one another, and after that they destroy themselves. Satan's primary work is death. Those who love Satan love death, and those who hate God love death.

BELIEVERS LOVE LIFE

Those who love God love life. What a precious gift God has given to us. We should cherish life. We should share it with others, especially those of us who have received life upon life—the gift of everlasting life from Christ, who freely offers us forgiveness and eternal life if we will trust in Him and repent of our sins. That is what God offers to us, and that is the life we should be rejoicing in, praising Him for, and sharing with other people.

Not only are we not supposed to be taking lives, we are supposed to be giving life to other people. We who are lighted by that life have the power to take the gospel and to share with others how they can come to everlasting life. Christ came to give us life and that abundantly, and that is the good news.

Christianity is about life—not death.

I DON'T TAKE PAIN LIGHTLY

I would not make light of pain. I know that life is not always easy. I know that sometimes it can be very painful indeed. I've had my share of pain. I rarely know a day without pain. I had more pain this morning than I knew how to handle. But I did not decide to throw my life back in the face of God. I did not decide to desert my post because of it. In Scripture the apostle Paul says, "I consider that the sufferings of this present time are not worth comparing with the glory that is to be revealed to us" (Romans 8:18).

What glories He has for us in that world where there will be no more tears, no more sorrow, no more death, no more pain! God uses our sufferings and trials and sorrows and pain in this life to perfect us and purify us and make us into what He wants us to be. Let us not be cowards, deserting our tasks, taking our lives against God's will, but let us cling to life and pray that God will use every part of it for our own good, knowing His promise that He will turn everything that comes to us to our good. Therefore, we can rest comfortably in His hands.

Have you said, "Lord, I don't care what comes to me—I know it comes from a loving Father's hand. I trust that You will give me the grace to endure whatever it is, and I will do it for Your glory as a witness for You"? Who knows how many people have been brought to Christ by the faithful, loving endurance of those who have trusted in a God who has promised to ultimately deliver them from their affliction, and also has promised that He will allow nothing to come that is more than they are able to bear. How marvelous are the promises of Christ, and how blind are the unbelievers of this world who are madly in love with death and are blind to God and a future world.

We should never forget that many great things have been accomplished in this world by men and women facing enormous difficulties. Thomas Edison lost his hearing as a young man, but he went on to become one of the greatest inventors in history (inventing, for example, the phonograph). Franklin D. Roosevelt was crippled and confined to a wheelchair, but that did not stop him from becoming one of our nation's most popular Presidents. John Milton was blind when he dictated *Paradise Lost* to his daughters. This is one of the great masterpieces of English literature. Whatever personal pain we may deal with, it is not our place to prematurely "check out" via suicide.

CONCLUSION

Several years ago a Presbyterian minister had to deal with life and death choices when his wife slipped into a coma. After several days everyone feared this could be permanent. Here's what *Time* magazine said about the incident: "The Rev. Harry Cole, a Presbyterian minister who faced the dilemma when his wife fell into a coma, admits the complexity of pressures. 'If she were to go on that way, our family faced not only incredible pain of watching her vegetate, but we also faced harsh practical realities.' The cost of nursing-home care was likely to top $30,000 a year. 'How could I continue to send three kids to college with the additional financial strain?'"

Harry then went to court to have her respirator removed. The judge refused, and six days later she woke up. She said, "I know he loves me. I know he was never trying to do away with me."

This true story reminds us that we should not play the role of God and choose life and death for others. Mrs. Cole has a problem with short-term memory loss, but other than that she is fine. She said, "When I look back at what the doctors said, I think, 'how wrong they were.' . . . What happened to me was truly miraculous."[6]

The issues are different, but the basic question is the same: Is God the giver, the taker, and the sustainer of life or not? What the secularists are debating is: Since there is no God, who decides life and death issues? We who believe in God can never allow anyone but God to hold the position of King over life and death.

PART III

THE SPHERE
OF THE
NATION

Introduction to Christianizing the Sphere of Government

We are being told today that religion may be dangerous to the American way of life. For some years people have been told that religion might be dangerous to their health, and so young people by the millions have abandoned it. We now find that our mental institutions are filled with these young people who, with no moral rudder to guide their lives, have found that everything has collapsed all around them. They are desperately seeking something on which to anchor their souls. Now it is not merely our health but our national health that is endangered.

We are also being told that religion and politics must be separate. We are being told that those who are serious about their faith will avoid politics altogether because "politics is dirty business."

Does the Bible have anything to say to the political arena? Does it have anything to say to economics? What happens when a nation is built on biblical principles? Let's explore such questions.

9

A CHRISTIAN VIEW OF POLITICS

And he put all things under his feet and gave him as head over all things to the church.

EPHESIANS 1:22

☩

"Government," said one person, "is a dangerous servant and a fearful master."[1] Those words were uttered by George Washington. The government he had in mind was that of the United States.

THE BIBLICAL CONCEPT OF GOVERNMENT

The founders of this country were imbued with a biblical concept of government because great teachings of the Word of God about government thundered forth from pulpits in New England and elsewhere. Unfortunately, today's pulpits have been silenced about these things.

Consequently, whole generations of Americans have grown up without the foggiest idea of what God has to say about government. In fact, they may even arrogantly affirm that God has no business saying anything about government.

THE BIBLE AND POLITICS

As we have been considering the Christian world-and-life view, we have noted that the cultural mandate found in the first chapter of the first book of the Bible requires that all phases of man's life are to be lived and exercised under the control of God and are all to be exercised for His glory. Man is to have dominion over all of the earth; he is to take all of the potentialities and possibilities of every phase of this world and culture it, improve it, and offer it all to God.

This includes all of the works of man's hands and mind. Included in this also is a very important area we call politics. Some would say that the church should never talk about politics; and it is no doubt true that some churches have lost sight of the gospel of Jesus Christ and have degenerated into simply political agencies.

Coauthor Jerry Newcombe often tackles political issues on the radio station that I founded years ago, WAFG, in Broward County, Florida. Often people will call whenever anything political is discussed, and they will ask, "How come you don't just preach the gospel? Why do you always talk about politics?" This is an exaggerated accusation. But it is a question that many in the church ask today: Why not just preach the gospel and forget about politics? It certainly is possible to overdo that or to do so without a proper balance. But the gospel has political implications. I never tell anyone how to vote, but I certainly try to inculcate a Christian perspective on the issues for my hearers.

Cal Thomas likes to say that salvation and the Savior will not come to us on Air Force One. That is correct, but I'm not sure if anybody said He would, although perhaps some preachers may seem to talk about politics to the point that one could surmise such.

In any event the psalmist says, "Put not your trust in princes" (146:3). Instead we should trust God alone. On the other hand, we have many examples in the Bible of important political leaders who were godly and who wielded influence for good—for God's people and even for the pagans. These leaders include Joseph, Pharaoh's right-hand man (the good Pharaoh), King David, and Daniel. Political leadership per se is not ungodly. It's how men or women rule that makes the difference. Does the Bible inform their politics, or does their politics inform their "bible," whatever that may be?

THE STATE AND TYRANNY

There is and has been a link between the state and tyranny. It was the tyrannical state of Egypt that brought the ancient people of God into hopeless bondage and sorrow. Pharaoh's agents brought the scourge upon their backs and committed them to the slime pits. The state of Assyria led the people of Israel into captivity, staked them out on the ground, and flayed them alive or impaled them on sharp-pointed, greased sticks. The state of Babylonia destroyed the southern kingdom of Judah, demolished the temple of God, and led the people into seventy years of horrible captivity.

The state of Rome crucified our Savior and decimated the early Christian church, drenching the earth with the blood of martyrs. China, under Mao

Tse-tung, killed between 55,000,000 and 72,000,000 Chinese and made Mao the greatest mass-murderer in the history of this planet. The state repressed the freedoms of the people of God in Poland for decades. Whether in Nazi Germany, the Soviet Union, China, Cuba, or Poland, the state has been and still often is the great persecutor of mankind.

We have forgotten the words of George Washington: "Government is a dangerous servant and a fearful master." Similarly, Ben Franklin once observed, "There is scarce a king in a hundred who would not, if he could, follow the example of Pharaoh, get first all the people's money, then all their lands and then make them and their children servants forever."[2]

THE PURPOSE OF GOVERNMENT

According to the Scriptures, government is a necessary evil. It would not even exist were it not for the fall of man. It was the sin and rebellion of mankind that brought government into existence in the first place. It was meant to restrain the evil tendencies and propensities in the hearts of men. Government was created by God to restrain marauders both within and without. It was established to protect citizens so they could live out their probation here on this earth in peace and safety and demonstrate whether they would submit to God and His law or whether they would rebel.

PRINCIPLES OF SCRIPTURE REGARDING POLITICS

Since government is a necessary part of our lives, I believe it is vitally important that Christian citizens be informed regarding the principles of Scripture as they relate to politics if they are going to exercise their rights and privileges as citizens and use their franchise in a wise and biblical manner. It is no doubt true that the church and the state should be separate institutions, but the church must proclaim the Word of God, the whole counsel of God, which includes in it some things about the state—its responsibilities and functions and our responsibility to it.

As Christians, we should be informed about these matters. One of the reasons we have problems is because the citizens of this country have acted and voted in an unbiblical way. Yes, the Bible can very definitely lead you as you exercise your vote at the poll. Not that it is going to tell you, nor is it the place of the church to tell you, which candidate to vote for. But there are basic biblical principles that deal with government and the state that every Christian should understand. They have a fantastic influence upon our lives.

"Whereas, the compass of the instituted church," Simon Kistemaker says, "is limited, the range of the Word of God is without limit." In fact, the area of politics governs most aspects of our daily lives—rent controls, wage minimums, taxes, inheritances, abortions, the right to work or the removal of that right, the national debt, inflation, subsidies, wheat prices, beef prices, wars, police actions, social security, Medicare, the United Nations, religious freedom, broadcasting, and a whole host of other areas. Therefore, no Christian can be rightfully ignorant of the biblical teachings about this.

Does the church have something to say about politics? Do Christianity and the church have something to say about politics, or should politics be completely separate from the purview of the church?

BIBLICAL PRINCIPLES OF THE STATE

What, then, are these biblical or Calvinistic principles that deal with the area of the state? The first is this: *the sovereignty of the Triune God over the whole of the cosmos in all of its spheres and kingdoms.* The Triune God is sovereign over everything—not merely over the church but over every sphere of life. Of course, that is the theme of this book: Christ is Lord over all these spheres, and we are to Christianize each one.

Listen to what the great Abraham Kuyper (1837-1920) had to say. Kuyper was the greatest theologian Holland ever produced. Not only was he a tremendous scholar, founder of the Free University of Amsterdam, an exegete of the Scriptures, and a minister of the gospel of Jesus Christ, but his talents were so outstanding that he became the prime minister of Holland. So effectual was his office as prime minister that the government declared a national holiday to celebrate the seventieth birthday of this man who had revived the biblical teachings involving the whole of the national life of Holland. He was a great Calvinistic theologian. He stated: "In the total expanse of human life there is not a single *square inch* of which the Christ, who alone is sovereign, does not declare, 'That is mine!'" (emphasis his).[3] That includes the realm of government.

This leads us to the second principle: *The ultimate source of all authority is not the state, it is not even the people—it is God.* As we read in the Scriptures, all authority is of God; all power is of God. Whatever power man exercises, he exercises it merely as a delegated power and authority from God. This is vitally important. Historically it has been true that every humanistic or nontheistic state that endeavors to place the authority for the right to govern (the right to govern is the right to coerce) in an all-powerful state or even in the people contains within itself, logically, the seeds of totalitarianism.

According to John Locke and Jean-Jacques Rousseau, the people give to the state, in a social contract, all of their rights. But do the people have the authority in the first place? Do they have any rights?

The authority of the state comes from God, and the state is answerable to God. Whenever that is lost sight of, eventually totalitarianism is going to result. The state, then, is an agency of God's common grace (not His special grace, which deals with our salvation), by which He restrains wickedness and does not allow it to run its greatest course, and by which He causes the sun to shine on the just and the unjust and sends rain on the wicked and the righteous alike. In the realm of God's common grace, He has given to us the state. Its purpose is to enact and execute the laws that God has given us in His Word, the moral laws He has written upon the hearts of men. It is, therefore, our responsibility to that state to honor it, for Scripture says that the powers that be are from God. We are to yield obedience to it, we are to pay tribute, and we are to pray for those in authority over us.

This leads us to a third principle, which is that *the state, then, is obviously limited in its authority and power.* God has placed a limit. The state does not encompass all things; there are other spheres. There is the sphere of the family, the sphere of the church, the sphere of education and of science, and the state is not to control these, as it endeavors to do in totalitarian states. Each of these has its own sphere of authority and responsibility, and men are to work out their lives freely in the various spheres in which they live.

This means, of course, that if anyone in any sphere of activity oversteps his authority, the Christian is bound to disobey. If the state commands the Christian to do that which is contrary to the clear teaching of God's Word, it is incumbent that he obey God and not man. There are and have been states that have forbidden Christians to pray and have forbidden believers to worship God and that to this day forbid believers to fulfill the Great Commission of Christ and to proclaim the gospel to others. (China, Vietnam, Cuba, and Saudi Arabia all fit this criterion.) In these and all other clear instances where the state is endeavoring to countermand the commandments of God, the Christian is bound to obey God rather than men because the state is limited in its authority.

THE RELATIONSHIP BETWEEN THE CHURCH AND STATE

What, then, is the relationship between the state and the church? In the Middle Ages the Roman Catholic Church taught that the state was under the church, and indeed in the eleventh and twelfth centuries it actually achieved such a position of dominance that it controlled all of the states of Europe.

There are today, and have been in the past, others who would put the church under the state, as is done in Communist lands where the church is completely controlled by the state—even to the electing of its officers and all of its various functions.

We believe there should be a separation of the institute of the church and the institute of the state, and such did John Calvin teach. This, however, is not to be a separation of God from the state, which we find going on in our country today. The Bible very clearly states that the nation that forgets God "shall be turned into hell" (Psalm 9:17, KJV). The Founding Fathers of this country by no means meant to establish a nation separated from God. The Declaration of Independence mentions God as the giver of inalienable rights to men. Benjamin Franklin arose during the writing of the Constitution of the United States and declared it was no more possible for men to build a political state without the help of God than it was for the builders of Babel.[4]

This shows the utter folly and ultimate fall of those who would say that we should do away with prayer before the opening of the sessions of the House of Representatives and the Senate on the premise that it is contrary to our Constitution. Nothing could be more ridiculous or ultimately more damaging to any nation. Prayer in Congress predates the Constitution

THE PURPOSE OF THE STATE

What is the purpose of the state? It was been instituted by God because of sin—to restrain the wicked and to grant justice. In a perfect world, it would not be needed. Its purpose is to control evildoers. The purpose of the state is that God may be glorified as citizens are free to go about their tasks and live for Him.

A frequent question is, what is the best form of the state? Well, that all depends on what the highest good for man is. Some say that the ideal and highest good is security. Theologian Gordon Clark states that some theorists say depressions are the worst things that can possibly happen to a nation, and to avoid them, a totalitarian control of money, prices, labor, education, and religion is justified. He said that two centuries ago there was a breed of political bird, now apparently almost extinct, that held that political freedom was the ideal.

For men like Thomas Jefferson and Patrick Henry, tyranny was the worst form of governmental evil, and a little economic competition was a small price to pay for that liberty. It all depends on what we mean by the "highest good." Humanists believe that this life is all there is, and that inevitably leads to a certain corollary that there is no future life; since this life is not a testing ground for eternity, then for them it is inevitably true that their form of the state must guarantee that man will not fail. He is continually propped up by the state.

The Bible sees this world as simply the foyer to eternity—a testing ground where talents, the abilities that have been given by God to man, are to be used and exercised. What is important is what man does in this life with his acceptance or rejection of Jesus Christ as Lord and Savior of his life, and with his improvement of the talents God has given to him and the offering of those to God for His glory. As He views this life as a prelude to eternity, he sees this world in an entirely different light, and this will affect, of course, his view of the state.

Another principle of the state that is so important from a Christian perspective is the idea that man is sinful, and because of that we must build elaborate political structures to protect us from power getting into the hands of the few. This idea is so important that we will explore it at length in the next chapter.

CONCLUSION

I think it is important that each one of us carefully consider the biblical teachings about man, society, the state, and the purpose of life while we still have the freedom to consider them at all. Government comes from God and is instituted for our good but, of course, can be abused—His principles should be applied to government.

10

CHRISTIAN STATESMANSHIP

Righteousness exalts a nation, but sin is a reproach to any people.

PROVERBS 14:34

✛

The whole concept of Christian statesmanship has almost been forgotten. But in the past, honorable leadership meant something in this nation. Our country was, indeed, conceived and birthed largely by Christian statesmen. Today I am afraid that such statesmanship is choking and dying at the hands of mere politicians, and I think it is vital that we rekindle the flame of Christian statesmanship in this country.

George Washington was a Christian statesman par excellence. For example, he was elected twice as President of the United States without opposition, unanimously. He refused ever to take any salary for that position. He set an unbelievable example. They tried to make him a king. He several times refused that offer. They would have had him continue running for office, but he said that for the good of his country, he would retire after his second term. He set before us a remarkable example of a statesman and of a Christian.

Sometimes modern skeptics want to lump him in with the Deists of his day. But the facts do not support that. He was an active member of his Trinitarian church. He wrote repeatedly about how God (whom he usually called Providence) had uniquely helped the American cause. He wrote to the Delaware chiefs: "You do well to wish to learn our arts and ways of life, and above all, the religion of Jesus Christ. These will make you a greater and happier people than you are. Congress will do everything they can to assist you in this wise intention."[1] Indeed, Washington was the model Christian statesman.

I believe a statesman is a person who takes office for the purpose of giving rather than for the purpose of getting. I think a statesman is a person whose soul is conscripted by a high and noble ideal—that his great desire is to benefit his nation. He (or she) is a true patriot. And I believe those are the kind of people who founded this nation. A Christian statesman, obviously, is a person who is a Christian. He or she is a civil servant.

The idea of servant-leadership comes from the Bible. Jesus said that He came to serve and to give His life as a ransom for many (Mark 10:45). Jesus said to Peter that the Gentiles lord it over each other, but it should not be that way with us. "But whoever would be great among you must be your servant" (Mark 10:43). We still say that people *serve* in office, but the servant-leader is rare today, and most politicians serve themselves and their special-interest groups.

"YOU CAN'T LEGISLATE MORALITY"

You probably have heard the cliché that you can't legislate morality. Well, that has to be one of the most foolish statements anyone has ever made. If you can't legislate morality, pray tell me, what should you legislate? Immorality? We have some in our country today who would like to do that, and they have made their attempts. Congress continues to wrestle with this, as do the courts. But historically speaking, you can't and shouldn't legislate immorality, and we have not, historically speaking, legislated anything but that which is moral. In every nation law is built upon morality and ethics, and ethics flow out of religion. Dr. Martin Luther King, Jr., pointed out that at the very least, the law could be used to prevent immorality: "While the law cannot change the heart, it can certainly restrain the heartless."[2]

The late great Dr. Francis A. Schaeffer said, "Show me the laws of any nation, and I will tell you its religion." It's just that simple. If you want a classic example of this, go to Lebanon. If you commit a crime in Lebanon, which is partially Christian and partially Muslim, they will ask you, "Do you want a Christian trial or a Muslim trial?" because they know there is a vast difference between the two. And there would probably be, depending on the crime, a vast difference in the outcome.

All legislation is based upon ethics and morality, and all morality stems from religion. What has happened in this country for the last half century is that the religion of secular humanism has been pushing aside the religion of Christianity upon which this nation was based, from which its ethics arose, and upon which its legislation was framed. So now today we have a dual foundation, and our legislators don't know whether they are voting for laws based upon humanism or based upon this nation's Christian foundation.

The humanists have done an amazing job in bringing this to pass. They have succeeded in passing into law many of their particular religious tenets and documents, such as abortion, gambling, free divorce, the freedom to have sex with any consenting person (no longer consenting adult), and many such things as that. You see, it is always some morality that is being legislated into law, and you will find that the person who is screaming the loudest, "You can't legislate morality" is with his other hand busily engaged in promoting the legislation of his own morality into law behind your back. That is what has been happening in America today. The people who have been most active in legislating humanist morality into law have also been the most vocal in screaming that you can't legislate morality. Do you begin to get some idea that a bit of a con game has been going on in our nation?

WHAT DO I WANT?

I once got a call from somebody on a newly-elected President's staff. He wanted to know what I wanted. At first I didn't understand what he meant. He said, "Well, you were a help in the campaign."

I said, "I never mentioned the candidate."

He said, "But you were a help, and we want to know what you want."

I was stunned. I said, "I don't want anything. The only thing I want is good, moral, godly government. That is all I want." And I'll say that again. I don't take any salary or honorarium or anything else from television or radio or from any political organizations. I just want to help this country, and I want to do as much good as I can while I am here. I just want to help lift up the idea of godly Christian men and women in places of authority who will put principle first.

THE GREAT EMANCIPATOR

I think of Abraham Lincoln. Why did he emancipate the slaves? Was that a political move? If it was, it was a very foolish one. He didn't need to do that when he did. He simply would have no doubt solidified the opposition to him. He said that he made a solemn vow to God that if He gave our troops victory in a certain battle, he would manumit the slaves. On the key occasion he picked up his hat and pulled out a battered piece of paper that contained on it The Emancipation Proclamation. "I made a solemn vow to God." That is a Christian statesman.

THE NATURE OF MAN

Christian statesmen recognize a truth that is not popular but is true nonetheless. It is very important to know that humanists and all nontheistic concepts of religion have always endeavored to declare that man is basically good. This is true of Communism, socialism, humanism, and all nontheistic concepts of the state.

Far from religious views being foreign and irrelevant to government and the state, Abraham Kuyper, that great theologian and statesman, declared, ". . . no political scheme has ever become dominant which was not founded in a specific religious or anti-religious conception."[3]

The United States was clearly based upon a religious, specifically Christian concept, whereas, for example, Nazism and Communism are very clearly based upon an anti-religious concept of materialistic humanism and anti-Christian and anti-God sentiments. All of these nontheistic views say that man is basically good. What did Karl Marx say? Essentially that once the workers achieve their revolution and set up a "workers' paradise," the government will wither away because government will be proven unnecessary. Try telling a Cuban today (or a Russian fifteen years ago) that he is living in "paradise." Marx got it wrong at the foundation of his theory because he had a false view of anthropology.

Here is the key issue: Are we perfectible (in our own strength), or are we corrupt? This is a theological concept, and it is vitally important in the outworking of one's view of politics. It should impact how we vote.

Dr. Gordon Clark, philosopher, in discussing the fact that all humanist views of government declare that man is good, states that socialists of all stripes are very inconsistent at this point. Psychologically they declare that man is good, but when they pass from psychology to politics, it turns out that only poor men are good, and somehow the rich have become evil. Then, if this is not inconsistent enough, in their demands for more and more governmental regulation, they clearly imply that not merely are poor people good, but politicians are even better. Since they apparently are immune from all temptation and evil and the profit motive, they can be trusted to regulate all of our daily affairs. This is an obvious contradiction.

WHICH CORRUPTS—WEALTH OR POWER?

It is vitally important to understand that in all humanistic and socialistic concepts of government, it seems that wealth corrupts, but power does not. Remember that. All of history would rise up with one voice to proclaim that thought to be a lie. It is axiomatic in history, as Lord Acton (1834-1902) pointed out, that "power corrupts, and absolute power corrupts absolutely." Notice how often you will be faced with a decision that deals with this very question—the humanistic concept that wealth corrupts, but power does not.

The founders of America, because of their clear understanding of the teachings of Christ, knew that man basically is evil; therefore, they designed the form of government that took into consideration their religious under-standing of the nature of man as being evil. Jesus said, "If you then, who are evil . . ." (Matthew 7:11). The Bible says:

- "None is righteous, no, not one." (Romans 3:10).
- ". . . for all have sinned and fall short of the glory of God" (v. 23).
- "The heart is deceitful above all things, and desperately sick; who can understand it?" (Jeremiah 17:9).

So, the founders of this government gave us a limited government, which is a basic, biblical, Calvinistic principle of government. Calvin stressed this greatly. They gave to the federal government certain specified powers and clearly stated that all of the rest were to be reserved to the states. Why did they do that? Because of the biblical doctrine that man is sinful. Furthermore, they even took the federal government and divided it into three parts to avoid the collection of power in too few hands. So we have the judicial, the leg-islative, and the executive branches of government. But today we find that the division between the powers of the state is being obliterated, the distinc-tions between the three branches of the federal government are being oblit-erated, and more and more power is being collected into fewer and fewer hands. Were the Founding Fathers of our country right? Or are men basically good? Does this really matter politically?

Not only did our founders separate the branches of government, but they ensured that the powers of government are to be divided between the federal and the states—and even some reserved unto the people.

And more than that, the powers of the federal government are to be def-initely limited and specifically enumerated.

And even more than that: There are to be other checks and balances, such as the veto, and the power of the Congress to override a veto, and the power of the courts to declare the acts of Congress unconstitutional.

These and many other things are all part of the American Constitution and system because man is evil.

James Madison, a man often called the chief architect of the Constitution, said that government was instituted among men because we are not angels (we are not basically good), and, furthermore, we need to protect the people from the government. This is what he wrote in *The Federalist*:

> But what is government but the greatest of all reflections on human nature? If men were angels, no government would be necessary. If angels were to govern men, neither external or internal controls on government would be necessary. In framing a government which is to be administered by men over men, the great difficulty lies in this: you must first enable the govern-ment to control the governed; and in the next place oblige it to control itself.[4]

In short, the founders of America recognized what the Bible, all of history, and today's newspaper attest to: the sinfulness of man.

We've seen that there are ramifications of this sin nature and the denial of it. A government like ours, which acknowledges man's selfishness and sinfulness, provides a system of government that allows for the greatest freedom and the greatest protection of our fellow human beings. But those who do not acknowledge the sinfulness of man, invariably, such as in the French Revolution, in which they said that man was good, ended up with a bloody horror and the terror of the guillotine. This is true also of the Russian Revolution, which led to the gulag; or consider the Nazi terrors of the Holocaust. In all these systems, all of these people believed man to be basically good, and they produced a hell right here on earth.

As we briefly mentioned above, Karl Marx assumed that though man was basically good, he was corrupted by capitalism and capitalism's class structures. He argued in *The Communist Manifesto* that once the proletariat (the workers) seized power and controlled the state, they would establish a social order that had no classes, and eventually no need for political power. So the state would wither away. He wrote:

> When, in the course of development, class distinctions have disappeared, and all production has been concentrated in the hands of a vast associa-tion of the whole nation, the public power will lose its political character. . . .
> In place of the old bourgeois society, with its classes and class antag-onisms, we shall have an association, in which the free development of each is the condition for the free development of all.[5]

Tens of millions of people have been murdered in the past century because of this view of man's nature. Marxism did produce a new Communist man—a man so cruel that he could commit the most barbaric crimes against his fellow human beings, without the slightest qualms of conscience, and go home and sleep at night. When we become aware of what took place in the ghastly labor camps, or gulags, we can understand the nature of the new Communist man, perhaps the cruelest man the world has ever seen.[6]

The system Marx helped create gives a false picture of man's true nature. This false paradigm has probably caused more evil than any system known to man. Recently a former Communist who became a convert to Catholicism summarized that all Communism really has had to show for its time in power is dead bodies. Eugene Genovese, who along with his wife Elizabeth Fox-Genovese used to publish *Marxist Perspectives* magazine, said this about the former Soviet Union in a recent interview:

> When it all collapsed, the question was, After seventy years, what do we have to show for it? Especially when it became clear that, even on a basic level, the system didn't deliver the goods, the one thing it was supposed to do. So what we had to show for it was tens of millions of corpses.[7]

Paul Johnson, the great historian and author of *Modern Times*, writes that the twentieth-century state "proved itself the great killer of all time."[8] The Communists bear the largest share of responsibility for that fact.

A RUDE AWAKENING

Let me give you an illustration. While I was at New York University in the late 1970s, there were about fifteen students in the very last course I took for the Doctor of Philosophy degree. These students were deans of colleges, professors in universities, and principals of high schools—the academic elite of our country. One day the discussion came around to national defense and the monies being spent upon armaments, and quite a lively discussion ensued. Seeing there was no point of agreement, I finally said to myself, "Well, I will make a point on which certainly everyone will agree, and then we can move on from there."

I said, "I assume that all of you would agree there is some degree of need for national defense. That is, if we scrapped all of our missiles, all our bombs, all our planes, and all our ships, tanks, and guns and disbanded our army, navy, marines and air force, I assume you would all agree that it would simply be a footrace to see whether Russia or China got to the Mississippi first." Silence.

"No, I don't agree with that," said one.

"Nor I," said another.

"Nor I," said a third and a fourth and a fifth.

To my utter astonishment, it turned out that there was not one single person in that classroom who felt that Russia or China or anyone else would move one little finger against us because actually the imperialism of America was the only cause of trouble in the world. If we did that which I suggested, it would simply usher in an era of universal peace. Now, that is based upon the concept that basically people are good.

You can see the political ramifications of that very unbiblical view of man. Even if you point out that history clearly refutes that view, people still do not seem to be impressed. You can point out to them, as a copy of the *Congressional Record* did, that rather than 60,000,000 people having been killed by Communism, the estimates run higher than 135,000,000 people who have been killed—20,000,000 to 40,000,000, according to the leading British expert on Soviet affairs, under the regime of Stalin alone. But that wouldn't change their mind.

It is interesting to notice the propaganda that Moscow and their allies put out years ago. For example, they used to trumpet the line that Fidel Castro was the George Washington of Cuba and Mao Tse-tung was simply an agrarian reformer. Of course (they claimed), neither of them was a Communist. Their fellow travelers in our media told us that Communism had mellowed and that the Viet Cong and the Cambodian Khmer Rouge were actually very gentlemanly folk. We saw one headline after another about their morality and their gentleness and friendliness and how things were much better under their rule—how life in Indochina without the American presence was much better, for example. No word about the link between America pulling out of Vietnam and the millions who were slaughtered in the killing fields of Cambodia as a result.

Every time John Lennon's song "Imagine" is heard on the radio, a certain nation leaps to mind. In the song he longs for the day when religion will have no more influence on society and where humankind will finally be free to make up its own rules instead. About the time of his song in the early 1970s, there was a nation on earth where a group of atheists seized power and remade society—totally free of religious superstition, totally free of God's rules about anything. The nation was Cambodia, and they ended up killing hundreds of thousands (at least one-fifth of the population) in an experiment of societal makeover. An experiment that failed, as Communism always fails because it doesn't conform to human nature. Lennon may argue, "Wait a minute. I envision a world of peace and love, free from the shackles of religion and thoughts of heaven." But given human nature as it is, such a world doesn't exist. In trying to get away from heaven in the next life, they created hell on earth.

The Word of God says, "for all have sinned and fall short of the glory of God" (Romans 3:23). Thus the biblical teaching about the nature of man is vital to our understanding of the state. Christians should not be naive about the danger of the all-powerful state. All we need to remember is how believers have been treated in all-powerful states and the role they played there: Egypt, Assyria, Babylonia, pagan Rome, Nazi Germany, Fascist Italy, Communist Russia, China, and Vietnam.

CONCLUSION

Someone said to me years ago, "Do you think as a Christian I should be involved in politics? That's dirty business." I said, "Of course not. You should leave it to the atheists; otherwise you wouldn't have anything to complain about." Well, we have plenty to complain about today because that is exactly what we've done.

Jesus Christ is not only Lord of our souls. He is Lord over politics. He is Lord over the White House, the House of Representatives and the Senate, and even the Supreme Court—although sometimes these institutions go against what He has clearly revealed. It is time for us to recognize His rightful place— yes, even in the political realm.

11

A NATION BUILT ON CHRISTIAN PRINCIPLES

Blessed is the nation whose God is the LORD.

PSALM 33:12

What happens when biblical principles are applied toward building a nation? I believe the United States of America has been such a nation. What made it great in the first place? Our Judeo-Christian heritage.

THE TRINITY DECISION

Did you know that the United States Supreme Court declared that America is a Christian nation? They did this in a 1892 decision, called the Trinity decision, which has never been abrogated. Lawyers like to say this is dictum—it is not binding. They were not deciding, is America a Christian nation, yes or no? But they arrived at their decision by marshaling arguments showing that Christianity played a unique role in the shaping of this country.

The High Court did not come to this decision lightly. After spending ten years reviewing all our founding documents, they finally made the incredible declaration that ours is a Christian land. Furthermore, this was the unanimous conclusion of those seven men (there weren't nine justices until F.D.R. packed the court in the 1930s). After reviewing major evidence, the 1892 court concluded: "These and many others which might be noticed, add a volume of unofficial declarations to the mass of organic utterances that this is a Christian nation."[1] It seems amazing that the Supreme Court could make such a ruling. Many decisions made since then have certainly ignored the Trinity case or have virtually stood the decision on its head.

THE CHURCH OF THE HOLY TRINITY VS. THE UNITED STATES

The 1892 Supreme Court decision (*The Church of the Holy Trinity vs. The United States*) concludes, virtually without controversy, that America was founded as a Christian nation. The details surrounding the case are rather complicated. The gist of the dispute was this: Is a church body exempt from some of the laws applied to other types of organizations? The court answered that it was, and its rationale comprises the bulk of the Trinity decision. Specifically, the controversy surrounded whether an Episcopal church in Ohio, the Church of the Holy Trinity, violated a law prohibiting the hiring of foreigners. The church hired a minister from overseas and was hauled into court for allegedly violating a law that restricted laborers from abroad from coming here, lest they take away American jobs. The case worked its way through lower courts all the way to the Supreme Court, where the church prevailed.

MAJOR PORTIONS OF THE TRINITY DECISION

Here are major portions of the Trinity decision, interrupted by my commentary on the same. I have assigned numbers to the arguments made, just to simplify the points.

1) Opening Overview—We Are a Christian People

The Trinity decision begins with all the specifics of the case. Then for page upon page it explores the deeper question as to why this church in Ohio, or any church in the United States, may possibly be exempt from this type of law: Are we or are we not a Christian nation? The Supreme Court weighs in on the issue: "This is a religious people. This is historically true. From the discovery of this continent to the present hour, there is a single voice making this affirmation."[2]

When the court wrote in 1892 that we are a religious people, they were saying we are a Christian people. Far more than 90 percent of the country at that time were professing Christians. (Even today the number is about 78 percent.[3])

2) The Commission to Christopher Columbus Mentions God

The commission to Christopher Columbus, prior to his sail westward, was from "Ferdinand and Isabella, by the grace of God, King and Queen of Castile," etc. and recites that "it is hoped that by God's assistance some of the continents and islands in the ocean will be discovered," etc.[4]

The Supreme Court takes us back to Columbus, who was so clearly motivated by Christ to undertake his death-defying voyage. As he wrote: "it was the Lord who put into my mind (I could feel His hand upon me) to sail to the Indies."[5]

3) The Earliest Charters and Grants All Mention God

The first colonial grant, that [was] made to Sir Walter Raleigh in 1584, was from "Elizabeth, by the grace of God, of England, France and Ireland, queen, defender of the faith," etc; and the grant authorizing him to enact statutes for the government of the proposed colony provided that "they be not against the true Christian faith now professed in the Church of England." The first charter of Virginia, granted by King James I in 1606, after reciting the application of certain parties for a charter, commenced the grant in these words: "We, greatly commending, and graciously accepting of, their Desires for the Furtherance of so noble a Work, which may, by the Providence of Almighty God, hereafter tend to the Glory of His Divine Majesty, in propagating of Christian Religion to such People as yet live in Darkness and miserable Ignorance of the true Knowledge and Worship of God, and may in time bring the Infidels and Savages, living in those parts, to human Civility, and to a settled and quiet Government; Do, by these our Letters-Patents, graciously accept of similar import may be found in the subsequent characters of that colony, from the same king, in 1609 and 1611; and the same is true of the various charters granted to the other colonies. In language more or less emphatic is the establishment of the Christian religion declared to be one of the purposes of the grant.[6]

Examine any colonial charter of America. Every one of them mentions a Christian goal as their reason for coming to these shores. Here's a small sample:

• The charter of Massachusetts Bay, granted in 1629 by Charles I: "Whereby our said people, inhabitants there, may be so religiously, peaceably and civilly governed as their good life and orderly conversation may win and incite the natives of the country to their knowledge and obedience of the only true God and Saviour of mankind, and the Christian faith. . . ."[7]

• The charter of Maryland, 1632, founded by Catholics, with the colony being named after Maria, the wife of Charles I: "Charles, by the Grace of God, of England, Scotland, France, and Ireland, king, Defender of the Faith, etc. . . . being animated with a laudable, and pious Zeal for extending the Christian Religion. . . ."[8]

• The charter of the Carolina colony (which eventually split into two).

Supreme Court Justice David Brewer, the man who wrote the Trinity decision, also wrote *The United States: A Christian Nation* in 1905, in which he
stated: "The charter of Carolina, granted in 1663 by Charles II, recites that
the petitioners, 'being excited with a laudable and pious zeal for the propa-
gation of the Christian faith . . .'"[9]

• Pennsylvania was founded by the devout Quaker William Penn, and
here is its Frame of Government (1682): "They weakly err, that think there
is no other use of government than correction, which is the coarsest part of
it; daily experience tells us that the care and regulation of many other affairs,
more soft, and daily necessary, make up much of the greatest part of government; and which must have followed the peopling of the world, had Adam
never fell, and will continue among men, on earth, under the highest attain-
ments they may arrive at, by the coming of the blessed second Adam, 'the
Lord from heaven.' And with the laws prepared to go with the frame of government, it was further provided 'that according to the good example of the
primitive Christians, and the ease of the creation, every first day of the week,
called the Lord's Day, people shall abstain from their common daily labor that
they may the better dispose themselves to worship God according to their
understandings."[10] Here he is marshaling the Bible to make the point that
government is an instrument of God for our good.

4) The Mayflower Compact Was Christian. . . .

> The celebrated compact made by the Pilgrims on the *Mayflower*, 1620,
> recites: "Having undertaken for the Glory of God, and Advancement of the
> Christian Faith, and the Honour of our King and Country, a Voyage to
> plant the first Colony in the northern Parts of Virginia; Do by these Presents,
> solemnly and mutually, in the Presence of God and one another, covenant
> and combine ourselves together into a civil Body Politic, for our better
> Ordering and Preservation, and Furtherance of the Ends aforesaid."[11]

The Mayflower Compact begins: "In the name of God. Amen."[12] Is it not
accurate to say that in a very real sense, America began in the name of God?
Amen.

5) . . . As Were "The Fundamental Orders Of Connecticut," One of Our Earliest Constitutions

The Supreme Court now shifts from the Pilgrims to the second full-blown
constitution written by American colonists, by the Puritans who established
the Connecticut settlement.

The fundamental orders of Connecticut, under which a provisional government was instituted in 1638-1639, commence with this declaration: "Forasmuch as it hath pleased the Almighty God by the wise disposition of his divine providence so to Order and dispose of things that we the Inhabitants and Residents of Windsor, Hartford and Wethersfield are now cohabiting and dwelling in and upon the River of Conectecotte and the Lands thereunto adjoining; And well knowing where a people are gathered together the word of God requires that to maintain the peace and union of such a people there should be an orderly and decent Government established according to God, to order and dispose of the affairs of the people at all seasons as occasion shall require; do therefore associate and conjoin our souls to be as one Public State or Commonwealth; and do, for our souls and our Successors and such as shall be adjoined to us at any time hereafter, enter into Combination and Confederation together, to maintain and preserve the liberty and purity of the gospel of our Lord Jesus which we now profess, as also the discipline of the Churches, which according to the truth of the said gospel is now practiced amongst us."[13]

The Puritans were not reticent to mention God or Jesus Christ—the very basis of their colonies—in their political charters, compacts, and constitutions.

6) Penn's Charter States That God Is the Source of Our Liberty

Next we see the Pennsylvania charter, allowing for religious liberty under God:

In the charter of privileges granted, in 1701, by William Penn to the province of Pennsylvania and territories thereunto belonging (such territories afterwards constituting the State of Delaware), it is recited: "Because no People can be truly happy, though under the greatest Enjoyment of Civil Liberties, if abridged of the Freedom of their Consciences, as to their Religious Profession and Worship; And Almighty God being the only Lord of Conscience, Father of Lights and Spirits, and the Author as well as Object of all divine Knowledge, Faith and Worship, who only doth enlighten the Minds, and persuade and convince the Understandings of the People, I do hereby grant and declare," etc.[14]

Next, the High Court jumps ahead to the time of the American Revolution.

7) The Declaration of Independence Proclaims God as the Source of Our Liberty

> Coming nearer to the present time, the Declaration of Independence rec-
> ognizes the presence of the Divine in human affairs in these words: "We
> hold these truths to be self-evident, that all men are created equal, that they
> are endowed by their Creator with certain unalienable Rights, that among
> these are Life, Liberty, and pursuit of Happiness." "We, therefore, the
> Representatives of the United States of America, in General Congress,
> Assembled, appealing to the Supreme Judge of the world for the rectitude
> of our intentions, do, in the Name and by Authority of the good People of
> these Colonies, solemnly publish and declare," etc.; "And for the support
> of this Declaration, with a firm reliance on the Protection of Divine
> Providence, we mutually pledge to each other our Lives, our Fortunes, and
> our sacred Honor."[15]

Four times the Declaration of Independence, our nation's birth certificate, mentions God, the source of our liberties. Notice how the court shifted from Penn's charter, which acknowledged their liberties as a gift from Almighty God, to the Declaration, written in Philadelphia, which also declares that our liberties come from God. Man can't take them away.

8) The State Constitutions Mention God and Often Have (Had) Specific Religious Requirements, e.g., for Those Running for Office

As the colonies shifted over to states, these new entities still recognized God:

> If we examine the constitutions of the various States we find in them a con-
> stant recognition of religious obligations. Every constitution of every one
> of the forty-four States contains language which either directly or by clear
> implication recognizes a profound reverence for religion and an assump-
> tion that its influence in all human affairs is essential to the well being of
> the community. This recognition may be in the preamble, such as is found
> in the constitution of Illinois, 1870: "We, the people of the State of Illinois,
> grateful to Almighty God for the civil, political and religious liberty which
> He hath so long permitted us to enjoy, and looking to Him for a blessing
> upon our endeavors to secure and transmit the same unimpaired to suc-
> ceeding generations," etc.[16]

Illinois is obviously just one example. The constitution of every one of the fifty states mentions God somewhere in the document (usually in the preamble). The Supreme Court continues to look further at state constitutions and the fact that they mention God:

> It may be only in the familiar requisition that all officers shall take an oath closing with the declaration "so help me God." It may be in clauses like that of the constitution of Indiana, 1816 Article XI, section 4: "The manner of administering an oath or affirmation shall be such as is most consistent with the conscience of the deponent, and shall be esteemed the most solemn appeal to God." Or in provisions such as are found in Articles 36 and 37 of the Declaration of Rights of the Constitution of Maryland, 1867: "That as it is the duty of every man to worship God in such manner as he thinks most acceptable to Him, all persons are equally entitled to protection in their religious liberty; wherefore, no person ought, by any law, to be molested in his person or estate on account of his religious persuasion or profession, or for his religious practice, unless, under the color of religion, he shall disturb the good, order, peace or safety of the State, or shall infringe the laws of morality, or injure others in their natural, civil or religious rights; nor ought any person to be compelled to frequent or maintain or contribute, unless on contract, to maintain any place of worship, or any ministry; nor shall any person, otherwise competent, be deemed incompetent as a witness, or juror, on account of his religious belief: Provided, He believes in the existence of God, and that, under His dispensation, such person will be held morally accountable for his acts, and be rewarded or punished therefore, either in this world or the world to come. That no religious test ought ever to be required as a qualification for any office of profit or trust in this State other than a declaration of belief in the existence of God; nor shall the legislature prescribe any other oath of office than the oath prescribed by this constitution."[17]

This Maryland state constitution, quoted at length by the High Court, demonstrates the importance of belief in God. And remember, for the vast majority of the lawmakers and the law-abiders, it was the Christian God under consideration. This Maryland constitution of 1867 had been written long after direct Puritan influence in New England had waned.

On the one hand, there was no direct religious test that could be applied for those running for office (e.g., no denominational boundaries). On the other hand, they had to believe in God. Why would they stipulate that? They tell us why directly: Belief in God implies moral accountability. We shall all stand before the judgment seat of God and give an account before Him. When people believe that, it makes them better citizens. When they don't believe it, then they often try to get away with whatever they can. As Dostoevsky pointed out, "Destroy a man's belief in immortality and not only will his ability to love wither away within him but, along with it, the force that impels him to continue his existence on earth. Moreover, nothing would be immoral then, everything would be permitted, even cannibalism."[18]

Returning to the Trinity decision:

> Or like that in Articles 2 and 3, of Part 1st, of the Constitution of Massachusetts, 1780: "It is the right as well as the duty of all men in society publicly and at stated seasons, to worship the Supreme Being, the great Creator and Preserver of the universe. . . . As the happiness of a people and the good order and preservation of civil government essentially depend upon piety, religion and morality, and as these cannot be generally diffused through a community but by the institution of the public worship of God and of public instructions in piety, religion and morality: Therefore, to promote their happiness and to secure the good order and preservation of their government, the people of this commonwealth have a right to invest their legislature with power to authorize and require, and the legislature shall, from time to time, authorize and require, the several towns, parishes, precincts and other bodies-politic or religious societies to make suitable provision, at their own expense, for the institution of the public worship of God and for the support and maintenance of public Protestant teachers of piety, religion and morality in all cases where such provision shall not be made voluntarily." Or as in sections 5 and 14 of Article 7, of the constitution of Mississippi, 1832: "No person who denies the being of a God, or a future state of rewards and punishments, shall hold any office in the civil department of this State. . . . Religion, morality and knowledge being necessary to good government, the preservation of liberty, and the happiness of mankind, schools and the means of education, shall forever be encouraged in this State."[19] Or by Article 22 of the constitution of Delaware, 1776, which required all officers, besides an oath of allegiance, to make and subscribe the following declaration, "I, A.B., do profess faith in God the Father, and in Jesus Christ His only Son, and in the Holy Ghost, one God, blessed for evermore; and I do acknowledge the Holy Scriptures of the Old and New Testament to be given by divine inspiration."[20]

We see here that some of the states, such as Mississippi or Delaware, stipulated a Christian belief system for those running for office. Like the Maryland state constitution, the Mississippi constitution of 1832 declared that man's accountability to God was an important condition to them for their rulers. They didn't want any rogue politicians.

9) *The U.S. Constitution Is Indirectly Christian*

Now the Trinity decision shifts over from some of the state constitutions, which were directly Christian, to the federal one:

> Even the Constitution of the United States, which is supposed to have little touch upon the private life of the individual, contains in the First Amendment, a declaration common to the constitutions of all the States, as follows: "Congress shall make no law respecting an establishment of religion, or prohibiting the free exercise thereof," etc. And also provides in Article 1, section 7, (a provision common to many constitutions,) that the Executive shall have ten days (Sundays excepted) within which to determine whether he will approve or veto a bill.[21]

Note what the court says here about the Constitution in general—it's "supposed to have little touch upon the private life of the individual." This is significant because it shows that in earlier times the Supreme Court did not view the Constitution as something that regulated what we believe or how we worship.

10) *Earlier, Lower Court Decisions Affirm This Is a Christian People*

Next the High Court reviews some earlier court decisions that affirm the inescapable conclusion that they are building up to:

> There is no dissonance in these declarations. There is a universal language pervading them all, having one meaning; they affirm and reaffirm that this is a religious nation. These are not individual sayings, declarations of private persons; they are organic utterances; they speak the voice of the entire people. While because of a general recognition of this truth the question has seldom been presented to the courts, yet we find that in *Updegraph v. The Commonwealth*, 11 S. & R. 394, 400, it was decided that, "Christianity, general Christianity, is, and always had been, a part of the common law of Pennsylvania; . . . not Christianity with an established church, and tithes, and spiritual courts; but Christianity with liberty of conscience to all men." And in *The People v. Ruggles*, 8 Johns. 290, 294, 295, Chancellor Kent, the great commentator on American law, speaking as Chief Justice of the Supreme Court of New York, said: "The people in this State, in common with the people of this country, profess the general doctrines of Christianity, as the rule of their faith and practice; and to scandalize the author of these doctrines is not only, in a religious point of view, extremely impious, but, even in respect to the obligations due to society, is

a gross violation of decency and good order. . . . The free, equal, and undis-
turbed enjoyment of religious opinion, whatever it may be, and free and
decent discussions on any religious subject, is granted and recurred; but to
revile, with malicious and blasphemous contempt, the religion professed by
almost the whole community, is an abuse of that right. Nor are we bound,
by any expressions in the Constitution as some have strangely supposed,
either not to punish at all, or to punish indiscriminately, the like attacks
upon the religion of Mahomet or the Grand Lama; and for this plain reason, that the case assumes that we are a Christian people, and the morality of this country is deeply engrafted upon Christianity, and not upon the
doctrines or worship of those imposters."[22]

Did you catch how politically incorrect all this is? The Supreme Court of
the United States is quoting with approval an earlier, lower-court decision that
dares to call followers of non-Christian religions "imposters." These days we
have become so accustomed to Christian-bashing that we become numb to
it, but in earlier times it was illegal and punished by U.S. courts.

And in the famous case of *Vidal v. Girard's Executors*, 2 How. 127, 198,
this court, while sustaining the will of Mr. Girard, with its provision for
the creation of a college into which no minister should be permitted to
enter, observed: "It is also said, and truly, that the Christian religion is part
of the common law of Pennsylvania."[23]

So we see that courts in the nineteenth century were much more favor-
able to Christianity than recent courts have been. Here's the essence of what
these three court cases cited:
   • "The people . . . of this country profess the general doctrines of
Christianity" (*Updegraph v. The Commonwealth*).
   • ". . . we are a Christian people . . ." (*The People v. Ruggles*).
   • ". . . the Christian religion is part of the common law of Pennsylvania"
(*Vidal v. Girard's Executors*).
   Now the Court is building up to its climax:

11) *The Climactic Conclusion: This Is a Christian Nation*

If we pass beyond these matters to a view of American life as expressed by
its laws, its business, its customs and its society, we find everywhere a clear
recognition of the same truth. Among other matters note the following: The
form of oath universally prevailing, concluding with an appeal to the
Almighty; the custom of opening sessions of all deliberative bodies and

most conventions with prayer; the prefatory words of all wills, "In the name of God, amen;" the laws respecting the observance of the Sabbath, with the general cessation of all secular business, and the closing of courts, legislatures, and other similar public assemblies on that day; the churches and church organizations which abound in every city, town and hamlet; the multitude of charitable organizations existing every where under Christian auspices; the gigantic missionary associations, with general support, and aiming to establish Christian missions in every quarter of the globe. These and many others which might be noticed, add a volume of unofficial declarations to the mass of organic utterances that this is a Christian nation.[24]

These may be fighting words today, but there it is in black-and-white. The United States Supreme Court declared that "this is a Christian nation."

OBJECTIONS TO THE IDEA OF AMERICA AS A CHRISTIAN NATION

One of the key objections is that America has not always lived up to Christian ideals. Shamefully, there have been some serious flaws in our history. The most notable of these in times past was the mistreatment of the Indians and the practice of slavery. The Founding Fathers didn't create a perfect government; but they created the means by which such evils could be corrected.

A serious blotch on the American experience was its condoning of slavery for so long. Dr. Martin Luther King, Jr., liked to point out that a year before the Pilgrim forefathers came over, the first batch of slaves arrived and were sold here. In 1619, one year before the disembarking of the Pilgrims at Plymouth, a handful of slaves was sold at Jamestown, and thus began "the peculiar institution" that was destined to tear the country in two some two and a half centuries later.

Dr. John Eidsmoe, respected historian, law professor, and author of the classic book *Christianity and the Constitution*, once told my coauthor on this book, Jerry Newcombe, that there never would have been a United States Constitution if the Founding Fathers had made slavery illegal right away. Some of the southern states, notably South Carolina, would not have agreed with the document.

Virtually from the introduction of slavery on American soil until its abolition at the end of the Civil War and the Fourteenth Amendment (1868), there had been strong opposition to slavery—mostly from Christian quarters. For example, in 1652 in Rhode Island, there was a move against slavery, as was true eventually in the other colonies of New England. Providence and Warwick made a law that "no black mankind by covenant, bond, or otherwise" was to be forced to perpetually serve. The master "at the end of ten years, shall set them free, as the manner is with English servants; and that man that will not let [his slave] go free, or shall send him away, to the end that he may be enslaved to others for a longer time, shall forfeit to the colony forty pounds."[25] Historian George Bancroft points out that forty pounds was twice the value of a black slave in those days. So the colony made slavery illegal and provided financial incentives to not own a slave. Bancroft adds: "The law was not enforced; but the principle did not perish."[26]

Even in the South there was some strong opposition to slavery. Notice what Patrick Henry said about the slave trade in a letter he wrote in 1773:

> I take this opportunity to acknowledge the receipt of Anthony Benezet's book against the slave trade. I thank you for it. . . . Is it not amazing, that at a time when the rights of humanity are defined and understood with precision in a country above all others fond of liberty, that in such an age and in such a country, we find men professing a religion most humane, mild, meek, gentle and generous, adopting a Principle as repugnant to humanity, as it is inconsistent to the Bible and destructive to liberty? . . . I will not, I cannot justify it. . . . I believe a time will come when an opportunity will be offered to abolish this lamentable evil. . . . It is a debt we owe to the purity of our Religion to show that it is at variance with that law which warrants slavery.[27]

While the Founding Fathers were not able to abolish slavery at the Constitutional Convention, they were able to stipulate that the slave trade would be abolished by 1808. And so it was. Unfortunately, it would take much longer to free the slaves already here. Of course, Christians helped pave the way—beginning with William Wilberforce's lifelong crusade to free the slaves in his native England, which helped inspire the abolition movement in America.

Obviously, these conflicts between pro-slavery and anti-slavery states were not resolved until the Civil War. Then for a hundred years after that, strong forms of racism still needed to be addressed. Racism is clearly wrong because the Bible teaches that through one man, God made all the people of the earth (Acts 17:26).

Regarding American Indians, how colonists treated them was commendable in some cases and deplorable in others. I hold up as positive examples in this realm the Pilgrims (who made a treaty of peace that lasted for more than fifty years), Roger Williams (who chided his fellow Puritans for not always paying for the Indian lands they took), and William Penn (who consistently treated the Indians in a Christian manner). Bancroft points out that justice for all, including the Indians, was important to the Pilgrims of Plymouth. "Murder had ever been severely punished by the Puritans: they had at Plymouth, with the advice of Massachusetts, executed three of their own men for taking the life of one Indian."[28]

The greatest travesties against the Indians took place in the nineteenth century. Many of those who most slaughtered the Native Americans were Indian-haters who had cut their teeth fighting in the Civil War. Some of these veterans may possibly have been professing Christians, but they certainly weren't known for their piety.

CONCLUSION

The Supreme Court decision of 1892 was very well-researched and well-written. It drew on innumerable primary documents of our nation's founding. But to even quote the Trinity decision today is politically incorrect. Yet the facts in the decision still stand, historical revisionism notwithstanding. The facts are the facts.

Apply biblical principles to government, and you end up with the best aspects we find in America. Despite all our flaws, we have a self-correcting system of checks and balances that gives people freedom—freedom that comes from the Almighty. As John F. Kennedy said at his Inaugural Address, "I am proud of the revolutionary beliefs for which our forebears fought . . . the belief that the rights of man come not from the generosity of the state but the hands of God."[29]

12

THE BIBLE AND THE ECONOMY

For even when we were with you, we would give you this command: If anyone is not willing to work, let him not eat.

2 THESSALONIANS 3:10

Christian author Mary Hunt felt deprived as she grew up; she could never get enough money, which—she confesses—she loved. Her childhood dream was to get rich one day. She married a banking executive with the assumption that her financial problems would be over. "After all, a man is supposed to take care of his wife," she reasoned, "handle the finances, and make sure she, whose job it is to spend the money, has plenty of it."

But her life didn't work out that way. Life seldom does.

In September 1982, after twelve years of marriage, the bottom fell out for Mary's family financially. Her husband had started a home business, which failed after only four months. What made matters worse was that they were 100,000 dollars in debt, which was mostly consumer debt that Mary had cheerfully run up.

The Hunts didn't take the easy way out. They eventually paid back the entire debt, plus all the interest, which took them at least thirteen years.

One of the things they had to come to grips with was Mary's spending habit. Mary says, "I've come to face my compulsive overspending problem and am learning one day at a time how to deal with that and depend on God to meet our needs, instead of looking to credit as a solution."

Today Mary Hunt is a financial counselor, helping couples and individuals get out of debt and stay out of debt. She even publishes her own newsletter, *The Cheapskate Monthly*.[1] Mary has learned how to hunt for and find a bargain. She says, "It is possible to become responsible in areas where irresponsibility is the order of the day."[2]

Mary Hunt came face-to-face with the cause of her financial irresponsibility, and by the grace of God, she was able to change. If we're ever to live under the lordship of Christ, we need to apply God's principles to our finances as individuals, as families, as churches, as communities, as cities, as states, and as a nation. Too often we live well today because we rack up major debts for tomorrow.

THE WONDER OF THE WORLD

America has always been a wonder in the eyes of the world: the home of the free and the land of the rich—a land of unparalleled opportunity. A city set upon a hill, shining in the noonday sun and sending forth its gleams to the ends of the earth—to the desolate, the destitute, the tempest-tossed, who have come by the millions to these shores of plenty. Yet today the dream seems to have faded. For a large number of Americans the opportunities seem to be gone. Something seems to have gone wrong, but most folks cannot quite put their finger on what that is.

What I am about to say is politically incorrect, but it needs to be said. I want to talk to you about what the Bible says about economics. Most of our politicians shy away from this subject like it was the plague. Economics may seem like an academic and theoretical subject, but I disagree—it is very practical. Each one of us lives life enmeshed in the world of economics. It is well that we understand it and perhaps see where this nation went wrong. This economic deviance has taken decades to transpire, and therefore it is difficult to perceive. So let us step aside and look at what is happening in America today through the lens of God's Word.

WHAT GOD SAYS ABOUT PRIVATE PROPERTY AND WORK

The Bible is not a textbook on economics. It is not a textbook on politics or science either. But Scripture has a great deal to say about all those subjects that is true and valuable. From those teachings we may erect certain systems and derive an understanding about those subjects. Certainly the Bible has much to say about private property. Man has a legitimate interest in the possession of his own property, Scripture says, and that interest is guarded by the flaming sword of divine vengeance and is guaranteed in the Decalogue: "You shall not steal" (Exodus 20:15).

God knows that for us to fulfill our probation in this world, it will be necessary for us to make use of the things of this world. If we are going to demonstrate our faithfulness in little things, if we are going to demonstrate our honesty, if we are going to demonstrate our charity, we will need to exercise private ownership. Therefore God has guaranteed it.

This rules out certain systems—for instance, systems that deny private property, such as Communism or various aspects of socialism that would deprive us of our property rights. The Bible has a good deal to say about other things that impinge upon economic matters, such as greed and covetousness and envy and jealousy. Scripture also has something to say about work.

GOD HAS ORDAINED WORK

Many people suppose that work is a curse to be avoided if at all possible, an activity to be involved in only when necessary. This is not the case. God ordained work before the Fall. Adam was commanded to tend the garden before he fell into sin; therefore it is not part of the curse (Genesis 2:15). Even after the first sin, work still occupies a very important position in man's life, though it is greatly aggravated by the results of the Fall and the curse (Genesis 3:17-19). Without work, it is impossible for any human being to fulfill God's purpose for his or her life.

The apostle Paul minces no words about loafers: "For even when we were with you, we would give you this command: If anyone is not willing to work, let him not eat" (2 Thessalonians 3:10). The apostle knew that man inclines toward evil and so will avoid all opportunities to work if he can.

This does not refer to a person who is not able to work. The Scripture has a great deal to say about caring for the lame, the blind, the sick, the infirm, the aged, and the very young. But if anyone will not work, if he refuses to work, then neither let him eat.

Most people feel a twinge of guilt when they hear those words, as if they were words without compassion. May I say to you that this is the most compassionate statement on the subject of economics that has ever been uttered. Were that not to a large degree followed, wholesale famine and starvation would plague the world. So let it be proclaimed to a deaf culture that is committed to a partial form of socialism based on what one scholar calls "the politics of guilt and pity": If anyone will not work, neither let him eat.

The Bible also says much about justice and charity.

JUSTICE AND CHARITY

The Bible does not equate justice with charity, as we do today, which results in a great source of confusion. Equating justice with charity slows down productivity and puts a damper on the growth of the Gross National Product, throwing people out of work and creating all sorts of economic chaos in the nation today. It is vitally important that people understand the difference between the two. Yet probably 95 percent of Americans cannot define justice or charity clearly.

Let us look closely at justice and charity for a moment.

JUSTICE: IMPARTIALITY

What is justice? Justice means fairness, impartiality. Justice is blind. We have been trying to tell people that for many centuries. Remember the famous statue of Justice with scales held high and a sword in hand but a blindfold over the eyes. Justice does not discriminate: It does not see whether one is of high or low class, rich or poor, black or white, working or not working. It does not see one's national origin, nor one's religion. It treats all men and women equally (Proverbs 18:5). That is the essence of justice. The sword in the statue's hands reminds us that justice is enforced by the coercive power of the state (Romans 13:4). The principal business of the state, law, and government is protecting the rights of all people equally.

CHARITY: DISCRIMINATING AND VOLUNTARY

On the other hand, charity is not blind, nor is it based on coercion. Charity is discriminating and voluntary. If you remove the voluntary aspect of charity, it ceases to be charity. What would you think if a rich man told his friends how charitable he had been to the poor after Robin Hood had placed his sword at that man's throat and deprived him of his purse, then scattered his coins to the poor? There was no charity on the rich man's part—not a penny's worth. If you take away the voluntary aspect of charity, it becomes despoliation, legal plunder, robbery, not charity.

Confusing justice and charity has produced something called "social justice," the basis for the welfare state. Even though we have had limited welfare reform recently, many premises of the welfare state still linger in the minds of millions as unspoken assumptions that we dare not challenge. Yet the irony is that social justice is having a tremendous negative impact upon the economic well-being of this country.

You cannot have charity or justice when you forcibly take money from

A and give it to B. You do not have charity because the money was not freely given. You do not act justly because you are not treating A and B equally. Instead, you are taking from one and giving to the other. The rights of each have not been protected but stripped.

SOCIAL JUSTICE AND THE REDISTRIBUTION OF WEALTH

Behind this notion of social justice lurks the idea that there must be a more equitable distribution of wealth. We have heard this so many times that I am sure the majority of Americans have accepted it. Sometimes the politicians talk about the wealthy "paying their fair share." These notions presuppose the idea of a static economic pie of one size that stays constant. Many think it obvious that if you have eight people and one pie, and one person ends up with a very large piece of this pie, that person is despoiling somebody else. Therefore we need to intervene with justice, which means we are going to take away part of that person's pie and give it to somebody who has less. This concept has become so prevalent in America that it needs to be carefully examined.

First of all, this notion accepts the static view of economics typical of Communism but is totally alien to the free enterprise system that made this country prosperous. Free-market economics postulates a growing economic pie and by no means indicates that if one person has more, another person must inevitably have less. It postulates exactly the opposite. If one person has more, in the process of getting more, this person has succeeded in contributing to the enlargement of every other piece.

For example, Henry Ford was born into this world a poor man. Yet when he left the world, he was worth hundreds of millions of dollars. From the static point of view, the Communist point of view, Ford obtained hundreds of millions of dollars by plundering everyone else. He despoiled all of us. If justice prevails, we should take that away from him and divide it among ourselves because he has impoverished us by his gain.

Is that true? No. Instead we are all richer because of Henry Ford. Would you prefer to walk to work or the store or ride a horse?

I find it fascinating to hear the latest starlet who wears a 5,000 dollar designer dress downgrade the capitalist system. She is then shuttled off in her limousine to her multi-million-dollar mansion. These are "limousine liberals," also known as "sofa socialists."

Unfortunately those who know little about economics often denigrate capitalism and the free-market system.

THE FREE MARKET AND ECONOMIC GROWTH

Adam Smith wrote his famous foundational work *The Wealth of Nations* in 1776, the year America was born. Though the Bible laid out some of the principles upon which such a free system should be built—for example, "You shall not steal" and "You shall not covet" (Exodus 20:15, 17)—people had never put them all together. In the popular parlance of today, Adam Smith was the first to connect the dots after the Reformers, particularly John Calvin, helped bring many of them to light. On that basis Adam Smith finally put the pieces together in his book, which has impelled scholars to say that modern capitalism began around 1780.

INITIAL DIFFICULTIES IN THE ADJUSTMENT

In the early days of implementing capitalism, there was unprecedented growth. But there were also abuses. Charles Dickens's novels often capture the dreary existence of the workers—children and adults—in the early factories. While a small group had begun to obtain great wealth and power, the masses often lived in tenement-like conditions. Meanwhile, a middle class began to emerge. Karl Marx and Frederick Engels fired their salvos on behalf of the workers. Later laws against monopolies began to emerge, as did unions, often born in bloody street battles outside factories. All of these attempted to correct abuses in the capitalist system.

However, in the long run free enterprise and capitalism produced wealth on a scale unknown to humankind. As the middle class grew, this wealth became available to millions more. Today the average Westerner has meals that are so lavish that they exceed what kings and queens ate in past centuries. We suffer from overeating, not starvation.

President John F. Kennedy gave us a memorable analogy in a slightly different context. At the time he was promoting tax cuts, which in today's political milieu may seem out-of-place. Imagine a Democrat leading the charge on behalf of tax cuts! Kennedy likened tax cuts to high tide in a harbor, which raises all boats and ships, no matter the size. The large cargo ship rises, and so does the rubber dinghy. I think President Kennedy was right on this one. Giving the taxpayers a refund to spend their own money just means we were overtaxed in the first place.

Similarly, capitalism and the free enterprise system have brought incredible wealth to tens of millions of people. Even the poor in capitalist countries do much better than the poor of countries with limited capitalistic development. The poor here rarely miss a meal. Yet in some countries—barely touched by the free enterprise system and modern capitalism—there are garbage-dump people—men, women, and children who live in the garbage dumps, foraging around for whatever morsels of food they can find.

And yet capitalism and the free enterprise system continue to get a bad rap.

SOMETHING FOR NOTHING

After the initial successes and growing pains of capitalism, statist concepts (the limited pie theory I described earlier) began to be proclaimed. Even Christians sometimes fell prey to this mistake. The problem with these concepts is that they presuppose that limited pie. But the socialist utopians began to weave their magic spells over people's minds. The old idea of something for nothing permeated thought and desire until they began, more and more, to interfere and to hamstring the type of economic system that had produced America, the land of plenty and opportunity, until today we have enormous economic problems and hop along with one foot tied behind our back.

Someone could argue that the prosperity we enjoy is so great, why worry about making a little bit more? Part of my point is that the poor are the ones hurt by the policies of those who promote the politics of guilt and pity. Welfare chased dads out of many poor households and condemned single-mom households to a hopeless life of poverty. The poor in America would be much better off had welfare never become so popular and widespread, since the family is the key to upward mobility.

Years ago Dan Quayle chided Hollywood for fostering the myth of the successful single parent. Oh, there are exceptions to that myth, but for the most part millions are trapped in a life of poverty because of their single-parenthood state. In fact, less than a year after Quayle was crucified for his infamous (but very wise) Murphy Brown speech, *Atlantic Monthly* did a cover story on the issue, declaring in bold words, "Dan Quayle Was Right."[3]

The point is, programs to help the needy inevitably throw gasoline on the problem.

We spent five trillion dollars on the War on Poverty, and we lost. The welfare state inevitably produces more of that which it sets out to cure. Fifty years ago there were practically no transfer payments (welfare checks, food stamps, national school lunch programs, and so on) or other forms of social spending in this country.

When I preached about this in the early 1980s, there were 283 billion dollars in transfer payments of one sort or another. Today if you add up the

U.S. Department of Treasury's outlays for Fiscal 2000, that number exceeds 900 billion dollars. This only applies to federal spending. This has nothing to do with state and local wealth-transfer programs.

Let me show where I come up with this number (which by no means includes all federal expenditures that are essentially transfer programs):

Food Assistance Programs	$32,687,000,000[4]
Public Health Service	$28,281,000,000
Health Care financing	$413,124,000,000
Housing and Urban Development Department	$30,830,000,000
Unemployment Trust	$24,149,000,000
Social Security Administration	$441,810,000,000
Total	$970,881,000,000[5]

This means that nearly one trillion dollars per year of taxpayers' money was spent on these different transfer programs, and again, this list is by no means exhaustive of federal spending alone for such purposes. Do we have less poor people today than when we began all these programs? I don't think so. These programs have hurt the very people they have purported to help, and they have partially hamstrung the economy for all of us.[6]

Anything the government subsidizes, increases. If chickens are selling for a dollar a pound, and the government subsidizes them for a dollar fifty a pound, what will inevitably happen? In five years you will be up to your armpits in chickens. The same is true with the welfare system. We are going to have more and more people on it.

The truth of this can be seen in the preliminary results of welfare reform. Such reform has helped many women not get caught in the vicious cycle of poverty, inherent in becoming a "welfare mom." For example, Cheryl Wetzstein writes in *The Washington Times*: "A new study in two states finds that welfare reform is discouraging single mothers from having more children and encouraging them to think 'more seriously about getting married.'"[7] Welfare reform is certainly a step in the right direction.

In the early 1800s, someone astutely predicted, "America will last until the populace discovers that it can vote for itself largesse out of the public treasury."[8]

Largesse is a term any sixth grader reading *McGuffey's Reader* would know. Yet the average American with his modern education probably does not know what the term means. What this saying means is that America will last until people realize they can vote gifts or handouts from the public treasury for themselves.

Much of the public has discovered this with a vengeance. And the politicians are bending over backwards to let the rest of the people know. Often politicians boast about how much money they've managed to steer from the public treasury to their state and their pet projects. What few people say is that this is the people's money, not the politicians' money.

THE SAD RESULTS OF SOCIALISM

The welfare state inevitably produces conflict. I remember one time when President Ronald Reagan spoke, and reporters interviewed a group of protesters afterward. Every one of them was angrier than a hornet because each wanted more money out of the public treasury for his little thing, whatever it was. "We want money for this, and we want money for that," they said. Gimme, gimme, gimme. If this trend grows unchecked, every segment of society could be at another segment's throat, until our nation degenerates into rancor, riots, and ultimately anarchy. What else could you expect when a government expropriates a huge pot of money and doles it out not to those most in need but to those who apply the greatest political pressure?

WHO ARE THE ULTIMATE BENEFICIARIES OF GOVERNMENT PROGRAMS?

I believe that the ultimate beneficiaries in public expenditure for welfare are not necessarily the intended recipients but the bureaucrats who administer it. Why is it that a county in Maryland and one in Virginia, bedroom counties for Washington, D.C., have the highest per capita income in the United States? Because that's where the bureaucrats live. Why is it that we gave money to help the Indians in the amount of 30,000 dollars per Indian, but they are barely scratching out a living? Yet, the people in the Bureau of Indian Affairs are doing just fine, thank you very much.

Furthermore, public charity leads to indolence, while private charity encourages a work ethic, because private charity discriminates. Private charity is not likely to benefit a twenty-two-year-old who is living with his parents and loses his job and then does not go out and look for work.

Also, public charity and the welfare state destroy private charity. Last year nearly one trillion dollars was expropriated from citizens—money that became unavailable for private charity. When all of these assets are taken by the government, it leaves precious little for private charity. Just think what could have been done with that money. All this leads to unbelief. God the provider is pushed aside, while the state becomes the provider for a disbelieving populace.

Furthermore, it leads to a loss of freedom as we sell our souls to the government store. More and more people are willing to sell their birthright for a mess of pottage, or as somebody said, a pot of "socialistic message." If this goes on unchecked, they will end up as a people totally dependent upon the state and without liberty.

Welfare also leads to a loss of meaning to life. The socialist says this is all the life there is. You only go around once; therefore, to fail here is to fail ultimately and totally, finally and forever. This materialistic worldview is contradictory to Christianity.

PRACTICAL SOLUTIONS

If we are to have a truly Christian worldview, and if we are to apply God's principles in the sphere of the nation, then we must surely get back on track in the financial realm. I'd like to propose four steps to help us do so.

Step One: Remember the Failed Socialism of the Pilgrims

Americans have forgotten one of the key lessons of the Pilgrims. When they first settled in America, they employed a form of socialism. (This system was imposed upon them by the London-based company that financed the whole venture.) The prevailing ideal was that they held all things in common, and the people would work for the common good. Yet even the Pilgrims, as godly as they were, had trouble getting some of their members to work diligently. This resulted in such meager food production that Governor Bradford decided to abandon this by 1623.

Instead, each man was given a small parcel of land that was his own to till. Production increased dramatically, and soon there was abundant food for all. Socialism didn't work in the beginning of the country. It doesn't work now. It never will work.

Step Two: Support the Ministries Helping to Wean People Off Welfare

The church at large can make a big difference in the realm of economics. Several inner-city churches have helped their members get off welfare. They have helped them learn a marketable skill, so they can go out and get a meaningful job.

I think of the example of Star Parker, Christian author and speaker—and former welfare recipient. As an African-American, she grew up believing that all the problems in the black community were the white man's fault. She got involved in gang activity, illegal drugs, and sexual promiscuity. After having four abortions, she decided to keep the next baby and go on welfare, which she remained on for about seven years.

Through the influence of some Christians, Star eventually accepted Christ as her Savior. About a year after her conversion, her minister found out she was on welfare. He asked her a question she couldn't answer: "What are you doing on welfare?"

She says, "I went home and asked myself the same question, looking in the mirror, and I still couldn't answer it. So I wrote my social worker and said I want off."[9] The church helped her through the transition, as they have helped many persons get off state aid.

Star Parker makes an excellent observation: "We have two economic systems working for America: capitalism for the rich and socialism for the poor. The problem with a government that lets both systems operate is that the middle class gets stuck working for the rich to support the poor."[10]

Step Three: Vote Your Conscience

I think we can make a substantial difference at the ballot box by studying the issues. We can avoid hurting our children's and grandchildren's futures by ringing up a large tab in social-transfer payments such as perpetual welfare and meaningless government programs that spend more and more of the taxpayers' money.

It still amazes me that millions of men and women who claim to be born again don't vote. Some of them are not even registered. Others vote but don't take the time to study the issues and vote in accordance with godly principles.

Step Four: Maintain Excellence in Work

In our professional work, we can shine like lights in the firmament as we work hard, not accepting bribes or kickbacks. The honest, hard-working Christian man or woman in the workplace who does more than he or she is paid for will stand out for Christ. Even if we get passed by for promotion, the question we each need to ask ourselves is: Have I been faithful to Christ, even in the little things?

I remember reading about a man who was turned down for a job as a junior executive. He seemed to have all the right qualifications and disposition, but he lost out in the job interview because of ten cents. His prospective boss took him out to lunch at a cafeteria. As they were in line, the potential employee took a ten-cent pad of butter and hid it under one of his plates. Then he showed his future boss how clever he was. But his "future boss" decided he would not hire a thief.

In this day when employers are constantly complaining about dishonest employees, we Christians have an opportunity to work hard as unto the Lord. Millions of Christians following this simple piece of advice could help revolutionize the workforce.

CONCLUSION

Summing up, perhaps the single most important principle from the Bible on the subject of economics is the idea of stewardship. God owns it all (Psalm 24:1). We are merely His managers of these things, and He will hold us accountable for how we manage them (Matthew 25:14-30).

Another key biblical principle is that God has granted us the right to have private property. If we decide to plunder our neighbor's goods, from a biblical point of view we have no right to do so.

Furthermore, God wants us to be generous with our material goods. He encourages voluntary generosity, not forced charity. Forced charity is not charity at all. It is plunder. God's Word has much to say about us caring for the poor and needy (e.g., Matthew 25:31-46).

PART IV

THE SPHERE
OF THE
SCHOOL

INTRODUCTION TO CHRISTIANIZING THE SPHERE OF THE SCHOOL

Did you hear about the time twelve-year-old Johnny brought home a not-too-good report card? He showed it to his father, who admonished him, saying, "Do you realize that when George Washington was your age, he was making straight A's?" Was Johnny properly admonished? Was he thoroughly contrite? Completely repentant? Determined to do better?

Well, hear his response: "Yeah, Pop, and when he was your age he was President of the United States."

All humor aside, the public school today is one of the least evangelized portions of our society. If we truly believe that parents are responsible to God for their children's education, we need to do something. Dr. James Dobson of Focus on the Family has pointed out repeatedly that we're engaged in "a civil war of values" in our culture, and the prize is our children. He writes: "Children are the prize to the winners of the second great civil war. Those who control what young people are taught and what they experience—what they see, hear, think, and believe—will determine the future course for the nation. Given that influence, the predominant value system of an entire culture can be overhauled in one generation, or certainly in two, by those with unlimited access to children."[1] The purpose of this section is to see what we can do to develop a Christian world-and-life view of education.

13

A TEACHING RELIGION

. . . and how from childhood you have been acquainted with
the sacred writings, which are able to make you wise for sal-
vation through faith in Christ Jesus.

2 TIMOTHY 3:15

✠

In a front-page story Michael Weisskopf of the *Washington Post* once said,
"Corporations pay public relations firms millions of dollars to contrive the
kind of grass-roots response that Falwell or Pat Robertson can galvanize in
a televised sermon. Their followers are *largely poor, uneducated and easy to
command.*"[1] Thankfully, they apologized. But still, the fact that this slipped
by so many editors indicates that many in the media elite view born-again
types as ignorant.

Here's a more recent example. After the 2004 election, CBS veteran commentator Andy Rooney continued to perpetuate the Christians-are-ignorant
stereotype. At a forum at Tufts University, he said that Christian fundamen-
talism is a result of "a lack of education. They haven't been exposed to what
the world has to offer." He also added, "I am an atheist. I don't understand
religion at all. I'm sure I'll offend a lot of people by saying this, but I think
it's all nonsense."[2]

It is amazing that some people still think of Christianity as being anti-intellectual or anti-education. The Reverend John Harvard certainly did not think
so. Nor did the Puritan Elihu Yale or the Presbyterian founders of Princeton.
For the first 200 years of this nation's history, education was explicitly
Christian, and it produced amazing results. In the early 1800s John Adams
observed that to find an illiterate man in New England was as rare as a comet.[3]

How interesting that along with the rise of secularism within our educational institutions has also come a sharp rise in illiteracy. While more than a

trillion dollars have been poured into the secular public education system in America at the same time that Christ has been taken out of it, the illiteracy rate has increased thirty-two times. Our literacy rate is rapidly plunging to that of Zambia. What a contrast to the era of the Founding Fathers, when education was Christian and literacy was widespread.

A TEACHING RELIGION

From its very beginning, Christianity has been a teaching religion. The Scriptures have been a major means of communicating Christian truth. To be able to read the Scriptures, one must be able to read. In this section we will consider Christianity and the sphere of education. Here we will get an overview on the subject. Next we will look at the issue of truth. Christianity believes in absolute truth—contrary to the views of millions today, even many professing Christians, who think that truth is relative. We will also look at what happens when humanistic ideas dominate in education. This has disastrous consequences, even shootings in the classroom in extreme cases.

Tragically, some of what is called "Christian education" today essentially has a secular worldview with a thin veneer of spirituality to make it appear Christian. In contrast, the Christian education the founders experienced was biblical at its core. Even the least religious of the Founding Fathers were biblically literate. If you are familiar with the Scriptures, you can see mini-quotations or biblical phrases throughout the founders' writings.

There has been a strong link between Christianity and education—in particular, Protestant Christianity because of the Protestant emphasis on reading the Bible for oneself. (Not until Vatican II in the 1960s were Catholics encouraged to read the Bible for themselves.)

BIBLICAL PRINCIPLES OF EDUCATION

The Scripture says, "Train up a child in the way he should go; even when he is old he will not depart from it" (Proverbs 22:6). This is a general principle, not a hard and fast rule. But it points to how important the formative years are for a young child. It reminds me of the Indian proverb: "As the twig is bent, so goes the tree." As much as is up to us, we do well to train our children in the Christian faith.

Furthermore, Solomon in his wisdom tells us:

> *The fear of the Lord is the beginning of knowledge;*
> *fools despise wisdom and instruction. (Proverbs 1:7)*

This point is so profound that we will dedicate the next chapter to plumbing its depths.

Who does the Bible delegate as the teacher? Or let's put it this way: Who does the Bible say is responsible for the education of children? The answer is not the teachers, not superintendents, not the state. The answer is very simple: the parents. They are the ones the Lord will hold accountable for their children's education. God commands in Deuteronomy 6—just after giving the great commandment where we are ordered to love the Lord with all our being—that parents (fathers in particular) are to teach their children about the laws of the Lord. Education is a means to an end. What end? Knowing the law of the Lord. Here is what God said through His servant Moses:

> *And these words that I command you today shall be on your heart. You shall teach them diligently to your children, and shall talk of them when you sit in your house, and when you walk by the way, and when you lie down, and when you rise. You shall bind them as a sign on your hand, and they shall be as frontlets between your eyes. You shall write them on the doorposts of your house and on your gates. (Deuteronomy 6:6-9)*

In short, don't forget the laws of God, and don't let your children forget them.

So what is the purpose of education? To get a good job? To secure a good future? To make more money? To help spread the gospel? That answer is getting closer. But the real answer is that our Christian faith will be passed on to our children. That doesn't necessarily mean all our children can receive a Christian education. That is not always feasible. But if they cannot, at least parents should supplement their children's education with biblical principles.

In the New Testament, Paul commends this instruction to fathers: "Fathers, do not provoke your children to anger, but bring them up in the discipline and instruction of the Lord" (Ephesians 6:4). Why is the father so instructed, when obviously the mother is with the child the most, when the mother has the most immediate and frequent requirements of discipline and teaching? The father is at the office most of the day. Why, then, are these words directed to the fathers?

The answer is that the father is the head of the household and is responsible for the spiritual welfare of that household. God holds him responsible for the nurture and admonition of his children. We are told that we are to manage our households well. If you manage a business, it doesn't necessarily mean that you do everything that needs to be done. There is such a thing as delegation; but there is also the matter of investigation of what has been delegated to see that it is done, and that is our responsibility as fathers. The buck stops here. The fact is that if children are not nurtured and if they are not disciplined, it is the father who is held responsible by God.

What does it mean to nurture our children in the Lord? It means to teach them line upon line, precept upon precept, a little bit here and a little bit there. We are to teach our children the things of God. We are to teach them the commandments of God. It is interesting to note that the overwhelming majority of adults in America today cannot name the Ten Commandments. I have no doubt that 90 percent of the children in this country cannot name them either.

Another point about the Bible and education is an implied one. We should know the Scriptures, which make us wise unto salvation (2 Timothy 3:15). How can you know the Scriptures if you can't read?

Certainly millions of Christians from the beginning of the church to the present have been illiterate. That does not mean they were or are bad Christians. But they certainly are dependent on others to help them learn the Bible. Even today missionaries go from place to place, for example, showing the *Jesus* movie. This introduces millions to specific verses in the Gospel of Luke (upon which the movie is based). This is like a modern-day proclamation of the Word of God. If we said that the only spiritual Christians are those who can read the Bible for themselves, we would not be fair to the millions and millions of Christians who have been (and even in our own day are) illiterate. But if you really want to know the Bible for yourself, if you really want to study the Scriptures, it is imperative that you be able to read. Christians who place much emphasis on reading the Bible for themselves are following in the footsteps of Martin Luther and John Calvin.

CALVINISM AND EDUCATION FOR THE MASSES

Calvinism, in particular, put the greatest emphasis on reading the Bible for oneself. So wherever Calvinism had the greatest sway, the school was not far behind. In fact, Loraine Boettner, a scholar who has been quoted by the U.S. Supreme Court, points out, "Wherever Calvinism has gone, it has carried the school with it and has given a powerful impulse to popular education. It is a system which demands intellectual manhood. In fact, we may say that its very existence is tied up with the education of the people."[4]

This certainly can be seen in the American scene, where Calvinists of one sort or another were among the first to settle the various colonies, especially in New England. In Puritan Boston, for example, they made a law within twelve years of settling the place that schools would be mandatory for children. Why? So they could become familiar with the Scriptures. And this had a profound impact on all levels of education.

THE *NEW ENGLAND PRIMER*

One of the most influential documents for educational purposes for some 200 years in the American experience was the *New England Primer*. Although this is a book to teach children, it includes the Lord's Prayer, the Apostle's Creed, and the text of hymns and prayers by Isaac Watts. This book was used extensively to teach children in the New England colonies and beyond.

When the children learned the alphabet, they learned it in a way that taught them key messages from the Bible. More biblical truth is imparted in the *New England Primer* for little schoolchildren than in the average liberal church today. They learned how in Adam's fall, all of us sinned. They learned that Christ was crucified for sinners. In short, their ABC's were based on biblical truths.[5]

Note how they also learned the catechism through the *New England Primer*. Thus the children learned God's truths as well as the alphabet.

> Who was the first man? Adam.
> Who was the first woman? Eve.
> Who was the first Murderer? Cain.
> Who was the first Martyr? Abel.
> Who was the first Translated? Enoch.
> Who was the oldest Man? Methuselah.
> Who built the Ark? Noah.
> Who was the Patientest Man? Job.
> Who was the Meekest Man? Moses.
> Who led Israel into Canaan? Joshua.
> Who was the strongest Man? Samson.
> Who killed Goliath? David.
> Who was the wisest Man? Solomon.
> Who was in the Whale's Belly? Jonah.
> Who saves lost Men? Jesus Christ.
> Who is Jesus Christ? The Son of God.
> Who was the Mother of Christ? Mary.
> Who betrayed his Master? Judas.
> Who denied his Master? Peter.
> Who was the first Christian Martyr? Stephen.
> Who was chief Apostle of the Gentiles? Saul.[6]

By the time a child finished his primary education, he knew more Bible doctrine than the average Christian today. Anyone who knows the Bible is well-educated.

THE NORTHWEST ORDINANCE

How important was education to the Founding Fathers? Very. Did religion play a part in education in their opinion? Absolutely. The first Congress under the new Constitution passed a law that ensured that each state and territory to be added to the new nation would also be committed to building schools. On August 4, 1789, Congress passed the Northwest Ordinance (a provision they had also passed a couple of years earlier, in 1787 when the Constitution was not the law of the land, but rather the Articles of Confederation).[7] They called it the Northwest Ordinance in reference to expanding territory north and west beyond the Appalachians. Initially it referred to the area west of the original colonies, but east of the Mississippi. The Northwest Ordinance is one of our key founding documents, and it applied to all new territory and states of the United States.

And what does Article III of the Northwest Ordinance stipulate? "Religion, morality and knowledge, being essential to good government and the happiness of mankind, schools and the means of education shall forever be encouraged."[8]

Too often the public schools of today have become what even Bill Clinton said they should never be: "religion-free zones." That's because some of the Supreme Court decisions have gone to ridiculous lengths to keep any kind of religious—no, I should say Christian—expression out of the public schools.

The modern secular educrat believes that the responsibility for the education of our children does not rest with the parents but with the state. However, the Bible teaches something different. Parents, not the government, are ordained by God and have the responsibility for their children. The government will not answer to God for the children's education; their parents will. Nowhere in the Bible does God ask the government to teach the children. Those duties were divinely assigned to the home and to the church. Over time parents have abdicated that responsibility to the state. Even many Christian parents have done that, and that helps explain the mess we're in today.

AMERICA'S FIRST COLLEGES

It's amazing that within the first year that the Puritans arrived in the New World, they set out to create a college. For what purpose? To create new ministers for the colony. The purpose of the school was the glory of Christ. Even to this day, you can see the name of Christ in steel and cement all around parts of Harvard, because the original motto, which was in Latin, was *Veritas Christo et Ecclessia*, means "Truth for Christ and the Church." Sometime in the twentieth century they secularized the motto to just Truth (*Veritas*). That change is a picture of our culture's abandoning its Christian heritage, which is what made it great in the first place. Modern man wanted truth separated from the Word of God. Eventually he abandoned the concept of truth itself.

Harvard was founded in 1636 and was named after a Congregationalist minister who died very young. Cambridge-educated Rev. John Harvard died of tuberculosis soon after he arrived in the New World. He left some books and some money for the purpose of the new college. To honor his memory and his gift, they named the school after him. Harvard's original mission purpose was a verse from the Bible: "Every one shall consider the main End of his life and studies, to know God and Jesus Christ which is Eternal life" (John 17:3).[9] So a quote from the Gospel of John, which glorifies Jesus Christ, provided Harvard's reason for being: to know God and His Son. Harvard University began to veer from its Christian roots in the nineteenth century. But it is entirely possible that it was Christian longer than it has been secular.

Long before it became apostate, a Puritan divine warned against anyone turning Harvard away from Jesus Christ. Puritan John Wilson wrote a poem dedicated to "the most pious and reverend John Harvard." Note what he said about anyone who would ever endeavor to lead the great school away from the Lord:

> *Chosen of God to found, through grace Divine,*
> *For Christian Learning an enduring shrine . . . .*
> *If darling heresies delight afford,*
> *And ye deny your conscience and your Lord,*
> *How will ye spurn the path your founder trod?*
> *How tempt a covenant-keeping God!*[10]

This is fascinating. Wilson's poem, published in 1702 and written at least a hundred years before Harvard began to become liberal and spiritually corrupt, reminds us that God never forgets and that Harvard was dedicated to the glory of God from the beginning, and woe to those who would lead that school astray. Harvard University, as great as it is in many ways, is by and large no longer fulfilling the purposes for which it was created. Those who have perverted such an important institution will have much for which to give an account to our "covenant-keeping God."

North America's second college, William and Mary, was also explicitly Christian in its founding. It was established by the Anglican Church and was geared toward training future Anglican ministers, particularly for the colony of Virginia. Note one of the purposes stated for the new school in its guidelines of 1727: "the Indians of America should be instructed in the Christian Religion, and that some of the Indian Youth that are well-behaved and well-inclined, being first well prepared in the Divinity School, may be sent out to preach the Gospel to their Countrymen in their own Tongue."[11] Not only was the school to train ministers for the gospel, but it was to train Indians to spread the Word of God to their own people. Like Harvard, William and Mary lost its Christian emphasis more than a hundred years ago.

When a group of Congregationalist ministers stood around a table one day in 1700 in Branford, Connecticut, a college was born. Each minister donated some of his own books, and as they went around the table, they stated, "I give these books for the founding of a college in this colony."[12] The college is named in honor of Elihu Yale (1649-1721), a wealthy Puritan who made his fortune through the East India Tea Company. He even served as the governor of Ft. Saint George in Madras, India. He returned to England and made generous donations to "churches, schools, and missionary societies."[13] Mr. Yale had been born in Boston but grew up in England. He donated books and other valuable resources to the Congregationalists of Connecticut, who named the school after him.

A PROPHETIC WARNING

One of the great presidents of Yale was a very godly man named Timothy Dwight (1752-1817). A grandson of Jonathan Edwards, Dwight helped spark a spiritual revolution on campus. Not only did many of the students profess to accept Jesus Christ, but a large percentage of them entered the ministry through his influence. He preached a message on July 4, 1798, in New Haven, called "The Duty of Americans, at the Present Crisis." Note that the crisis he is referring to is spiritual crisis—the threat of unbelief:

> About the year 1728, Voltaire, so celebrated for his wit and brilliancy and not less distinguished for his hatred of Christianity and his abandonment of principle, formed a systematical design to destroy Christianity and to introduce in its stead a general diffusion of irreligion and atheism. For this purpose he associated with himself Frederick the II, king of Prussia, and

Mess. D'Alembert and Diderot, the principal compilers of the Encyclopedie, all men of talents, atheists, and in the like manner abandoned.[14]

". . . in the like manner abandoned" means that these atheists were all committed to the goal of destroying Christianity.

The principal parts of this system were:

1. The compilation of the Encyclopedie: in which with great art and insidiousness the doctrines of natural as well as Christian theology were rendered absurd and ridiculous; and the mind of the reader was insensibly steeled against conviction and duty.

Dwight is observing that these atheistic writers were taking Christian doctrines and reducing them to the absurd, thus causing readers to doubt the Christian faith.

2. The overthrow of the religious orders in Catholic countries, a step essentially necessary to the destruction of the religion professed in those countries.

3. The establishment of a sect of philosophists to serve, it is presumed as a conclave, a rallying point, for all their followers.

4. The appropriation to themselves, and their disciples, of the places and honors of members of the French Academy, the most respectable literary society in France, and always considered as containing none but men of prime learning and talents. In this way they designed to hold out themselves and their friends as the only persons of great literary and intellectual distinction in that country, and to dictate all literary opinions to the nation.

5. The fabrication of books of all kinds against Christianity, especially such as excite doubt and generate contempt and derision. Of these they issued by themselves and their friends who early became numerous, an immense number; so printed as to be purchased for little or nothing, and so written as to catch the feelings, and steal upon the approbation, of every class of men.[15]

This unbelief culminated in the formation of a group where:

The being of God was denied and ridiculed. . . . The possession of property was pronounced robbery. Chastity and natural affection were declared to be nothing more than groundless prejudices. Adultery, assassination, poisoning, and other crimes of the like infernal nature, were taught as law-ful and even as virtuous actions. To crown such a system of falsehood and horror, all means were declared to be lawful, provided the end was good. . . . The great and good ends proposed . . . are the overthrow of reli-gion, government, and human society, civil and domestic. These they pro-nounce to be so good that murder, butchery, and war, however extended and dreadful, are declared by them to be completely justifiable if necessary for these great purposes. With such an example in view, it will be in vain to hunt for ends, which can be evil.[16]

We can see all this as the forerunner to the French Revolution and later the Communist movement. We can see it also as the forerunner to the secu-larist movement, which has steered Yale away from its Christian course. Tragically, the same thing has happened over and over at the Ivy League schools, all of which were explicitly Christian, but none of which is explic-itly Christian today.

Dwight saw what was happening in contemporary Europe, where unbe-lief was beginning to spread all over, even among the universities, all of which were Christian in origin. This unbelief was spreading like cancer in different segments of European society. But, argued Dwight in the early 1800s, it couldn't make inroads to America because of the godliness of this land:

Where religion prevails, Illumination cannot make disciples, a French directory cannot govern, a nation cannot be made slaves, nor villains, nor atheists, nor beasts. To destroy us therefore, in this dreadful sense, our enemies must first destroy our Sabbath and seduce us from the house of God. Religion and liberty are the two great objects of defensive war. Conjoined, they united all the feelings and call forth all the energies of man. . . .

    Religion and liberty are the meat and the drink of the body politic. Withdraw one of them and it languishes, consumes, and dies. If indiffer-ence to either, at any time, becomes the prevailing character of a people, one half of their motives to vigorous defense is lost, and the hopes of their enemies are proportionally increased. Here, eminently, they are inseparable.

    Without religion we may possibly retain the freedom of savages, bears, and wolves, but not the freedom of New England. If our religion were gone, our state of society would perish with it and nothing would be left which would be worth defending.[17]

It's not too subtle when the president of Yale College warns us against the ravaging effects of unbelief—when he warns against ever losing our religion. I have quoted him at length because this was one of the great presidents of Yale (perhaps the greatest it ever had). Furthermore, he was a part of the Second Great Awakening.

CONCLUSION

A genuine Christian world-and-life view puts a high premium on education. It is from this tradition that our colleges and universities were born. During the Second Great Awakening, in particular on the frontier, there began to develop a new type of Christianity. It was still biblical, but it had an anti-intellectual bent. In trying to prevent dry intellectualism that was spiritually dead, it went too far the other way.

This trend got worse when liberalism swept through the seminaries. Suddenly young men who went to seminary to be trained to serve Christ instead ended up losing their faith. This is so tragic, and it is so needless because the truth is on our side. But, of course, it is not always presented that way. Sometimes people are exposed only to arguments against the Scriptures, and they never hear the evangelical rebuttal. Meanwhile, to avoid the tragedy of people losing their faith, many evangelicals have tended to avoid seminary or even college. Sometimes people will joke, "I never went to cemetery—I mean, seminary." Thus there is an anti-intellectual strain within some portions of Christianity even today. How tragic and ironic—especially when we consider the Christian origins of virtually all the great colleges, universities, and seminaries of America. A well-rounded Christian worldview places a high premium on education, for God is the source of all truth.

14

WHO STOLE THE TRUTH?

And you will know the truth, and the truth will set you free.
JOHN 8:32

☩

Peter Jennings, the host of the ABC evening news, has produced a couple of prime-time specials dealing with Jesus and with Paul. I have been vocal in my opposition to the first of these programs and parts of the second, in that he stacked the deck against the conservative side. His producers wanted to promote that second program (on Paul) to a Christian audience. So they arranged a discussion between Jennings and me to air on my radio program, *Truths That Transform*. There was an interesting exchange during a portion of that program on the issue of truth—relative or absolute. Here is that portion:

> Peter Jennings: I'm looking for as many opinions and ideas and reference in all this regard as I can. Your truth I fully wholeheartedly accept. But it's not everybody's truth and you know that.
> D. James Kennedy: Well, of course I believe that there are such things as absolutes and that there is an absolute truth, and the fact that it was true before I ever believed it, and I was almost 25 years old before I ever believed. But when I was 22, it was still true and I didn't believe it. I mean I did not believe Christ rose from the dead, and I was 23, and then I'm 26 and I do believe that Christ rose from the dead and nothing changed except me.[1]

Whether we believe truth is relative or absolute is another watershed issue. Our world-and-life views will be world's apart from each other depending on what we believe on this point.

TRUTH HAS BEEN STOLEN

Someone has stolen the truth. And it is amazing that there is very little out-cry at all. Indeed, if it had been our purse or our wallet that was stolen, surely the cry would ring throughout the room, "Stop! Thief!" And yet someone has stolen the truth. Even more tragic perhaps is the fact that most people do not even realize it is gone. Nor do they know who took it or, in fact, how this rather amazing feat was pulled off at all. Who stole the truth?

"TRUE TRUTH"

As we continue to examine a Christian worldview of education, we turn to the whole issue of truth—or perhaps I should say Truth with a capital T. Is there such a thing as absolute truth that is true no matter what our percep-tion about it may be? The late, great Francis Schaeffer often used the phrase "true truth," which sounds like a phrase coined in the Redundancy Department of Redundancy. But the idea he was communicating was abso-lute truth, or what Nancy Pearcey calls "total truth."[2]

Is there such a thing as absolute truth? Surely, this relates to the whole area of education because from the Christian perspective, the belief that there is such a thing as truth is the starting point for education. Putting it another way, "the fear of the LORD is the beginning of wisdom" (Proverbs 9:10; cf. 1:7).

"WHAT IS TRUTH?"

Truth is a foundational issue. While Jesus Christ says, "You will know the truth, and the truth will set you free" (John 8:32), much modern education says, along with Pontius Pilate, "What is truth?" (John 18:38). The very notion of objective truth is now questioned in many educational institutions.

Alan Keyes, former ambassador to the U.N. and perennial candidate for political office, notes, "It's quite obvious that if we abandon the idea that truth exists, that there is a basis for it apart from expediency, and relativism, and circumstances, then we are abandoning the foundation of our whole way of life, including the claim that each and every one of us makes to be respected in our individual dignity."[3]

TRUTH AND OUR PUBLIC SCHOOLS

Though more public money than ever is being poured into education, many of our nation's schools have become more dangerous and academically defi-cient places. How can this be?

Keyes continues, "What did the courts do? They drove God out of the public school. They took out prayer from the public school. What has been the consequence? We have seen a rising tide of crime and violence and drug abuse in our schools, where discipline has become the major problem."[4]

Though much public education in America's history was explicitly Christian, many courts, led by such groups as the ACLU and Americans United for the Separation of Church and State, now say that public education must be completely divorced from any religious foundation. Barry Lynn, head of the Americans United for the Separation of Church and State, argues, "Simply to be neutral about religion, which is what public schools are, is not a demonstration of hostility. It's simply a respectful recognition that, indeed, religion is not appropriate to be promoted within public schools."[5]

Alan Keyes counters, "I think when you divorce faith from education, you have, in fact, taken the soul out of it. And as we know, when you take the soul out of a living thing, it dies. And that's what we have been seeing."[6]

Or as commentator and columnist Pat Buchanan puts it, "Now, the idea that religion and government and belief in God and government should be separate is like trying to separate blood from the body and have the body still live."[7]

Because of the growing secularism in the schools, many parents are now opting for a safe, truth-based education for their children that begins with God—an approach that is producing noticeable results—homeschooling. Dr. Michael Farris, president of Patrick Henry College in Purcellville, Virginia, formerly headed the Home School Legal Defense Fund. He notes, "Christianity has everything to do with Western civilization. . . . Those who teach the principles and the history of Western civilization, and the literature of Western civilization, will inherently produce a better product."[8]

One child who has successfully been homeschooled is Sindy Quinonez, a twenty-year-old immigrant from Guatemala who lives with her family in Reston, Virginia. Sindy's father Hugo, a pastor, wanted to move his family away from the instability of Guatemala to America, the land of opportunity. A land he says, in broken English, that was founded on Christian principles: "This country is what it is, because it's Bible principle based."[9]

But the Quinonez family found their children in an American school system that was systematically removing God from the curriculum. In sixth grade Sindy faced a bizarre situation one day. The teacher took the class outside, "and she had laid rocks on the grass, and she told us to pick up a rock and think about it. I don't remember the exact terms, but that by touching the rock we would be one with nature. I remember it very clearly, because one boy raised his hand and asked the teacher, 'Do you really believe this?' Because to me, it seemed silly, and I guess it wasn't only me; it was other students around us. I thought she would say, 'No,' but she said, 'Yes,' that she did believe it. . . . It was very strange."

Eventually Hugo Quinonez made the difficult decision to take his children out of the school and teach them at home, from a biblical perspective. Through her studies, Sindy began to realize that the removal of God from school had affected all of her subjects.

"There's No Such Thing as Absolute Truth"

What the Quinonez family discovered firsthand was a clash between those who believe in absolute truth and those who don't.

So again I ask, who stole the truth? Or perhaps you are one of those who have not noticed that it is gone. Many parents have begun to get some sort of inkling that something is amiss. Their children go off to high school or college, and when they come back, something is different about them. When you try to carry on a conversation, something is different. There are no values anymore, and absolutes are smiled at, and the realities of the spiritual world and of God are considered, somehow, to have become irrelevant to life. Though the parents know something is wrong, they do not quite know what has happened.

In stealing the truth, these perpetrators have affected almost everything else. You see, the humanist educators who have pulled this coup have a number of things they are interested in getting rid of, and getting rid of the truth is the beginning. That pulls the rug out from under everything else. As they state in one of their texts, there are certain things that education needs to get rid of. Perhaps you did not realize that when your children went to school there were certain things some of their teachers were bent on ridding from your children, extirpating them as it were from their minds. And these include the concept of absolute, fixed, unchanging truth.

The first thing to be gotten rid of is the concept of absolute truth. Second, the concept of certainty must be removed. Third, the concept that knowledge is given—that it emanates from a higher power. Now you see the implications of this, which are very clear. There is no absolute truth, they say. Consequently there can be no certainty about anything. Gray probabilities are all we have left. And certainly there is no one above who can give us any knowledge of any truth. These things are at the top of the list of things to be gotten rid of in the education of your children.

As it is stated in the textbook by Neil Postman and Charles Weingartner, education is to help children "learn a new set of beliefs and a new set of values." This statement is taken from a book that has the interesting title, *Education as a Subversive Activity*.[10] As one man said, "Let me publish this textbook and I do not care who writes the songs or writes the laws of any nation."

Here's what I want to know. Who asked them to give our children a new set of beliefs and a new set of values, which turn out in most cases to be diametrically opposed to the beliefs of their parents and the values of their parents? Who asked them to do this? Indeed, who authorized them to do this at all? May I ask you: Is that why you send your children to school? Why, you thought they were there to learn the three Rs. The top priority in education today is to change the thinking of children concerning truth and values and basic beliefs. That is why the teachers today like to call themselves, in some cases, "change-agents" in the schools.

How was this brought about, and by whom? This is part of a great silent revolution that has been taking place in the Western world for the last fifty years or so thanks to the humanists in America and in the West. I suppose that if any single person could be credited with this, it would be the influential John Dewey. It was done so subtly and so cleverly that the average person never even knew it had happened. It was simply done by the redefinition of truth and fact.

To show you how successful they have been, let me ask you, what is a fact? Ultimately, all truth and all knowledge and all belief rest upon facts. Therefore, if we can change the meaning of facts, we can change the meaning of everything, and they have done precisely that.

Again I would like to ask you, what is a fact? Can you define it? A fact is "a statement that can be verified," we are told. If you believe that, you are a victim of brainwashing. That is not what a fact is at all. Yet I am sure that millions of people in our culture today would swallow that like a sugarcoated pill and not realize that the whole superstructure of knowledge, truth, and reality hinges upon this.

What is a fact? If you were to get an older dictionary, you would find that the word *fact* comes from the Latin *facere*, which means "to do," and from the past *factum*, which means "a thing done; an act done." A fact is simply that which is done, something that was done. A fact has reference to that which has actual existence; it is an event, the quality of being actual.

Some facts were verified by the verification processes of science, and other facts were unverified. Many things that have been done have been verified, and many things that have been done have not been verified. But they are all facts. You still do not see the significance, do you? For example, around the year A.D. 1000, if a person stated that the earth was round, was that a fact or not? Why, of course that was a fact. And yet it was entirely beyond the capability of being verified for another 500 years. When it was verified 500 years later, it did not then become a fact; it then became verified. It had always been a fact. Eternal facts arise out of the great Creator—God— and they do not depend upon a man to establish them as such.

This reminds me of a problem that philosophers were having many years ago with the Logical Positivism philosophy. If you ever studied it in school, you will know that the whole philosophy was derived from one great theory: "The only statements which are true are those which can be proved by empirical science." To its adherents, science was the only source of any truth.

This philosophy spread across the world for decades, but it collapsed virtually overnight in the mid-twentieth century. *The Cambridge Dictionary of Philosophy* asserts, "there are notorious problems for logical positivism."[11] It goes on to point out: "Ironically, the positivists had a great deal of trouble categorizing the very theses that defined their view, such as the claims about meaningfulness and verifiability."[12] For example, their basic defining statement—namely, that the only statements that are true are those that can be proved by empirical science—could not be proved by empirical science. I would like to believe that the whole philosophy fell to the ground at that time, but it still exists, though it is not as nearly as powerful as it once was.

We hear people say, "Well, things are changing, and what was true ten years ago is no longer true. What was true a hundred years ago is no longer true. We believe in progress. Everything is relative; nothing is certain or definite or absolute. All we deal with are probabilities."

There is a fact I hope you will never forget, because ten thousand times ten thousand mistakes have been made in people's lives because they don't understand this truth. To wit: Knowledge is derived from two different sources in our world today. The first (and I don't put them in any order of priority) is science. Science is man's attempt to wrest from nature whatever truths he can about its manner of operation. Science started with very few facts, and it has been growing over the centuries until we come to the place we are today. We will never learn everything; and when the world ends, there will still be vast volumes of our ignorance. Science is a progressive system.

A second source of knowledge is revelation, where God has revealed certain truths to us through His Scripture and, ultimately, through His Son. That revelation has not increased one iota over the centuries since its completion in the first century. God gave us a perfect revelation, and it continues as it was from the beginning.

But, unfortunately, our young people today are being exposed to a fallacy. They are being taught that the only thing that is true is that which can be verified by scientific verification. Can that statement be verified by scientific verification? Absolutely not! The whole thing is a fraud that is being perpetuated upon our youngsters in our schools.

Some, at least, know this. Philosophers have realized this, and they have stated that this is a fallacy, and they have burst the whole bubble. But it continues on in our educational system in this country today.

Sir James Jeans, one of the greatest astronomers of the twentieth century, a Britisher, said in effect that there is a growing conviction that the ultimate realities of the universe are presently well beyond the reach of science and perhaps forever beyond the comprehension of the human mind.[13]

Does all this really make any difference? If truth is only that which can be verified and only that which is based upon facts, and if facts are only those things that can be verified by scientific investigation, and if nothing else is true, what about God? God is a Spirit, eternal and unchangeable. He is not matter to be placed on a slide under a microscope or boiled in a test tube or beaker. He is not subject to the verification processes of science. Ergo, God is not a fact, God is not true, God is not real, and God is irrelevant to life. That is precisely the conclusion of secular humanism today. That same thing holds true of eternal life, the eternal salvation of man, heaven and hell, Jesus Christ, and all other things we hold true, including the moral absolutes.

If there is no absolute truth, there are no absolute morals, nor absolute values. This is so clearly seen in modern textbooks today. For example, a fifth grade textbook is entitled *Man: A Course of Study*. This very famous textbook is known by the acronym Macos and is funded by the National Science Foundations. One chapter has students spend a week discovering the lifestyles of various people. For one week they study the lifestyle of the Netsilik Eskimo of Canada. You see, they are told to get outside of themselves in their own culture, and they are to look at the cultures of other people, and, of course, the overall result of this is to show them that there are no absolute values for cultures and that there are no criteria upon which we may judge the cultures of other people. Every culture must be judged within that culture, and we have no standard by which to judge it from outside that culture. So our fifth graders study the lifestyle of the Netsilik Eskimos of Canada. This lifestyle includes infanticide, cannibalism, the murder of grandparents, wife swapping, and sex with animals. Very edifying subjects for fifth graders.

In this book they learn in detail about one of the Netsilik Eskimos by the name of Tuneque, who took his wife by the sides and felt for some skin. She became panicky and ran, and he chased her with a knife, caught her, and stabbed her repeatedly until she died, at which time he then ate her. This is being read in fifth grade. There is another lovable character by the name of Itqilik, whose brother's feet were frostbitten, and Itqilik ate them because they were no longer of any use. After eating his brother's feet, he said, "Oh, what the heck," and he ate the rest of him. After all, he was only his brother.

Do you wonder what is happening all over this country? You do not know what your children are being taught.

In another text, *A Teacher's Guide to an Introduction to the Behavioral Sciences: The Inquiry Approach*, published by Holt, we read in the teacher's guide: "As they do this exercise, the student should be developing the concept of cultural relativity—the idea that the 'rightness,' 'goodness' or 'badness' of a particular kind of behavior can only be judged in terms of the culture in which it is found. For instance: Is it 'bad' for people to eat the flesh of other human beings? How can we become so horrified at this in America; we who cook people in electric chairs, though we do not eat their flesh." What an incredible comparison. And we wonder why there has been so little patriotism in our country for the last several decades. Is that an accident, a quirk of some sort? How did this happen?

In the American history text *Many Peoples, One Nation*, published by Random House, we read: "No nation on earth is guilty of practices more shocking and bloody than is the United States at this very hour. Go where you may and search where you will, roam through the kingdoms of the Old World. Travel through South America. Search out every wrong. When you have found the last, compare your facts with the everyday practices of this nation. Then you will agree with me that for revolting barbarity and shameless hypocrisy, America has no rival." Now, students, we will recite the Pledge of Allegiance to the flag. This isn't a Michael Moore "documentary" I'm talking about—it is a textbook that has been used in some of our schools.

Perhaps you did not know what your children were learning in school. Perhaps you did. Is it any wonder they turn out like they do? Jesus said, "And you will know the truth, and the truth will set you free" (John 8:32). Having the truth denied to them, our children are being brought more and more into a condition of bondage. Our freedoms are in jeopardy.

Yet we know that far above man's poor pitiful search for truth has been God's revelation of absolute truth. Truth is conformity with reality, and God is the greatest reality in the universe. Truth is harmony with facts, and the fact of the resurrection of Jesus Christ is the greatest and best attested fact of history. The God who made us can make Himself known to us by the power of His Holy Spirit, can break through our darkness and ignorance, and can cause us to know that these things are true. That knowledge, that certainty, that has caused millions of Christians to be willing to die a martyr's death, even in this very century, is what is so infuriating to the unbelieving world of the humanists or the Communists, who even today are torturing and killing Christians because they know whom they have believed and are persuaded that He is able to keep that which they have committed unto Him against that day. The unbeliever cannot understand that. Again, like Pilate, they cynically sneer, "What is truth? No man can know the truth." To which sneer comes the reply of Jesus, eternally, "I am the truth." Specifically, He said, "I am the way, and the truth, and the life. No one comes to the Father except through me" (John 14:6).

Ah, the hour is late. The time has come when Americans need to wake up to what is being done to our children—to the perversion of the truth and the facts and values and meaning and reality by which their minds are being warped from the very earliest ages. This entire bucket of worms needs to be thrown out of the life of this country. Our children need to know the truth of Jesus Christ, which alone can set them free from the ignorance that says that truth is not true if the myopic see it poorly or if the blind cannot see it at all. Set them free from the bondage of their sins, which keeps them from even seeking the truth; set them free from the darkness of moral blindness through which so many are staggering today; and set them free from the fear and terror of death and the grave. Set them free to eternal life when they come to know Christ by faith, who is the Truth. Then the Spirit of God will make them know that this is eternal life: to know the true God and Jesus Christ, whom He has sent.

The Trinity is truth. God is the God of truth. The Father is the truth. Jesus is "the truth" (John 14:6), and the Holy Spirit is called "the Spirit of truth" (John 14:17). God is the absolute truth and reality from which all reason has its root and all understanding its source. That is why the knowledge of God is the basis for all sound education. 2 + 2 always = 4 because God made it that way. For this reason the pursuit of truth is in one sense the pursuit of God. Because God is truth, have not countless colleges and universities dedicated themselves to the pursuit of truth? Think again of the glorious truth that undergirded Harvard at the beginning: "And this is eternal life, that they know you the only true God, and Jesus Christ whom you have sent" (John 17:3). The real purpose for education is to know God and to know His Son.

This is the tragedy of modern education. It has been cut off from the ultimate source of truth. In the long run, truth and God cannot be separated. All education that tries to separate God and truth will eventually lose both.

NO LIARS IN THE KINGDOM OF HEAVEN

The matter of truth vs. lies is far more serious than the humanists would have us believe. Note what the Bible says happens to liars (and other sinners): "But as for the cowardly, the faithless, the detestable, as for murderers, the sexually immoral, sorcerers, idolaters, and all liars, their portion will be in the lake that burns with fire and sulfur, which is the second death. . . . But nothing unclean will ever enter it [heaven], nor anyone who does what is detestable or false, but only those who are written in the Lamb's book of life" (Revelation 21:8, 27). God takes lying seriously.

Perhaps you've heard about the children in Sunday school who had been learning Scripture verses. The day had come for the big quiz, and they were to answer various questions with the Scripture verses they had learned. The question was asked: What is the definition of a lie? Little Johnny popped quickly to his feet, all smiles. He had it. "A lie," he said, "is an abomination unto the Lord and a very present help in time of trouble." Johnny was a little confused.

The sad thing is that a great many other people, older and supposedly wiser, are also confused about that. In fact, a survey not long ago revealed that 60 percent of the people in America believe that although telling the truth is the best policy in general, there are times when a lie is excusable.

What are your thoughts about the matter? The New Testament makes it very clear that Christians are under a categorical imperative to tell the truth at all times. Further, though society as a whole has been most tardy in this department of morals and seems to have learned very slowly the value of truth, the Scriptures make it plain that this is no trivial matter—honesty is a very significant imperative. The Bible teaches that this whole universe was created by God through the vehicle of words and speech, and when God became incarnate, He was the incarnate truth—the One who was the way and the truth and the life. Furthermore, God desires truth in the inward parts of man.

Also, we see that when sin first entered into this world, it did so embodied in a lie: "You will not surely die" (Genesis 3:4). In the New Testament, when sin was first recorded in the Christian church, again it was enshrouded in a lie. Ananias and Sapphira held back part of what they had to give and then lied about it. Peter said to them, "[W]hy has Satan filled your heart to lie to the Holy Spirit? . . . You have not lied to men but to God" (Acts 5:3-4). And God struck them dead.

At the very onset of the Christian faith, God made it clear that He is a God of all truth and that He abhors all lying. As with all of the commandments of God, not only is the negative prohibited, but the positive aspect is enjoined. Furthermore, the worst form of the particular sin involved is usually stipulated, but all similar sins are also included under the prohibition.

CONCLUSION

God is the God of truth. Therefore, truth is the beginning of education for the Christian. Our starting place often determines where we end up. That is why so much truly Christian education excels, compared to worldly education—because it believes in absolutes.

I'm reminded of the hymn that declares in one of its verses:

> *Holy, holy, holy!*
> *Though the darkness hide Thee,*
> *Though the eye of sinful man*
> *Thy glory may not see,*
> *Only Thou art holy;*
> *There is none beside Thee*
> *Perfect in power, in love, and purity.*[14]

Amen. God's truth is the starting point of a truly Christian education. There may be much in common between Christian schooling and public schooling, but because the starting point is so radically different, so also will be the overall conclusions.

15

THE HUMANISTS AND EDUCATION

Train up a child in the way he should go; even when he is old he will not depart from it.

PROVERBS 22:6

Have you ever heard of the Janissaries? At one time it struck fear in the hearts of men to hear that the Janissaries of the Turks were coming. Now that is not a familiar word, but one that we might do well to learn. In the 1400s, *Janissaries* was the name given to the children of Christians who were abducted by the Ottoman Turks in the Byzantine Empire and from Constantinople in particular. These Janissaries had been taken as young children and had been taught the doctrines of Islam, and when they grew older, they were taught the arts of warfare by the Ottoman Turks. By 1453 the Janissaries were part of the army of Mohammed II that surrounded Constantinople, the remaining bastion of Christian influence.

The Turks had taken all of Byzantium except the capital city, and in 1453 they surrounded that city. A siege of many weeks took place. Finally, in utter weariness, the defenders were no longer able to defend the city, and the Ottoman Turks broke through the walls. As the defenders were endeavoring to flee out the back of the city, Mohammed II, in charge of the Ottoman army, decided that the Janissaries, the children of Christians, 20,000 strong, armed with shining blades, should lead the charge. So these 20,000 once-children of Christians, now fanatical soldiers of Islam, attacked the defenders, and hundreds and hundreds fell in agony and died in the despairing posture of their fall, stricken by the hands of their own children. The Janissaries had come.[1]

So what, you say? Well, there are Janissaries among us today—not this time abducted by the Ottomans, but by the humanist schools of our own country. Students have been taught the doctrines of atheism and godlessness and immorality, and they have often gone back to oppose vehemently the teachings of their own parents. Many a parent has asked, "What has happened? Where did I go wrong? How could my child have so completely turned his back on what I taught him when he was a little boy?" Our children have learned well from their teachers.

THEIR PURPOSE

This struggle for the minds and hearts of young people has been going on for a good while. Now it is almost complete in the public schools. What was the teachers' plan? What were they trying to do? Wasn't it just to provide a more progressive and more excellent education for our students?

First of all, the reason Horace Mann started the public school system back in the 1820s and 1830s was to take education out of the hands of the church and clergymen, where it had been for over 200 years at that time. Listen to the prophetic words of one of their own leaders, Orestes Brownson, one of the humanist socialist educators of America, writing back in the late 1820s:

> The great object was to get rid of Christianity and to convert our churches into halls of science. The plan was not to make open attacks upon religion, although we might belabor the clergy and bring them into contempt where we could; but to establish a system of state—we said national—schools, from which all religion was to be excluded. . . . The plan has been successfully pursued . . . and the whole action of the country on the subject has taken the direction we sought to give it. . . .[2]

Does that sound familiar? It reminds me of the former Soviet Union. The battle is long-standing. Let me quote from a more recent humanist educator, a man who has been widely read, Paul Blanshard: "Our schools may not teach Johnny to read properly, but the fact that Johnny is in school until he is sixteen tends to lead toward the elimination of religious superstition."[3] That "religious superstition," dear folks, is what you and I believe. They have succeeded in producing a system of national schools that have rid our country—our public schools, at least—from every vestige of religion.

THE RESULTS

The results? I think they are twofold. One, the educational standards of this country have plummeted. For the past forty years or so, the SAT (Scholastic

Aptitude Test) scores have gone down like a safe falling from an airplane. It began the year after prayer and the Bible were taken out of the public schools. Second, this has produced a tidal wave of immorality that could hardly have been imagined fifty years ago. So education has suffered, and morality has suffered with it.

I received two cartoons recently that I thought were quite apropos to the subject. The first one shows little Johnny, about ten years old, standing in front of the open door of the school bus one morning, reluctant to get on. His mother, stooping down near him, says, "I want you to learn to read and write and do arithmetic," and Johnny says, "So why are you sending me back to school?" That really isn't funny when you think about it.

When John Adams was the second President of the United States, a study of the educational level of America demonstrated that only one American in a thousand could not read and write neatly. Today there are almost 24,000,000 illiterates in America. These are people who can't read the instructions on a bottle of medicine if their life depends on it, and sometimes it does. They can't read a map or a road sign. They can't look up a name in the telephone directory. They can't read the names of products in grocery stores or drugstores. They are almost incapable of living in the modern world. This has been one of the results of ridding our schools of God.

The other result concerns morals and is again, I think, portrayed very poignantly in another cartoon given to me. It shows two grossly overweight soldiers wearing what looks like World War I German helmets inscribed with the letters ACLU. They are shining a flashlight into the locker of a young student and reciting the contents of his locker: "Handgun, cocaine, condoms . . . but no Bible. This one's clean." Now there the real tragedy comes through.

You probably have heard of the *McGuffey's Readers*. William H. McGuffey was a Presbyterian clergyman, an educator and president of a college, and had many other accomplishments. But the *McGuffey's Readers* he produced had an enormous impact on this country in the nineteenth century (and first part of the twentieth century). Published in 1836, over 122,000,000 copies were sold, and they indeed held back the tidal wave for almost a century. He said:

> If you can induce a community to doubt the genuineness and authenticity of the Scriptures; to question the reality and obligations of religion; to hesitate, undeciding, whether there is any such thing as virtue or vice; whether there be an eternal state of retribution beyond the grave; or whether there

exists any such being as God, you have broken down the barriers of moral virtue and hoisted the floodgates of immorality and crime.[4]

Fortunately for this country, McGuffey did a great deal toward holding on to the Christian foundations of this country, as did Noah Webster, who produced the *Blue-backed Speller*, which, like the *McGuffey's Readers*, contained Christian teaching, doctrine, morality, and ethics. Those sold 100,000,000 copies during the nineteenth century. At that same time, though, termites like Brownson were working to totally transform our schools into godless, irreligious schools where there was no moral standard at all.

MORAL COLLAPSE

Today we hear a great deal about "values clarification." Sad to say, many parents have never figured out what that is. Let me tell you very simply: It means that children are taught to make up their own moral standard—anything they want that is important to them—and then to live by that standard, whether that is following the Golden Rule or snatching purses. The teachers can't tell them that anything is wrong or right because nothing is wrong or right. Everything is relative.

One recent book stocked on the shelves of a grade school library was picked up inadvertently by a young Christian girl. *King and King* told the story of how the queen desired a bride for her son, the prince. He meets candidate after candidate and is not satisfied with any of them. He does not find his true love—until he meets another young man. The two even kiss at the end. This is homosexual propaganda, and it was found in a North Carolina grade school library. "Now, who are you," says the educrat, "to judge that prince?" There are no absolutes. What is right for them is right for them. It may not be right for us, but what is right for us may not be right for them. There are no absolutes at all, they claim.

So today we have millions of illiterates and millions more young people who have never been taught any moral standard whatsoever. Yet the founder of this country, George Washington, said something that we need to hear over and over again: "Let us with caution indulge the supposition that morality can be maintained without religion."[5] That has never happened. Anybody can make up a moral code—but getting people to live by it, that's a horse of several different colors. He went on to say: "Whatever may be conceded to the influence of refined education on minds of peculiar structure, reason and experience both forbid us to expect that national morality can prevail in exclusion of religious principle."[6] Thus said George Washington, the father of our country in his Farewell Address, one of the most important documents in American history. (He never delivered it as a speech, but rather it was circulated throughout the country in the newspapers.) We have attempted, supposedly, in our schools to do just what he warned us against, and the results have been catastrophic.

EDUCATIONAL COLLAPSE

So not only do we have a moral collapse, but we have an educational collapse as well. What do the schools say? They say the problem is very simple: We need more money. America spends far more money per student than any other nation in the world. In recent comparative tests of American students with the seventeen industrialized nations of the West, we scored last in two categories and first in none. We have passed the level of Albania and have reached the educational level of Zambia and the Ivory Coast.

One of the ironies of this is that a great deal of attention is put on building up American students' self-esteem—even if that is not in any way correlated with achievement. For instance, a recent study found that American students have higher self-esteem but lower academic achievements simultaneously. For example, in one international test of thirteen-year-olds, Korean children ranked first in math, and Americans ranked last. Yet 68 percent of the Americans felt they were "good at mathematics" compared to only 23 percent of the Korean students.[7] Thus the American youngsters ranked first in self-esteem and last in actual skills. This is a result of misguided emphasis on boosting self-esteem without any base in reality.

Meanwhile, one scholar has pointed out that on average we have lost one month's educational level per year. That is, the level at which students graduate from high school has dropped one month per year. That means that every decade we drop a whole school year. So we are five years behind where we were fifty years ago. You say, "Well, now, that can't really be true, can it?" Let me quote a few questions from a college graduation exam:

• In what state and on what body of water are the following cities? Chicago, Duluth, Cleveland, and Buffalo?

• Who built the Panama Canal?

• Name five republics and three monarchies.

• What is the length of a rectangular field 80 rods wide that contains 100 acres?

• A wagon is 10 feet long, 3 feet wide, and 28 inches deep; how many bushels of wheat will it hold?

• A rope 500 feet long is stretched from the top of a tower; it reaches the ground 300 feet from the base of the tower. How high is the tower?

• Write a brief biography of Evangeline.[8]

How did you do? Let me tell you something. That is not a college graduation exam. That is not even a college entrance exam. That is not a high school graduation exam. That is an entrance exam into high school in 1911. Let's face it. The average American couldn't even get into the high schools of 1911, and we're running around with college degrees.

One lady writes about the examinations she took when she was eleven years old in 1908. Avis Carlson says this:

> The orthography quiz asked us to spell twenty words, including elucidation and animosity. . . . An arithmetic question asked us to find the interest on an eight percent note for nine hundred dollars running two years, two months, six days. [Today we have high school graduates who can't make change in the grocery store.] . . . In reading, we were to give the meanings of words such as panegyric and eyrie. . . . Among geography's ten questions was: "Name two countries producing large quantities of wheat, two of cotton, two of coal." . . . In history, we were to "name the principal political questions which have been advocated since the Civil War and the party which advocated each."[9]

We are dropping one year every decade in academic achievement in this country, but we have gotten God out of our schools. Aren't we smart, and aren't we wonderful? I hope those responsible are very proud of their achievement.

A 1955 textbook on journalism makes this statement: "While crime news must be published, it should be balanced with the reporting of positive events. School news, for example is almost always good news."

Contrast that remark made in 1955 with school news from a recent year:

"High school girls active in prostitution ring."
"Scanners installed to deter guns brought to school."
"Student dead after shots ring out in stadium."
"Broward schools fight sexual harassment."
"Student who wanted 'A' fatally stabs teacher."
"SAT scores hit all-time low."
"Pupils held hostage by knife-wielder."

"Drug pusher arrested on high-school campus."
"Condoms distributed to seventh graders."

And on and on it goes.

Yes, the Turks, the humanists, have been very busy, and they have been turning our students into Janissaries of their own. In the very community where I minister, the greater Ft. Lauderdale area, there is a small community of Coral Springs. One of the members of my congregation who lives there told me about a five-year-old neighbor who had just attended the first day of kindergarten. The teacher reportedly had told the class, "No one can know for sure whether Jesus ever really lived." Whether the teacher actually said this or not, we don't know. What we do know is that the five-year-old said that the teacher said this. Interestingly, the historicity of Jesus Christ is well documented; we can reconstruct the highlights of the life of Christ through non-Christian writers of the first century.[10] After this incident, my church member thought to herself, *His first day in public school . . . and all of that in one morning. Imagine what they can accomplish in twelve years.*

Ah, they don't waste any time producing their modern Janissaries. How many parents have said, "Where did I go wrong? I provided them the best education. I sent them to Harvard." You might as well have shipped them to Saudi Arabia in 1450. Obviously, some Christian young people can handle going to Harvard or other highly secular schools, in part because of the outstanding student ministries on campus. But all too often young people lose their faith because of the one-sided, anti-Christian propaganda.

Parents want their children to have a good financial future, but often they destroy their souls in the process. How many parents have sent their children to public schools and colleges because it was going to look good on their vitae and help them get a good job, only to find they come back unbelievers who want nothing to do with Christianity. Yes, there are many Janissaries among us in our time.

What Should We Do?

Again, the Scriptures say, "Train up a child in the way he should go; even when he is old he will not depart from it" (Proverbs 22:6). That involves beginning that training when our children are in the cradle. In the first few days and weeks of their lives we should begin to train them. During those first months and early years, some of the most important training is being given to a child.

Certainly one of the first names a child should learn is the name of Jesus.

The first song they learn to sing ought to be "Jesus loves me, this I know, for the Bible tells me so."

They should hear the Bible read from the very earliest age.

Children should see their parents pray and daily read the Word of God.

They should not hear bickering and fighting in their homes; instead, they should see love dwelling there.

They should see that their parents are truly concerned with the things that are talked about on Sunday, that they have a passion for lost men and women, that they have a desire to share the gospel and to live a godly life, that they are honest, and that their conversations reveal an integrity that is consonant with the Christian faith they profess.

At bottom, your children are going to become what you are at heart, unless you deliver them over to mind-twisters who are going to turn them into something else—in which case you probably are still making them what you are at heart. What you are, they most likely will become.

We hear husbands lament that their wives will not submit to them, will not be obedient to them. Then the same wives lament that their children are disobedient to them. Their children have learned disobedience in the home from their mothers.

Do you pray with your children and for your children? Do you teach them the doctrines of your faith? Do you read the Bible with them? Are you bringing them up in the nurture and admonition of the Lord?

Are you training them up in the way they should go? Granted, that is a narrow way, and if there is one thing that our modern academicians do not like, it is anything that is narrow. They want their students to be broad—to accept all cultures, all religions, and all ideas. That they should discriminate between anything good and anything evil is absolutely the unforgivable sin in their view. Yet God tells us, "Enter by the narrow gate. For the gate is wide and the way is easy that leads to destruction, and those who enter by it are many. For the gate is narrow and the way is hard that leads to life, and those who find it are few" (Matthew 7:13-14). We must be able to discriminate, not between skin color of different people, but between evil and good. But modernists have maintained that everything is broad, everything is good—there is nothing basically evil.

We are to train our children in the way they should go. We are to teach them the commandments of God. We are to teach them the gospel of Jesus Christ. Abraham Lincoln was said to be the most honest lawyer east of China. Lincoln said he could always hear his mother's voice as he sat upon her knee (and she died when he was nine), saying, "Thou shalt not steal. Thou shalt not bear false witness. Thou shalt not covet." That had a lifelong impact upon his life. Teach your children the commandments of God; teach them the gospel of Jesus Christ, which can change the heart forever.

Speaking of "east of China," a survey of seventeen-year-old students in one city found that half of the students did not know where the Pacific Ocean was. This study was done in San Francisco. Half of the seventeen-year-olds surveyed in California could not tell whether New York was east or west of California. Concerning Russia, one student said it was near the Panama Canal, but he wasn't quite sure where.

Yes, secular humanists have taken over the schools, and that is why Christian education and homeschooling are so vital in our time. I am so happy that the church I pastor has founded a godly Christian school. Westminster Academy is an outstanding school and is noted as such all over the country. I thank God for all of the teachers, the headmaster, the principals, and all of the workers there and in all the truly Christian schools of the country that have taught so many young people in the way that they should go.

I would say to you, it may require some sacrifice, but I urge you to send your children to godly schools, to Christian schools, so they will receive a godly Christian education. If you send them off to some public school, keep in mind that you are shooting dice with your children's eternal souls. That is a gamble no Christian should be willing to make.

Does this mean that all Christian schools are good and all public schools are bad? No. Some Christian schools have failed to do what they ought to do, and some public schools are still doing a good job. Many godly teachers are teaching in them, and I thank God for those godly men and women in our public school system. But their hands are tied, and their mouths have been shut.

Does that mean that everyone who goes to a public school is going to end up overwhelmed by the evil forces that underlie its teaching? No. Some will get through and will survive because of the strength of what they are getting through their church and through the teachings in their homes. But I say to you that the overwhelming odds are in favor of your training up the child in the way he should go.

Unfortunately, some students who are turned out of the Sunday schools and into the secular high schools and colleges are overcome by the unbelief, the immorality, and the ungodliness that prevails. As the twig is bent, so goes the tree, and we, as Christian parents, are responsible for determining how that twig is bent.

"But," say some, "shouldn't we send our children into the public school system to witness for Christ?" You don't take eight- and ten-year-olds and send them off to Vietnam or Guadalcanal to fight in a war. I say yes to having Christian teachers in a public school, yes to having Christian principals in public schools, yes to having Christian administrators in public schools. Wonderful. I thank God for all of the Christian teachers in our public schools who are doing their very best to counter this flood of immorality and godlessness and humanism that has come into our schools. They testify to me, one and all, that it gets more and more difficult with every passing year. I thank God for their steadfastness. The thing would be even far more rotten than it is now if it weren't for such people as that.

But you don't send an eight-year-old out to take on a forty-year-old humanist. Train up a child in the way that he should go, and if we don't, in our old age that will be our greatest heartbreak. I have never seen any people more unhappy than fathers or mothers who have come to me and said, "Where did we go wrong? We gave him everything, and now he's turned his back completely on everything we believe." They gave him everything but a Christian education.

CONCLUSION

Martin Luther once said, "I am much afraid that schools will prove to be the great gates of hell unless they diligently labor in explaining the Holy Scriptures, engraving them in the hearts of youth."[11] He also added, "I advise no one to place his child where the Scriptures do not reign paramount. Every institution in which men are not increasingly occupied with the Word of God must become corrupt."[12]

16

VIOLENCE IN THE
SCHOOLYARD

There is no fear of God before their eyes.
ROMANS 3:18

Because God has been so systematically removed from America's public schools, there has been a spree of school shootings, and Americans ask, "Why?" I'll tell you why—because God has been so systematically removed from America's public schools. We've known for decades that America's schools are in decline—plummeting test scores, high dropout rates, graduating seniors unable to read their own diplomas. But the horrific school violence we have seen in the past several years is something new. Many believe it's not over yet. But what underlying elements are combusting to produce America's new zone of violence—our schools?

In the past few years there have been more than seven separate school shootings by students themselves, leaving a toll of more than twenty-five dead and seventy-four severely wounded. On top of that there have been many more killings (usually one victim at a time) that have not made the headlines.

Wayne Steger, who lost his daughter in the West Paducah, Kentucky, school shooting, notes, "Just one shooting should have been a wake-up call."[1] Dr. George Grant, coauthor of *Kids Who Kill*, remarks, "When we strip our culture of its traditional moorings and biblical Christianity, we are making way for some alternative vision of culture in society. We're catching a glimpse of what that alternative vision is, and it's a horrifying sight."[2]

These shootings occurred in various parts of America, beginning in Moses Lake, Washington, in February 1996, leaving one teacher and two students dead. There was another shooting in Pearl, Mississippi, in October

1997, leaving two students dead. The sixteen-year-old killer, part of a satanic cult, also stabbed his mother to death. In West Paducah, Kentucky, at Heath High School in December 1997, another student opened fire. That shooting claimed the lives of three girls and left another student paralyzed. All of this took place after a voluntary before-school prayer meeting.

Jonesboro, Arkansas, was the next town to be rocked by a school shooting, leaving one teacher and four students dead. The shooters were only eleven and thirteen. Linda Graham, school psychology specialist in Jonesboro, says, "I remember the night of the Paducah shooting that I was folding clothes at home—you know, watching on TV—absolutely horror stricken and sick for these people. But at the same time, just like everybody else does, if you see a car wreck or you're hearing about something you're saying, 'You know, I'm so glad that would never ever happen here,' and it did."[3]

Another school shooting occurred in Edinboro, Pennsylvania, in April 1998, leaving a teacher dead. The next major school shooting took place in Springfield, Oregon, where two students were killed and more than twenty students were injured, after the fifteen-year-old shooter had first allegedly killed his parents. Then there was the shooting at Columbine in Littleton, Colorado, which claimed the lives of twelve students, one teacher, and the two killers.

Conyers, Georgia, was the site of a school shooting that had no fatalities but left six students wounded. Then there was a shooting in Santee, California, in March 2001. Two were left dead and thirteen wounded. In the most recent school year as of this writing (2003-2004), the National School Safety and Security Services based in Cleveland, Ohio, reported that there were forty-nine "identified school-related violent deaths" across the United States.[4] Most of these were a shooting here or a stabbing there. They did not garner the headlines like the slaughter at Columbine. Taken as a whole, all of this indicates there is a serious problem afoot.

Wayne Steger says, "We need stiffer penalties; we need places to put the kids who don't want to be in school in the first place, who are just there until they reach an age until they can quit. We need counseling programs so that maybe one or two of these kids can be saved, instead of winding up in prison."[5]

COLUMBINE

Of course, the most notorious of these incidents is what happened at Columbine High School on April 20, 1999. Two of the better-known victims were the devout Christian students Rachel Scott and Cassie Bernall.

The killers had been planning the rampage for about a year; they chose April 20 to honor the birthday of their idol, Adolf Hitler. They set bombs up that never went off; their intention to slay over 500 victims that day fell short by 485. Many attribute that to answered prayer.

Misty Bernall, mother of Cassie, points out, "I also think that there could have been much more damage and many more lives lost, but I think at a point, God just put His hand down and said, 'Enough.' And it stopped."[6]

Meanwhile, part of the ongoing tragedy of all these school shootings is the pain the parents feel that just won't go away. Cassie's mother says, "We miss her very, very much. I wish that when a student thinks about taking another student's life, that they could see that these aren't just students; these kids are a participating and contributing member of a family."[7]

Wayne Steger observes, "It's for a fact that the public schools are not safe anymore. There are drugs, there are guns. You name it, it's in the public schools now."[8]

WHAT A CONTRAST TO THE 1950S

Democratic Senator Joe Lieberman of Connecticut, former presidential and vice-presidential candidate, states, "If you gave me a choice of being a teenager today, in school, or being a teenager back in the fifties, when I was, I would choose that earlier time. Sometimes I say to people that when I look back at my upbringing, it really does seem like happy days with Richie Cunningham, and it was. It was a time when people from all religions, ethnic groups, races were in our school. We all got on well together. Of course there were cliques, as there have always been cliques, but they were not divisive."[9]

It's amazing that when you look back at the 1940s and 1950s you see that a survey showed that the major problems in the public schools were:
- talking out of turn,
- chewing gum,
- making noises,
- running in the halls,
- cutting in line,
- dress code infractions,
- littering.

But today teachers report that the major problems schools face are:
- drug abuse,

- alcohol abuse,
- pregnancy,
- suicide,
- rape,
- robbery,
- assault.

These statistics are confirmed when we look at the results of another, more recent survey. It reveals that more than half of the students in grades six through twelve say they have threatened to harm a teacher. Nearly two-thirds say they have threatened another student. Almost 40 percent say they have carried a gun to school at least once. Nearly two-thirds say they are monthly users of illicit drugs. Public pollster George Gallup, Jr., says that these trends did not just happen overnight: "The Gallup Youth Survey, which started 22 years ago, has consistently shown that they are afraid, fearful of being in school in a given day; the figure can be as high as a fourth, and that proportion has grown over the two decades, so the situation has gotten worse."[10]

Certainly no time in history was perfect. Schools in the 1940s and 1950s had their problems too. But make no mistake—those problems were mere fleabites compared to the crisis we're in today where killing in the classroom has become all too common a possibility. I want to examine specific factors behind this rampage of violence. We begin with the issue of God and the schools. Is there any link between removing Him from our schools and our crisis today?

Benjamin Rush

In the 1830s Dr. Benjamin Rush, one of America's Founding Fathers, warned us that if the Bible should ever be removed as a textbook, crimes in school would increase, and we would have to waste lots of money to try and prevent them.[11] One can only wonder what Dr. Rush would say about far too many of today's public schools.

Murray vs. Murray

In addition to the ACLU, one of those involved in the removal of prayer from the schools was the well-known atheist, the late Madalyn Murray O'Hair. In the center of that lawsuit was fourteen-year-old William J. Murray. Today he is an evangelist, fighting to bring prayer back to the schools. He was in total disagreement during the last fifteen years or so of her life. (She disappeared in 1995 and was later found to have been murdered by a fellow atheist.)

William J. Murray says, "I would like people to take a look at the Baltimore public schools today vs. what they were when I went to those schools in 1963 and my mother took prayer out of the schools. We didn't have armed guards in the hallways when we had God in the classroom, but I'll guarantee you there are armed guards. In fact, the city school system of Baltimore now has its own armed police force."[12]

TO PRAY OR NOT TO PRAY

What have been further results of this change in the educational environment? Author David Barton found that since 1962, for the first time ever, S.A.T. scores went down, and they declined for eighteen straight years in a row. Furthermore, violent crime in the United States radically increased during the same period. Also, from 1962 on, teen pregnancies in America rose dramatically, so that today we have roughly one million teen pregnancies a year—the highest figure for an industrial nation. Meanwhile, divorce rates also increased dramatically, and in 1962, the year prayer was thrown out of schools, the divorce rate in America started to escalate.[13]

How did America as a nation degenerate to this level? David Barton has documented the correlation between the ACLU-initiated ban on prayer and Bible reading in our public schools and the nation's moral decline in his book *America: To Pray or Not to Pray?* Here's what he says about the link between kicking God out of the public arena and the denigration of our society:

> Having, by our own abdication, transferred a nation which was so firmly built on Godly principles into the hands of unGodly men, should we really be surprised by what has happened? The problems we have created for ourselves are evident.[14]

Surely, a multitude of factors have combined to create these problems, but the very heart of the question is: Are we going to follow God's Word and His ways, or will we explicitly reject Him in the public arena? Again, George Washington himself asked how a nation could maintain its morality without religion.[15]

A DISTORTION OF THE FIRST AMENDMENT

I believe that the ban of prayer and Bible reading in schools, led by the ACLU and their minions, is all based on a distortion of the First Amendment—interpreting it to mean the strict separation of church and state—that our Founding Fathers would neither recognize nor agree with.

David Barton observes, "On the floor of the Constitutional Convention, they talked about [how] a nation accounts to God for its stands. Prior to 1962, our official stand was that God was welcome in the affairs of the nation. In 1962, for the first time, we told God He was not welcome in the lives of our students or in our classrooms, that we wanted Him to stay out."[16]

And the results have been devastating.

Gwen Hadley, mother of one of the shooting victims in West Paducah, Kentucky, says, "I think there's definite correlation between not having God in school and just the problems with the whole country, not just to mention the schools. You take morality and God out of anything and you're going to have problems."[17]

The irony of the shooting in Kentucky is that in 1978 the Kentucky legislature passed a law calling for privately funded copies of the Ten Commandments to be posted at schools throughout the state. However, the ACLU sued to stop this law because of the alleged violation of the separation of church and state. By a 5-4 margin, the Supreme Court sided with the ACLU. Writing for the majority, Justice William Brennan wrote: "If the posted copies of the Ten Commandments are to have any effect at all, it will be to induce the schoolchildren to read, meditate upon, perhaps to venerate and obey, the Commandments. However desirable this might be as a matter of private devotion, it is not a permissible state objective under the Establishment Clause."[18]

George Grant says, "When Justice Brennan feared that children might actually obey the Ten Commandments, what he was really saying, was not that we don't want children to have a standard for behavior. He was saying, we want an alternative standard for behavior. A secular standard for behavior. Today we're reaping the harvest of that new standard."[19] Wayne Steger, again a man who lost a daughter in the West Paducah shooting, says, "Across the country, we have taken God out of the schools, God is out of the families. The first step would be to get God back in the schools."[20]

Yet, after the Columbine shooting the late syndicated columnist Mary McGrory intoned, "When it comes to preventing violence in our schoolyards, some fathead is bound to say that prayer is the solution."[21]

Meanwhile, George Gallup, Jr., of the Gallup Poll, based in Princeton, New Jersey, says there is a scientifically demonstrable link between good behavior and what he calls "the faith factor." Says Gallup, "The single most reliable indicator of whether or not a youngster will do well in school and get in trouble or not get in trouble really is the faith factor, and the stronger and deeper that faith, the less likely this person is to get into trouble."[22] And he adds, "In fact, the faith factor is more important as a determinant in how a person behaves than other background characteristics, such as level of education, even the strength of family, and a host of other factors."[23]

Darryl Scott lost his daughter Rachel in the Columbine shooting. He laments, "Because we've totally removed every shred of spiritual influence from our schools and godly influence, it's opened a void and a vacuum. And in that vacuum has just surged in so much secular education that's promoted—where anything goes."[24]

A month after the Columbine shooting, Darryl Scott was invited to address Congress on school violence. He read a poem he'd been inspired to write after the tragedy. Here's a portion of that poem:

> *Your laws ignore our deepest needs,*
> *Your words are empty air.*
> *You've stripped away our heritage,*
> *You've outlawed simple prayer.*
> *Now gunshots fill our classrooms and*
> *precious children die.*
> *You seek for answers everywhere,*
> *And ask the question why?*
> *You regulate restrictive laws*
> *Through legislative creed.*
> *And yet you fail to understand*
> *That God is what we need.*[25]

Wayne Steger agrees. He says, "If we can just introduce God back into our schools, that would be just such a great step in the right direction. Because, without God, I'm sorry, but it's going to be a losing battle."[26]

CONCLUSION

This is incontestable. Faith matters, and it matters deeply. So when every reference to God has been systematically outlawed from our schools, is it any wonder they're in crisis? That young people have no reference for good and evil, for right and wrong? If we're to see real change, God and his truth must be brought back to our schools.

We have seen in this chapter what happens when a Christian world-and-life view is totally removed from our education. A true Christian worldview sees Christians actively involved in applying biblical principles in the sphere of our schools.

I trust you will pray for America's schools and America's youth. It's never too late to reclaim them for Jesus Christ.

PART V

THE SPHERE
OF THE
CHURCH

INTRODUCTION TO CHRISTIANIZING THE SPHERE
OF THE CHURCH

Somebody once said, "If you ever find a perfect church, don't join it. Then it won't be perfect anymore."

It may seem strange to talk about "Christianizing the church," but I believe this is certainly another sphere that needs to be brought under the lordship of Christ. I recognize that some people profess to believe in Christ but are not officially a part of the outward body of Christ. I do not think they are right in their attitude. The church is something Jesus Christ created—it is His body. With all of the imperfections of the church—past and present—it is still His bride.

To Christianize the church, we have to make sure we ourselves are Christians. We need to learn to obey God's first and last commands. And we need to be sure that we don't abandon the instructions He Himself gave us.

In the parable of the ten virgins (Matthew 25:1-13), they were all waiting for the bridegroom, but only five were ready when he came. May God grant us the grace that we will be among those waiting, not those turned away.

17

THE BIBLE AND
THE SOUL

. . . as it is written, "None is righteous, no, not one."
ROMANS 3:10

✛

As we consider a full Christian world-and-life view and as we consider Christianizing the sphere of the church, we must consider what the Bible says about the soul. For the church is not mortar and brick. The church is comprised of its people.

What does the Bible say about man? Apart from the redemption available only through Jesus Christ, are we whole? Are we sick? Are we dead? Is man basically good? Maybe a little sick here and there, but basically good?

I believe that, as with just about everything related to a true Christian worldview, the truth as found in the Bible runs contrary to what millions in society believe. We need to explore what the Bible says about the soul because being in Christ is the starting point of a true Christian worldview.

MODERN MYTH: MAN IS BASICALLY GOOD

A plethora of modern myths plague the American church today. A tremendous shift has taken place in the thinking of Americans on basic religious issues. It is a witches' brew—partly secular humanism, partly New Age theology, and partly the remnants of biblical teaching.

One recent study found that 83 percent of Americans believe that man is basically good. A great many Americans deny original sin. Shockingly, this includes many professing Christians. Now, to me this is astonishing because it not only flies right in the face of biblical teaching, it flies in the face of all Western Christianity and civilization. It also flies in the face of 5,000 years of recorded history.

Karl Menninger, the famed founder of the Menninger Psychiatric Clinic, wrote a book some years ago entitled *What Ever Became of Sin?*, and he mused over the question of the use of the word *sin*. "It was once a strong word, an ominous and serious word. It described a central point in every civilized human being's life plan and life style. But the word went away."[1]

DID AMERICA STOP SINNING?

But today it seems that we never hear the word anymore. Menninger said, "Eisenhower mentioned it in one of his proclamations—Thanksgiving proclamation—quoting Lincoln, who said that we should 'repent of our sins' and turn to the Almighty.'"[2] But after that, he never mentioned it again. Nor did the three succeeding Presidents. So said Dr. Menninger in the early 1970s, and it seems that America "officially ceased 'sinning' some twenty years ago."[3]

Certainly if you listen to the media today—the news shows, the talk shows—you would suppose that sin has indeed ceased to exist in America. You never hear the word, do you? Oh, you see an awful lot of it on the screen, but it's just never called sin anymore. We like to call it lots of other things.

IS NOTHING WRONG ANYMORE?

Meg Greenfield wrote an article in *Newsweek* that was reprinted several years ago in *Reader's Digest*, entitled "Why Nothing Is 'Wrong' Anymore." She says, "it used to be that things were right and wrong. It was very clear, but it seems that we don't even call it wrong any more, much less 'sin.'" In fact, today we have substitutes, like we have "Right and . . . Stupid."[4] Correct? Especially if it is we who have done it, or some of our friends.

We don't talk about the fact that an act was wrong or sinful, instead calling it dumb. Consider a classic example from more than a decade ago: Magic Johnson—applauded all over our country, and certainly for his athletic prowess he should be—was a veritable ballet dancer in basketball shoes. He dropped balls in baskets like some of us drop donuts in coffee cups—with great ease. A decade ago he made his "brave" announcement that he had contracted the HIV virus. This was from his exposure to perhaps hundreds of anonymous lovers. In his announcement of having the disease, what he actually said, in essence, was not that he was wrong, but he was dumb. He should have practiced "safe sex," he stated. There wasn't anything immoral about what he did—certainly it wasn't sinful—just dumb.

I Wasn't Wrong—Just Dumb

I was troubled when one commentator, who was waxing positively euphoric, said, "young people, keep your eyes on Magic. Listen to what he says." What did he say? Not, avoid sin or flee fornication or turn away from immorality, but "practice safe sex." It seems today that we're not concerned whether something is sinful, wrong, or immoral. The only thing we're concerned about is that it's safe. We want to have "safe sex" so we don't have unpleasant consequences. We want to have "safe" abortions. We don't want to talk about whether the sex is immoral or the abortions are murder; we just want to have them safe and neat—not those messy, back-alley, "unsafe" kind, but the nice, clinical, safe ones.

We even want to have "safe" suicides. You know, if you do it yourself, it can be awfully messy; sometimes you just foul the whole thing up and you—you live. So we need to have a professional standing by to assist us—physician-assisted suicide. Nobody asks if suicide is murder. We just want it safe.

We are plagued with scandals. This is nothing new. But perhaps some of the excuses are new (although I wonder even if that is true):

- "But, officer, I wasn't driving drunk—I was merely overserved."
- "I had that affair for no other reason than this: because I could."
- "I didn't do anything wrong—I merely made a bad choice."

Loss of the Puritan Ethic

For centuries we have retained a Puritan ethic that helped set the tone for our nation. Through the years many politicians and some Presidents have been indiscreet—wait a minute, even that phrase is a euphemism to cover up sin, so let's reword it. Through the years, many politicians and some Presidents have committed adultery. Because of the Puritan ethic that was dominant for so long, Americans did not like this to be publicly known. If it were known to definitely be true, often the politician was drummed out of office.

This seemed to change with Bill Clinton. The Puritan ethic took a major beating. No longer was it a major problem to lie to the American people or even to lie under oath if "it was only about sex." When Bill Clinton appeared ubiquitous on the American mass media to promote his memoirs, he admitted his mistakes. But in light of the harsh words he reserved for Ken Starr, it seems the ex-President was more upset and sorry about having gotten caught than about having sinned in the first place.

It seems that we have lost the concept of right and wrong, of sin and righteousness. So instead things are "right and stupid," as Meg Greenfield puts it. Or maybe they're "right or sick." They're not wrong—they're just sick; they're not evil—they're just sick. When somebody shoots a President or murders a half a dozen people, "He must be sick. We ought to put him in a hospital for sick minds because, you see, people are basically good. So this nice fellow must be sick. When he gets well, he'll be good again."[5]

Or maybe they're "right and only to be expected," because, after all, it's not the person that's the problem—it's the circumstances, it's society. Growing up in that kind of environment, surely we are to expect that kind of thing. As one of our Presidents a few decades ago said, when the riots took place in New York, when the lights went out, the problem, he said, was unemployment—there was nothing wrong with the individuals, society was wrong.

What ever happened to right and wrong, and what ever happened to sin? Is man really basically good? It is to the Scripture, to the Word of God and the testimonies of the Lord, that we should turn. We must go back to the beginning: When God created man, He created him in His own image. He made Adam and Eve male and female, and it was very good. Man was good. He was God's crowning glory of all creation. Man was good in body, mind, and soul. That is how God created us—perfect. But the Fall happened, and our bodies became vulnerable to sickness and death. Our minds became darkened, so we could not see clearly. Our will was turned away from God and toward evil. Our soul came under Satan's dominion. Adam and Eve and all their unborn children died spiritually that day (Genesis 3:3). The rest of the Bible is essentially the story of our restoration (regeneration).

It is interesting, I think, that the greatest of saints down through the centuries have all acknowledged themselves to be the greatest of sinners. The closer you draw to God, the more clearly you see the uncleanness and filth within you.

A UNIVERSAL PROBLEM

And so it was with Job and Isaiah and Peter and Paul, who acknowledged their sin as they gained a glimpse of God. Job said, "I had heard of you by the hearing of the ear, but now my eye sees you; therefore I despise myself, and repent in dust and ashes" (Job 42:5-6). After being ushered into the presence of the Lord, Isaiah confessed: "Woe is me. For I am lost; for I am a man of unclean lips, and I dwell in the midst of a people of unclean lips; for my eyes have seen the King, the LORD of hosts!" (Isaiah 6:5). Peter said directly to Jesus, "Depart from me, for I am a sinful man, O Lord" (Luke 5:8). Paul called himself the chief of sinners: "Christ Jesus came into the world to save sinners, of whom I am the foremost" (1 Timothy 1:15).

Augustine, whose name is always attached to the word *saint*, wrote his most famous book, *Confessions*, to confess his sins. It is interesting that the unregenerate live in darkness; so they don't see their sin and uncleanness. People involved in prison work find that many inmates—although convicted in a court of law—maintain their innocence. (Perhaps some are, but the majority are not.)

Sin is the only thing I know of that the more you practice it, the less you are able to even discern its existence. So the people most enmeshed in sin are the people most vociferous in their denial that they have any such thing at all.

What the Scriptures Say

But what does the Word of God say?

- "[T]he hearts of the children of man are full of evil" (Ecclesiastes 9:3).
- "From the sole of the foot even to the head, there is no soundness in it" (Isaiah 1:6).
- "We have all become like one who is unclean, and all our righteous deeds are like a polluted garment" (Isaiah 64:6).
- "The heart is deceitful above all things, and desperately sick; who can understand it?" (Jeremiah 17:9).
- "I know that nothing good lives in me. . . . So I find it to be a law that when I want to do right, evil lies close at hand" (Romans 7:18, 21).
- "If we say we have no sin, we deceive ourselves, and the truth is not in us." (1 John 1:8).
- "[T]he whole world lies in the power of the evil one" (1 John 5:19).

Yes, but that is so negative and so pessimistic, some would object. We need something lighter than that to chew upon. Christ was so loving. We were told that Jesus didn't believe people were sinful, that Jesus had a more positive view of human nature and never would say anything as negative as what we just read. Again let's turn to the text itself and see exactly what Jesus Christ did believe about men, because the Scripture says that He knew what was in man. What did He think, and what did He say, and what did He declare? Listen to His words:

- "You serpents, you brood of vipers, how are you to escape being sentenced to hell?" (Matthew 23:33).
- "Then he will say to those on his left, 'Depart from me, you cursed, into the eternal fire prepared for the devil and his angels'" (Matthew 25:41).

- "For out of the heart come evil thoughts, murder, adultery, sexual immorality, theft, false witness, slander. These are what defile a person. But to eat with unwashed hands does not defile anyone" (Matthew 15:19-20).
- "Truly, truly, I say to you, everyone who commits sin is a slave to sin" (John 8:34)
- "You are of your father the devil, and your will is to do your father's desires" (John 8:44).

These and many other texts by Jesus show that what He said about mankind were such things as these: Men are sinners. They are the servants of sin. They are the children of Satan. They are wicked. They are hypocrites. They are transgressors. Their hearts are filled with evil thoughts, murders, adulteries, fornications, and thefts. They are workers of iniquity. They are serpents, a generation of vipers. They are fools and blind, and much more. Jesus Christ, who intimately understood the heart of man, knew that man's heart was indeed wicked from his youth.

This is the same Christ who said: "[T]his [cup] is the blood of the new testament, which is shed for many for the remission of [their]. . ." Their what? Their basic goodness? No. ". . . for the remission of [their] sins" (Matthew 26:28, KJV). Jesus Christ came into the world so that our sins might be forgiven.

The Scripture teaches that man is not basically good, Christ taught that man is not basically good, and history confirms that man is definitely not basically good. Some experts have noted that one-third of all human beings who have lived on this planet have died at the hands of their brothers—that mankind has killed one-third of the human race in war and so on.

THE TWENTIETH CENTURY

Consider even the last century. We saw the Armenian holocaust, the Spanish Civil War, the Nazi Holocaust, the Japanese prison camps, the Gulag Archipelago, the atrocities of Idi Amin in Uganda, the massacre in Cambodia, and 135 million people slaughtered by the Communists. Consider in more recent times Rwanda, 9/11, and the slaughter in Sudan. These and many another atrocities do not attest that man is basically good. It is utterly astonishing to me that any person with an ounce of intelligence or even common sense could hold to such an idiotic position.

Mike Wallace of *Sixty Minutes* once did a piece about Adolf Eichmann, one of the chief architects of the Holocaust, and as part of that he interviewed a survivor of the Holocaust, a man by the name of Yehiel Dinur, a Jewish man. He showed a clip from a motion picture taken at the Nuremberg trials when Dinur came to testify against Eichmann. When Dinur walked into the courtroom, he walked past where Eichmann was seated and turned to look at him. He suddenly began to sob out loud, and a moment later he fell in a dead faint on the floor. When he was revived, he was asked, "Did the sight of this monster, this monster of evil, so overwhelm you that he caused you to faint?"

Was Dinur overcome by hatred? Fear? Horrid memories? No; it was none of these. Dinur explained to Wallace that all at once he realized that Eichmann was not the godlike army officer who had sent so many to their death. This Eichmann was an ordinary man. "I was afraid about myself," said Dinur, "I saw that I am capable to do this. I am . . . exactly like him."[6]

There is, said the commentator, a little Eichmann in each of us. I would add that not only does history attest to this, but the Bible declares it, and Christ affirms it, and even common sense ought to be enough to demonstrate it. You don't need to be a historian; all you need is the front page of your newspaper.

READ THE NEWSPAPERS, WATCH THE NEWS

If man is basically good, as 83 percent of Americans now believe, why have so many churches been burned to the ground, as has happened in record numbers recently?

Why, if man is basically good, would an intelligent graduate student, envious of the academic honor bestowed upon a friend, take a gun and shoot his friend and four others and then himself?

Why, if man is basically good, would two youths make a video showing themselves with a room full of stolen goods, bragging, "We are high school dropouts, and we steal for a living"?

Why, if man is basically good, have 100,000 brochures been distributed in South Florida in recent years saying, "If you have a rented car, don't get lost"? I mean, if they get lost, surely some of these basically good people will help them find their way, or did I miss something in the paper? (There was a wave of killings of foreign tourists killed in South Florida who made a wrong turn. Thankfully, this trend has been largely curbed.)

Why, if man is basically good, have some of our public schools become battlegrounds where school shootings take place?

Why, if man is basically good, are there so many murders in convenience stores throughout the country?

Why, if man is basically good, did a woman leave her months-old baby in a garbage can?

Why, if man is basically good, did a woman throw her infant out of her car as she was speeding along an interstate highway?

Why, if man is basically good, is there such a growing demand for alarm systems for homes?

Why, if man is basically good, did Jeffrey Dahmer, in Milwaukee, dismember and even eat parts of seventeen victims that he killed in his home?

Why, if man is basically good, was one of the choir members from my church recently held up at gunpoint?

Indeed, even common sense would seem to shout that man is not basically good. Take just a little stroll with me near my church and you will see a policeman standing on the corner. Why? To help basically good people cross the street?

Or go into the bank to deposit a check, and you will notice the eighteen-inch steel doors behind which the money will be placed at night and the alarm buttons on the floor by the tellers. Why? Because they want to be able to sound an alarm in case the wind comes in and blows the money away?

Or stop by the bank vice president's office and ask for a loan, and you will raise the whole question of the subject of sin in his mind. He will have some very interesting questions to ask you that wouldn't be needed at all if men were basically good.

Uncle Sam has a bit more levelheaded idea about that. Why do we spend billions of dollars on courts and judges and prosecutors, on jails and prisons, if men are basically good? Why have we spent trillions of dollars on defense—to protect ourselves from those basically good folks on the other side of the ocean? Every missile and every silo is a silent and eloquent testimony to the fact that man is basically evil.

We are being misled and deceived by false teachers and prophets of all kinds from every direction.

Oh, it is certainly good for the pride and the ego to be told that we are all good. But, to paraphrase Henry Van Dyke, I would rather believe that most miserable fact of our sinfulness than to be deceived by the merriest lie. And the idea of man being good is, indeed, just that—a lie.

Chuck Colson has said that in recent decades popular, political, and social beliefs have all but erased the reality of personal sin from our national consciousness. How true that is. We are told that the evil does not lie in us but in society. As William Saroyan claims very succinctly: "Every man is a good man in a bad world, as he himself knows."[7]

Is It Society's Fault?

You see, that's where the evil is—out there—in society—in the environment. we are told. So we must repress all efforts to change the hearts of men. We must get rid of religion—get it out of the schools, out of the government, out of every public place—and focus all our attention on externalities.

Dr. Louis Evans put it very well when he said, "you may take the man out of the slums, but only God can take the slums out of a man." The problem lies in the human heart, as the eagle eye of Christ saw when He said that out of the heart proceed murders and thefts and adulteries and fornications and blasphemies. It's out of the heart that the evil of this world comes, and it's only by changing the heart that we have hope.

But not only do we have the reality of sin and the ramifications and the consequences of it, but also, thank God, we have redemption from sin in Jesus Christ, whom God has sent to be a propitiation for our sins. John the Baptist announced, "Behold, the Lamb of God, who takes away the sin of the world!" (John 1:29). Yes, we are born in a fallen state, a state of sin and depravity. But God so loved the world that He gave His only begotten Son, and God was willing to take all of that sin and place it upon His Son. God was willing to punish that sin not upon us in hell, but upon His own beloved Son on the cross. God was willing to come and take that blood and cleanse us and make us whiter than snow, so that we could be restored—that restoration beginning here on earth and being completed in heaven. Thus, ultimately He will restore His redeemed to the state in which He made us—good, perfect, and holy.

The Redemption of Christ

But, you see, if we deny that we are sinful, if we deny that we have this iniquity within us, then we cut ourselves off from the redemption of Christ. Jesus Christ came, as He said, to save that which was lost. He came to save sinners—not to call the righteous, but sinners to repentance (Matthew 9:12-13).

"The world has many religions," said George Owen, "it has but one Gospel."[8] There are hundreds of religions in this world; there is only one gospel. All of the religions of this world are simply good advice; only Christianity is Good News. When people say, "Well, all religions are the same," they are simply saying, "I am ignorant of the nature of religion altogether, and I really know nothing about it," because Christianity is diametrically opposed to all of the pagan religions of this world.

DO VS. DONE

In all of the world religions, man is endeavoring to reach up and somehow find God. In fact, the word *religion* means "bind oneself to." Only in Christianity, however, is God reaching down to man. Only here does the Lord reach down to find fallen and helpless rebels. Only here does God do Himself that which is necessary for us to be reconciled to Him.

All of the world's religions could be boiled down into one single two-letter word: *do*. This is the essence of the message of every pagan religion in the world. Do this, do that, don't do the other. Because people are blinded to the truth of the gospel and do not see that the basic message of the Bible is the gospel, they suppose it is nothing but law and that Christianity is simply do— do this and don't do that.

However, the basic message of Christianity is not do but *done*. "It is finished" were the last words of Christ before commending His soul to the Father (John 19:30). It is done. It is finished. It is complete. It is enough. It is accomplished. *Tetelestai* is the Greek word used there ("paid in full"; the debt of our sin was fully paid). The penalty has been paid; the purchase is made; the atonement is completed. And now those who trust in Him have eternal life freely as a gift.

THE GIFT OF ETERNAL LIFE

Dear one, have you ever truly yielded your life to Christ? Have you ever truly surrendered yourself to Him? There is life through a look at the crucified one. Won't you come and yield your heart to Him? If you have never accepted Jesus Christ alone as your Savior and Lord, we encourage you to pray something to this effect:

> *Lord Jesus Christ, I ask You to be my Savior. I want to be Your child. Forgive me for assuming that I am good enough on my own merit to get into heaven. Wash me and make me whiter than snow. Come into my heart, Lord Jesus Christ. I repent of my sins. Please cleanse me from all my unrighteousness. O Christ, I yield my life to You. Amen.*

If you prayed that prayer sincerely, then I encourage you to write for a free book to help you get started in your Christian life. It is entitled *Beginning Again*. (To receive a free copy of *Beginning Again,* please write to me at Box 40, Ft. Lauderdale, FL 33302. God bless you as you do.)

Eternal life begins here and now, and it is a gift for time and eternity.

When we surrender our will to Christ's will, eternal life begins through the power of the Holy Spirit.

CONCLUSION

The Bible says that the soul that sins will surely die (Ezekiel 18:4). It also says that we are all sinners (Romans 3:23). As Christians today, we cling to a truth recognized in Western civilization in times past—that all men are sinners. We must rid ourselves of the dangerous myth that man is basically good.

So what is the Christian view of man? We were created good, but through the Fall, our mind, body, will, and soul were eternally affected. In our fallen state we are evil. But God sent Christ to restore us not only to our former glory, but to a righteous state in which we can live with Him.

The 83 percent of Americans who think we are all good have an instinctive feeling that it should be so. We ought to be good. What they don't know is that only Christ can make us so. The story of the Bible is the story of man: creation, fall, restoration or generation, degeneration, regeneration.

THE OLD LAMPLIGHTER

. . . for at one time you were darkness, but now you are light in the Lord. Walk as children of light.

EPHESIANS 5:8

✠

How do we fulfill the purpose for which we were created? In particular, how does the church of Jesus Christ fulfill its purpose for being placed here on earth?

GOD'S FIRST AND LAST COMMANDS

How we are to do that is spelled out in the first and last commands that God has given, the beginning and the end of God's mandates for the human race. The first one is given in Genesis 1:28, which says that God created us in His image so we could subdue the earth and have dominion over all things in it. As the vice-regents of God, we are in His place to bring to pass His will in all of the various spheres of life.

The last commandment Christ gave, right before being taken up, was that we were to go and make disciples of all nations. "You will be my witnesses" (Acts 1:8). This is repeated four times in four slightly different ways (Matthew 28:18-20; Mark 16:15; Luke 24:46-49; Acts 1:8), but it is clear that we are to take the gospel of Jesus Christ to a lost and needy world. Ah, that is something that so desperately needs to be done, and I thank God that so many of you are eagerly and joyfully doing it through the witnessing training offered in your church. I rejoice in that. But I know that others have not and do not. If I ask the question, "How many people did you share the gospel with recently?" I'm afraid many would have to say, "None." None this year, this decade; some, alas, never.

In this chapter and the next we want to explore command #2 and command #1 (in that order). In this chapter we will discuss winning the world to faith in Christ, and in the next chapter we'll discuss reclaiming the culture for Christ. Thus the two chapters combined will present what some people call "the salt and light solution."

THE OLD LAMPLIGHTER

Sir Harry Lauder, the famed Scottish humorist and comedian at the turn of the twentieth century, was a Christian. One evening, at the Hotel Cecil, he told about an incident that might have been spoken from the pulpit. He said:

> I was sitting in the gloamin', an' a man passed the window. He was the lamplighter. He pushed his pole into the lamp and lighted it. Then he went to another and another. Now I couldn't see him. But I knew where he was by the lights as they broke out doon the street, until he had left a beautiful avenue of light. Ye're a' lamplighters. They'll know where ye've been by the lights [ye have lit].[1]

I think that is one of the most beautiful descriptions of the Christian life I have ever heard. That is exactly what we are. We are all lamplighters. Jesus Christ said, "I am the light of the world. Whoever follows me will not walk in darkness, but will have the light of life" (John 8:12). He also told us, "the light has come into the world, and people loved the darkness rather than the light because their deeds were evil" (John 3:19). All those in whom burns brightly the Light of Life of Jesus Christ are to bring light to those who sit in the shadow of darkness, so that upon them the wondrous light of Christ might shine as well.

The symbolism in Lauder's comments is clear. As believers in Christ we are lamplighters. The darkened lamps are the lives and souls of lost men and women who sit in a dark world, far from the life and light of God, lost in sin's dark night. The flame is the love of Jesus Christ burning by His Spirit in our hearts. The pole is the presentation of the gospel of Jesus Christ, and the light that keeps shining is a life lit by the love of Christ and empowered by the Holy Spirit.

It is the evangelization of men and women by the power of His Word and Spirit that takes that flame and causes those who once were in darkness to come into the light. Wonder of wonders, when all the lamps are lighted, the city becomes aglow with their light.

Indeed, we live in a dark world where there are so many who do not know the Savior. We increasingly see the results of this as more and more of them sink our society into the depths of depravity and sin—the ultimate consequences of which were seen when we heard the confessions of men like Ted Bundy. Like those creeping, crawling things that hide in the dark shadows of a rotting log, so all kinds of vice and viciousness haunt the darkness of a world without Christ.

Are you a lamplighter for Jesus Christ? They will know where you have been by the lights you have lit. Every new light brings a glow with it. The light illuminates and comforts, and the people around can bask in its glow, until it shines as "a "city set on a hill" (Matthew 5:14). I am happy to say that I know many believers of whom it can be said: If we could take but one heavenly snapshot of their entire pilgrimage through this life, we would see that everywhere they have gone, they left people lighted for Christ. When they visited in this home or that home, or spoke across the fence with their neighbor, or talked to someone at the store or at the front door, or went on vacation, or went to dinner or lunch, or shared with someone bereaved or in the hospital, or shared with loved ones—wherever they have been, they lighted men and women for Jesus Christ, and we can see a trail of light that has followed them throughout their lives as Christians.

Ah, yes, they are indeed true lamplighters. On that great day, in that glorious Assize, when judgment is set and the tomes of judgment are open, they will know and we will know and all the world will know where they have been. Let us spread the light around us and not place it under a barrel.

Closet Christians

One of the sociological phenomena of our day is called the "emptying of the closet." The closet used to be full in America—as full as that famous one owned by Fibber McGee on old-time radio. Today it is empty. The prostitutes have left the closet and are marching down the streets demanding their rights. The homosexuals are out of the closet and now are having their own parades. Even the fornicators have left the closet and have put both of their names on the mailbox where they cohabit apart from the blessings of marriage.

Ah, the closet is empty indeed—unless you move aside some of the heavy winter coats and perhaps push a suitcase or two away, and there, cringing in the darkness in the corner, clinging to his lamplighter's pole, can be found a church member who professes to be a follower of the Light of the World. Ah, that is tragic indeed.

I think in many places the church symbol should not be a burning bush but rather a flapping chicken. Where is that courage and boldness that so typified Christians in past ages so that men could tell they had been with Jesus? If you profess to be a believer in Jesus Christ, you cannot trust in Jesus Christ and care for others without sharing with them the light of eternal life.

One businessman asked his friend, "How long have we known each other?"

"About fifteen years."

"And you believe, I understand, that no man can go to heaven except through faith in Jesus Christ. Is that correct?"

"Oh, yes, I believe that very definitely."

"Do you really care about me?"

"Indeed I do."

"Sir, I beg to differ with you. You actually do not care for me at all, for in fifteen years I have heard you talk about hundreds of subjects, but you have never yet once talked to me about Christ."

This reminds me of the poem entitled "You Forgot My Soul":

> *You lived next door to me for years;*
> *We shared our dreams, our joys, our tears.*
> *A friend to me you were indeed,*
> *A friend who helped me in my need.*
> *My faith in you was strong and sure;*
> *We had such trust as should endure.*
> *No spats between us e'er arose;*
> *Our friends were like—and so, our foes.*
> *What sadness then, my friend, to find*
> *That after all, you weren't so kind.*
> *The day my life on earth did end,*
> *I found you weren't a faithful friend.*
> *For all those years we spent on earth*
> *You never talked of second birth.*
> *You never spoke of my lost soul,*
> *And of the Christ who'd make me whole.*
> *I plead today from hell's cruel fire*
> *And tell you now my last desire.*
> *You cannot do a thing for me;*
> *No words today my bonds to free.*
> *But do not err, my friend, again—*
> *Do all you can for souls of men.*
> *Plead with them now quite earnestly,*
> *Lest they be cast in hell with me.*[2]

CHRIST'S COMMAND

You cannot believe Christ and love men and not share with them the Light of Life. Jesus, in His last command, said that we are to be witnesses to Him. He came to this earth and suffered and agonized and bled and died and purchased eternal life for all who would trust in Him. He left that great treasure, that great legacy, in your hands and mine. What have we done with it? We must spread the Light of Life, as Christ commanded.

Can we be so disobedient, so rebellious, to Him who so graciously and eternally loved us—even unto the cross? Oh, if we could but see a friend, a loved one, an acquaintance, a business partner five minutes after his death, we would surely lament if we had not told him about the Light of Life. If our lives are going to have any real significance, we must be witnesses for Him.

Michelangelo, the great Italian painter and sculptor, carved several statues out of ice one cold winter day—perhaps for the amusement of friends. With his genius, they were magnificently done, and many came to admire them. But, of course, soon the sun rose higher in the sky, and as the day passed, very soon those statues melted completely away.

We would think it extremely foolish for someone to spend his life doing something like that. To leave a legacy in ice that will turn to water and mud would be folly indeed. Some of you have spent your whole life carving in ice. What have you spent your life doing? Making a living? Fixing a house? Making sure your lawn is impeccable? What will it amount to 500 years from now? Five hundred million years from now? What will it amount to in eternity?

John Wesley said that a wise man builds on that which will be of value in eternity.[3] Michelangelo, fortunately, fashioned some statues out of marble or we would never remember him at all. And even marble is consumed by the teeth of time and will disappear altogether.

MAKING YOUR LIFE COUNT FOR ETERNITY

Those who are truly wise will sculpt in human souls and fashion those souls into the image of Jesus Christ. Ah, to know that you are building something that is eternal in the heavens, something that never dies. The stars will burn into cinders and fall from the sky, but the souls of men will have just begun to live. That is why we should go and make disciples.

What are you making of your life, and what will it amount to a million years from now? I urge you to work with the souls of men. Do something that will give to your life significance and meaning that will be glorious. So many people, it seems, think that being a witness for Jesus Christ is some great burden, some huge responsibility. It is that, but ah, it is also the greatest joy.

Just the other night I heard a beautiful young lady tell about the ecstatic joy she had found in leading an acquaintance to the Savior, Jesus Christ. What a wondrous joy was in her eyes. It radiated from her entire being. It is a great joy to be a witness for Him. Once one has overcome fears and trepidations and has become a confident, joyous witness for Christ, it is the most gladsome thing I know of to do.

In our church, by the grace of God, thousands of people have been trained to work in souls, trained to light the lamps of those who are now in darkness. They have discovered that with but a little training (compared to most things in this world that are vastly more difficult), they can, with joy, set forth before lost men and women the glad tidings of Jesus Christ. It gives significance and satisfaction to life.

Do you really have satisfaction with what you have spent your life doing, or do the words of this well-known hymn speak to your heart:

> *Must I go, and empty-handed?*
> *Must I meet my Savior so?*
> *Not one soul with which to greet Him:*
> *Must I empty-handed go?*[4]

If so, that need not be your plight. You can learn to rejoice and to share the gospel and to light the lives of men that shall be lighted down through the unending ages of eternity.

Many a time I've heard someone tell me about a friend who died, and his great remorse was that he had never talked to that friend about Christ. Of course, not all who hear it accept the gospel—that is their responsibility. But at least they should be given the chance to hear.

THE JOY OF SHARING

Some people in this world will never hear the gospel of Jesus Christ unless they hear it from you. If every person reading this book were to become truly a lamplighter for Jesus Christ, there would be a new level of excitement in their lives—and joy and ecstasy. Could you imagine the impact on this country if each Christian this year would commit to leading just one person to Jesus Christ and discipling that person? We could change this land in a very short time.

Nothing I have ever done has given me as much satisfaction as sharing the gospel—unless, perhaps, it is the equal joy of seeing a person I have trained come to the place where they, too, are rejoicing in having lighted the lamp of another. I guess that is the joy of being a spiritual grandparent.

So many people need to hear the gospel. Fred Hawkins, a layman, while in a town in Missouri, the heartland of America, one day decided to find out how many people really needed to hear the gospel. He went out onto a street corner, and as people passed by, he simply asked them this question: "How do you get to heaven?" He asked twenty-nine people that question and got only seven right answers. Twenty-two people right in the heart of America had no idea how to get to heaven. From where he was standing, he could see the spires of five churches.

Millions are perishing right in the very shadow of the steeples of churches. Perhaps you think that people aren't really interested, that they wouldn't really want to know. I think of another businessman who was on a trip. His plane stopped for a layover in Dallas. Being a genuine lamplighter for Christ, he wondered how he could use the hour-and-twenty-minute wait to good purpose.

He had some tracts in his briefcase. So he took them out, inserted a business card in each one, and gave one to every person in that particular section of the airport. He said to each one, "Here, this will tell you how to become a Christian. If you would like to know more, I will be sitting right over there [pointing across the waiting room] until my plane leaves in about an hour. Or if you would like to write me, here is my business card."

What do you think happened? Before his plane left, men were standing four deep around his seat trying to find out more about how to become a Christian, and for weeks he was answering letters from those who inquired. Ah, many people want to know about Jesus.

CONCLUSION

If we are ever to truly Christianize the sphere of the church, we must learn to mobilize the army of God to share the faith. We are privileged to share in joy and satisfaction and fulfillment and meaning in life by leading others to Christ and discipling them.

"And those who are wise shall shine like the brightness of the sky above; and those who turn many to righteousness, like the stars forever and ever" (Daniel 12:3). How glorious that we should be rewarded for doing that which is the most gladsome thing I know of to do. How amazing, indeed, is the grace of God.

Yes, we are all lamplighters, and people will know where we have been by the lights we have lit.

19

WILL THE CHURCH FORGET?

Therefore render to Caesar the things that are Caesar's, and to God the things that are God's.

MATTHEW 22:21

✤

So we see that the church is to fulfill God's last command. But we are also to fulfill God's first command—to be fruitful and multiply and subdue the earth. We are His vice-regents here on earth. But have we forgotten that call?

Every year at Memorial Day we take the time to remember all those who have fallen in the great fight for freedom, those who have given their lives or limbs in order that we might live in peace. The first freedom is the freedom to worship. The original settlers of this land came for religious freedom. Therefore, on Memorial Day it is appropriate that we recognize those who have survived the battle and who have served in our armed forces—Army, Navy, Air Force, Marines, Coast Guard, and in any other capacity. I trust that each of us will not forget those who have sacrificed to make our freedom possible.

My question in this chapter is, will the church forget? I don't think it will forget those who have served, unless the church should be taken over by the radical liberals of the 1960s who said, at a time when the world was being confronted by an increasingly aggressive and hostile Communism, that they stood foursquare against all anti-communism. Believe it or not, those were Americans. Those were the radical liberals of the sixties. Some people think they went away. They didn't go away; they simply went underground. Today they are still in our universities, but they are tenured, and they are teaching in our schools.

The question I would ask is, will the church forget those who fought to defend, including those who gave the last full measure of devotion? Will the church forget the principles upon which this nation was founded—principles of liberty, and not license; of godliness and piety and morality? That is what this nation was built upon. Will those things be forgotten? Alas, I am afraid that not only will the church forget them, but to a large degree the church has already forgotten them.

SILENT PULPITS

Rev. Don Wildmon, a gentleman who has done an amazing job with the American Family Association, wrote about a decade ago something that I think is even more true today. He said this:

> Today, 4,000 innocent precious lives of unborn babies were snuffed out. . . .
> And 300,000 pulpits are silent. . . .
> The networks make a mockery of Christians, the Christian faith, and Christian values with nearly every show they air. . . .
> And 300,000 pulpits are silent.
> Teenage suicide is the highest it has ever been. . . . Christian morality cannot be taught in schools, but atheistic immorality can. . . .
> And 300,000 pulpits are silent.
> Rape has increased 700 percent in the last fifty years, and that takes into consideration the population growth. . . .
> And 300,000 pulpits are silent.
> Rock music fills the airwaves and our children's minds with music which legitimizes rape, murder, forced sex, sadomasochism, adultery, satanic worship, etc.
> And 300,000 pulpits are silent.
> A majority of states now have lotteries. . . .
> And 300,000 pulpits are silent.
> What important matters are being dealt with in our churches?
> The church bulletin says there will be a meeting to plan the church-wide supper. We are raising money to put a new floor cover on the kitchen. (The old one doesn't match the new stove and refrigerator.) The sermon subject last Sunday was "How To Have A Positive Attitude." We are organizing a softball team.[1]

Isn't the church relevant to our age?
It hasn't always been silent, by any means. Down through the centuries

churches have been the ones who have moved to get rid of most of the great evils of our world. It was through the work of Christians in churches that slavery was eliminated from Great Britain, and two-thirds of the members of the Abolition Society in New England were Christian clergymen.[2] No, the church was not always silent. The church spoke out on issues such as child labor laws, wives being beaten and abused, and many other such issues. The church has been responsible for getting rid of cannibalism and head-hunting, the binding of feet of women in China, and numerous other terrible social issues. The church has spoken out about prison reform, reform of asylums for the insane, and many other things.[3] But today that seems to no longer be the case.

DOES IT MAKE A DIFFERENCE?

Does it make any difference? Well, how about Reverend Jonas Clark? You remember Jonas Clark, don't you? We owe so much to Jonas, but alas and alack, the vast majority of Americans—even Christians—have forgotten who he was. He was a very influential pastor. He was the parson in a little town called Lexington. As was the case so often then, he was one of the few people, sometimes the only person, who had an education beyond high school. Therefore, he was the parson. He was the most influential man in town. Most of the people attended his church.

One particular night in 1775 he was having dinner with some folks you will remember: John Hancock and Samuel Adams. It was a very distinctive night because it was the night when Paul Revere made his famous ride. These two great patriots asked Clark the question, if war came, would the men of Lexington fight?

What did Jonas Clark say? "Uhhhh, oh my goodness gracious me oh my. We've never talked about such things as fighting for our liberties. I don't know. I would have to give this my consideration." That is not what he said. When asked, "Would the men of Lexington fight?" Rev. Jonas Clark replied that he had trained them for that very hour.

The next day "the shot that was heard around the world" was fired in the parking lot of his church, only a few yards from his parsonage. The people who were killed were members of his congregation. Clark looked down with great anguish on the bodies of those who had died and made this statement, which we should never forget: "From this day will be dated the liberty of the world."[4] The date was April 19, 1775.

Furthermore, Rev. Clark, reminding us that this slaughter occurred

before war had even been declared, said this of the marauding British troops
who slew many of his congregants:

> And this is the place where the fatal scene begins! They approach with the
> morning light; and more like murderers and cutthroats than the troops of
> a Christian king, without provocation, without warning, when no war was
> proclaimed, they drew the sword of violence, upon the inhabitants of this
> town, and with a cruelty and barbarity, which would have made the most
> hardened savage blush, they shed INNOCENT BLOOD. . . . Yonder field
> can witness the innocent blood of our brethren slain! There the tender
> father bled, and there the beloved son![5]

It began in a church—with a congregation. It began with a parson not
afraid to speak out on the great issues of freedom and liberty and oppression
and tyranny. So it was that he was a part of what is called by some "the Black
Regiment" because of the black robes these pastors wore—these pastors who
preached resounding sermons that resonated throughout New England about
the evils of tyranny and the importance of liberty. They set the stage for the
liberty of America, which is a liberty that has indeed spread across the world
to hundreds of other nations. "From this day will be dated the liberty of the
world," said Rev. Jonas Clark.

Recently, at a convention attended by people from all over the United
States, the speaker asked this question: "Do your pastors speak out on the
great issues of our day?" Though there were hundreds of people from
churches all over the country of various denominations, not one that I saw
raised his hand. "Are you satisfied about the way your pastors are addressing the great issues of our time?" Not one hand went up.

I would like to say directly to the ministers reading this right now,
"Brethren, gentlemen, God needs men who will speak out on the issues of the
day." As I pointed out earlier, Martin Luther said something to the effect,
"Though we be active in the battle, if we are not fighting where the battle is
the hottest, we are traitors to the cause." May God grant you courage.

I have asked people why their pastors do not speak out. The answers are
always the same: They are afraid. Be not afraid. Christ is with you. And I believe
your people will be supportive. That doesn't mean all of them, of course.

I will no doubt get comments from readers complaining about what I'm
saying. I want you to know right now, I don't really care. The only thing those
comments tell me is that people do not understand what the Word of God is
supposed to be accomplishing. They do not understand that we are not only

to render to God what is God's, but we are supposed to render to Caesar the things that are Caesar's. They do not understand that our whole culture is going to hell in a handbasket, and most people in the churches are doing nothing about it. Most preachers are very guardedly saying nothing about it. May God have mercy upon us.

THE END OF WESTERN CIVILIZATION AS WE KNOW IT

We are literally seeing the end of Western civilization. In most of the major colleges today there is not a single course on Western civilization. If any mention is made, it would be sluffed off with, "Oh, you're talking about those dead white guys—those European white men. Unimportant." There are a lot of classes on feminism, many classes on homosexual rights, but nothing about Western civilization. You will get nothing in college about the Christian foundations of this country. If the church doesn't speak out, who will? We are growing a nation of pagans.

Recently the National Alumni Forum (NAF) conducted a study that confirmed what I am saying about the death of Western civilization:

> Shakespeare and other Great Authors have been dropped from English major requirements at two-thirds of the 67 colleges and universities responding to an NAF survey. The survey contacted the *U.S. News [& World Report's]* "top fifty" schools as well as others for added balance.[6]

This is a tragic trend. Jonathan Yardley, writing in *The Washington Post*, commented on this NAF study: "The final piece of evidence that the lunatics are running the academic asylum is now firmly in place."[7] Literally, instead of Shakespeare, some courses are studying such noteworthy subjects as soap operas, Graceland, "White Trash," and gangster films. I believe this is further evidence of the anti-Christian (and anti-Western) bent found among our cultural elites. Modern academics are apparently trying to distance themselves even further from the culture that the Bible was instrumental in shaping.

SLOUCHING TOWARD GOMORRAH

One of the pivotal books in recent years is by Judge Robert Bork. You remember Judge Bork, professor at Yale University Law School, whose name was placed by the President for appointment to the Supreme Court. But the radical left attacked him in every conceivable way, and he was not approved.

When you look at the morals of some of the men who were on that judicial committee, that they would have the gall to disapprove of this man is unconscionable!

Judge Robert Bork wrote his monumental blockbuster book *Slouching Toward Gomorrah*. If you haven't read it, you ought to. I don't think the title needs much elucidation. *Slouching Toward Gomorrah* speaks volumes in itself. He has an incredible way of saying things and bringing into focus things you may have thought or vaguely or dimly understood, but not clearly. In the very first part of the book, in talking about the decade of the 1960s, he says that the activists politicized everything. They saw all of culture and life as political. Do you realize that before the sixties, politics was something completely set apart from the rest of our life? The most important thing in the world wasn't politics. People had lives to live. There was a culture to experience. There were things to do. But the radical leftists of the sixties politicized the culture.

Because of the influence of the 1960s, Bork writes, "The idea that everything is ultimately political has taken hold. We know its current form as 'political correctness,' a distemper that afflicts the universities in their departments of humanities, social sciences, and law. . . . A corollary to the politicization of the culture is the tactic of assaulting one's opponents as not merely wrong but morally evil. That was, of course, a key stratagem of the New Left, and it remains a crucial weapon in modern liberalism's armory."[8]

Now that means that politics has more and more left its own proper realm and has obtruded itself into every realm of culture imaginable—for example, abortion. By the way, politics always obtrudes itself in the same way. Its proponents pick out a particular sin, give it their imprimatur, and declare it to be legal. Since most people in America feel that if something is legal, it must be right, therefore they have license to go ahead and do it.

THE EXAMPLES OF ABORTION AND HOMOSEXUALITY

Consider the matter of abortion. For almost 2,000 years abortion has been a moral and spiritual issue within the church. In the early church it was considered such a heinous sin that if anyone had an abortion, they were excommunicated with no possibility of reinstatement. Is that a serious matter? Then the government comes along and says it is legal. So now it is all right. It is all right to pull a baby three-fourths of the way out of its mother's womb, stick a pair of scissors in the back of its neck, and kill it. So we see the politicizing of culture.

Similarly, homosexuality has always been a moral and spiritual issue. I have looked through a number of nineteenth-century commentaries on passages dealing with homosexuality. You know what I found? Nothing. The word cannot be found. The closest you can come to it is passages in books on Scripture dealing with it as "that unspeakable sin." It was a sin so vile, so heinous, as to not even be mentioned by name.

I read recently that every new sitcom on all of the major networks has at least one homosexual writer on staff, and there are twenty-six homosexuals in prime-time television playing the parts of homosexuals. Indeed, things have grossly changed, and our politics have been culturalized.

PASSIONATE INTENSITY OR A LACK OF ALL CONVICTION

Returning to Judge Bork's book, at the very beginning he quotes William Butler Yeats's poem entitled "The Second Coming." Since it is a fairly long poem, I won't quote it in its entirety, but I will quote just two lines because they are so important. It is talking about the Second Coming. It is talking about "slouching towards Bethlehem." With apologies to Yeats, Bork borrows the phrase and changes it to "slouching towards Gomorrah." It is talking about these times when Western civilization is moving and being pushed more and more to the edge of the abyss and, in this time of great conflict of tremendous issues, the greatest battle in history. Yeats says: "The best lack all conviction, while the worst are full of passionate intensity."[9]

I have been all across this country. I have debated and confronted face-to-face and eyeball-to-eyeball the leaders of the abortionist movement, the leaders of the homosexual movement, the leaders of the feminist movement, atheists, evolutionists, and all of the left-wing cadre, and I want to tell you something I have noticed about them: They are all "full of passionate intensity," while "the best lack all conviction."

Which side are you on? Are you one who is filled with passionate intensity for the great cause of Jesus Christ, the only cause worthy of getting excited about? Or are you more interested and do you get more excited about who is going to win the semifinals in the basketball playoffs? I am saddened to say that, with few exceptions, I think Yeats is right: "The best lack all conviction."

Where is the intensity? Let me tell you. *They* have it. One historian said that the people who have that intensity are the people who always win. Ultimately it is going to be a decision as to which side lacks conviction and which side is filled with passionate intensity—intensity for the kingdom of

Jesus Christ. "Seek first the kingdom of God and his righteousness" (Matthew 6:33).

Charles Spurgeon, the great pastor, said that Christ did not simply tell us to seek the kingdom of God. This is what He told us: "Seek *first* the kingdom of God. . . ." Above all else, is that the most important thing in your life, or is it your job, your business, your home, your family, your finances, your vacation? What is first in your life? Jesus said, "So, because you are lukewarm, and neither hot nor cold, I will spit you out of my mouth" (Revelation 3:16).

"The best lack all conviction, while the worst [of men] are full of passionate intensity." They are determined to bring their view of the world into existence, and I want to tell you, it is an ugly, ugly thing. Already, like a frog in a kettle, we have sat passively as the temperature has gone up.

OUR ROLE AS SALT AND LIGHT

Jesus said, "You are the salt of the earth, but if salt has lost its taste, how shall its saltiness be restored? It is no longer good for anything except to be thrown out and trampled under people's feet. You are the light of the world. A city set on a hill cannot be hidden" (Matthew 5:13-14).

Peter Marshall, chaplain to the Senate, said that when the apostles preached, there were either riots or regeneration. Today we get a pat on the hand and a "nice sermon, pastor."

Today there is a new brand of Christianity around, Vance Havner tells us. It is a non-irritating brand of Christianity. It is without offense and without effect. But Jesus didn't call us to be "the sugar of the world." He called us to be "the salt of the earth."

I want to tell you something—I would much prefer to be the sugar of the world. I would be delighted to have all men think well of me. I want you to know that I don't like it when people carry signs that say I am a Nazi and a hatemonger, a Fascist, a Khomeini, and all sorts of other lies. I don't like it when the newspapers print nasty things about me. I really don't like that at all. Would you? I would much rather be Uncle Candy Man, and then everybody would love me. But "woe to you, when all people speak well of you, for so their fathers did to the false prophets" (Luke 6:26). "Blessed are you when others revile you and persecute you and utter all kinds of evil against you falsely on my account. Rejoice and be glad, for your reward is great in heaven, for so they persecuted the prophets who were before you" (Matthew 5:11-12).

SALT HEALS

We are also not called to be the vinegar of the world—neither the sugar nor the vinegar. We are called to be salt, because salt not only stings, it also purifies and cures and heals. There is nothing like hot saltwater for a bad throat, as every speaker and singer knows, and many others as well. So we should not only irritate, if need be, but also we should be healing balm. Salt is healing. In the first part of Matthew 5 Christ described all the virtues and qualities of the Christian life. If we possess these qualities that Christ has given us, we will be a healing balm to others, and people will come to us.

CHRISTIANS CAN MAKE A DIFFERENCE

Let's note a few examples where the church acted as salt in the culture and the incredible difference that made.

A few years ago the state of Alabama was poised to adopt a state lottery. That state was one of the last holdouts. It seemed a foregone conclusion that it was going to adopt the lottery because the voters rejected a governor opposed to the lottery and voted in his opponent, who was in favor of it. But the people had one last chance in 1999 to directly vote for or against the lottery.

This gave the Christians of Alabama a new chance to oppose this expansion of legalized gambling. The odds, so to speak, were completely against them. But, as *Citizen* magazine points out, the church made all the difference on this issue: "Hundreds, if not thousands, of Alabama pastors preached against gambling from the pulpit in the weeks leading up to the vote. Churches conducted prayer vigils, registered voters, and even contributed significant amounts of money to help counter the pro-gambling propaganda. Five days before the election, 460 ministers from various denominations gathered on the statehouse steps to denounce the lottery plan."[10]

On October 12, 1999, the people voted 54-46 percent against the lottery referendum. The Associated Press reported: "The proposal—a constitutional amendment to allow gambling—had once enjoyed a 20-point lead in the polls, but came under increasing fire from church groups, who said it would exploit the poor."[11] Because of this vote and a defeat against video poker machines in South Carolina (where Christians also played a key role), gambling expert William Thompson, a professor at the University of Nevada in Las Vegas, called it "the biggest anti-gambling week in American history."[12]

This reminds me of the Methodist minister Rev. Tom Grey, who retired from his pulpit in picturesque Galena, Illinois, to fight the expansion of legalized gambling. It all began for him when a riverboat casino became a fixture in his town through a backroom deal. We featured Tom on our program, *The Coral Ridge Hour,* and he credits our initial exposure as a platform that launched his message nationwide.

Tom Grey chafes at comparing gambling to harmless entertainment like going out to a movie or taking in a play. The gaming establishment makes this argument all the time. Here is Tom Grey's response to that: "You could see *The Sound of Music* 100 times and you wouldn't walk out in the parking lot and blow your brains out."[13]

Tom Grey has been most successful in mobilizing communities, churches, and individuals across the country against the expansion of legalized gambling. Because he is a Vietnam vet, the gambling forces derisively call him Riverboat Rambo. Would to God there were more godly men and women just like him.

CONCLUSION

Earlier we heard from Rev. Don Wildmon, another Methodist minister who has done so much to reclaim the culture in his own way. We close this chapter with a stinging piece he wrote, entitled "That's What Christians Do Now":

In 1973, the Supreme Court said it was okay to kill unborn babies. Since then, we have killed more than the entire population of Canada. And it continues. A woman's choice? Half of those who have died in their mothers' wombs have been women. They didn't have a choice. It is called abortion.

Me? I go to church, the minister preaches, I go home. That's what Christians do now.

First it was in dingy, dirty theaters. Then, convenience stores. Then, grocery stores. Then on television. Now it is in the homes of millions via the Internet. It is called pornography.

Me? I go to church, the minister preaches, I go home. That's what Christians do now.

They called it no-fault. Why should we blame anyone when something so tragic happens? Haven't they already suffered enough? . . . The children suffer. The family breaks down. It is called divorce.

Me? I go to church, the minister preaches, I go home. That's what Christians do now.

At one time it was a perversion. We kept it secret. We secured help and hope for those who practiced it. Now it is praised. We have parades celebrating it, and elected officials give it their blessing. Now it is endowed with special privileges and protected by special laws. Even some Christian leaders and denominations praise it. It is called homosexuality.

Me? I go to church, the minister preaches, I go home. That's what Christians do now.

It used to be an embarrassment. A shame. Now a third of all births are to mothers who aren't married. Two-thirds of all African-American children are born into a home without a father. The state usually pays the tab. That is why we pay our taxes, so that government can take the place of parents. After all, government bureaucrats know much better how to raise children than parents do. It is called illegitimacy.

Me? I go to church, the minister preaches, I go home. That's what Christians do now.

At one time it was wrong. But then the state decided to legalize it, promote it and tax it. It has ripped apart families and destroyed lives. But just look at all the money the state has raised. No longer do we have to teach our children to study and work hard. Now we teach them they can get something for nothing. We spend millions encouraging people to join the fun and excitement. Just look at the big sums that people are winning. They will never have to work again. It is called gambling.

Me? I go to church, the minister preaches, I go home. That's what Christians do now.

Not long ago, Christians were the good guys. But now, any positive image of Christians in movies or on TV is gone. We are now depicted as the bad guys—greedy, narrow-minded hypocrites. The teacher can't have a Bible on her desk, but can have *Playboy*. We don't have Christmas and Easter holidays—just winter and spring break. We can't pray in school, but can use foul language. It's called being tolerant.

Me? I go to church, the minister preaches, I go home. That's what Christians do now.

Yes, all these things came to pass within 30 years. Where were the Christians? Why, they were in church. All these things were for someone else to deal with. Times have changed. Involvement has been replaced with apathy.

But don't blame me. I didn't do anything. I go to church, the minister preaches, I go home. That's what Christians do now.[14]

I hope you aren't that type of "Christian," but rather the kind we find in the book of Acts who was instrumental in turning the world right-side-up.

THE FIGHT FOR
GOD'S WORD

All Scripture is breathed out by God and profitable for teaching, for reproof, for correction, and for training in righteousness.

2 TIMOTHY 3:16

In the very opening of this book, we spoke about the Great Divide. Again, picture two drops of water next to each other, before they go their separate ways. First, they are beside each other. Next they are only an inch apart, then a foot, soon a hundred yards, then a mile, then ten miles. Eventually one drop ends up in the Atlantic Ocean and the other in the Pacific. The different pulls on the water—one to the east, the other to the west—are imperceptible at first, but in time the full implications are made manifest.

So it is with our view of the Bible. Whether or not you believe the Bible to be the true, inspired Word of God, without error in its original form, has vast implications. Belief in the Bible leads to vibrant, healthy spiritual growth. Unbelief in the Bible spreads like a cancer from the liberal seminaries, reaching even to the person in the pew, leaving a wake of spiritual destruction and in many cases eternal judgment. A truly Christian world-and-life view has a very high view of Scripture as the very Word of God.

"I don't believe the Bible is the inspired Word of God." I have on numerous occasions heard people make that statement. They often do it while being blissfully ignorant of the fact that this view creates more numerous and more serious problems than it solves. They don't seem to realize that if the Bible is indeed not the Word of God, they are back to ground zero, having to deal again with the old college questions—who are we, and why are we here?

These and many other questions remain huge question marks in a life filled with those enigmas. Such persons also seem to be oblivious to the reality that there are evidences that support the fact that the Bible is indeed the inspired Word of God. They seem to assume that Christians who believe that do so out of blind faith, or else out of ignorance and superstition, or perhaps prejudice and bias, or mere credulity and gullibility.

But I have never yet met such a skeptic who has so much as read one book that sets forth the evidences for the inspiration of the Word of God.

Why is it so important that we believe that the Bible is the Word of God? It is crucial because when theologians and pastors and seminary professors question what is true and what is not, all of a sudden the student of the Bible becomes its judge and jury. Scholars start to decide—like a cafeteria—what they like and dislike and what they think is acceptable for today.

First, such critics said the Bible contains the Word of God but only in spiritual matters—not in history or geography and especially not science. The end of this type of thinking is groups like the Jesus Seminar—a group of liberal scholars who sat in judgment on the words of Christ. These scholars voted anonymously that Jesus only said for sure 18 percent of that which is attributed to Him in the Gospels.[1]

Christianity unravels with the denial of the Bible as God's Word. If we are going to hold to a Christian world-and-life view, we have to stand on the firm foundation of the inerrancy of the Scriptures.

IS THE BIBLE THE WORD OF GOD?

So the question before us becomes: Is the Bible the Word of God? Several thousands of times the Bible itself claims to be the Word of God. "Thus says the LORD" appears hundreds and hundreds of times (e.g., Exodus 4:22), as does, "The word of the LORD came to me" (1 Chronicles 22:8). In the New Testament we are told: "All Scripture is breathed out by God" (2 Timothy 3:16).

Many people say, "Oh, I believe the Bible is a good book, but there are other good books as well." The Bible is not merely a "good book." If it is not the very Word of God and is merely a human book, then it is a book crammed full of lies and is obviously not a "good book." It is rather a cruel hoax, a gigantic fraud perpetrated upon the human race.

IS JESUS GOD?

We have a similar situation in regard to Christ. Either He is the living Word of God, the Son of the Almighty, or else He most certainly is not a good man.

He never left us the alternative of believing that He is a good man. He claimed to be divine: "And now, Father, glorify me in your own presence with the glory that I had with you before the world existed" (John 17:5).

Those are not the words of a merely good man. They are either the words of the Son of God or the words of a lunatic who should be classed with those who suppose themselves to be Napoleon or a poached egg, to use an old C. S. Lewis argument.[2] He is either who He claimed to be, or He is a deceiver of the most satanic type, for millions of people have died because of His claims. They have given their lives willingly and gladly and suffered the most horrible tortures.

Therefore, Jesus was not a "good man." In Matthew 19 we read of one who came running to Him and said, "Good Master . . ." (v. 16, KJV). Jesus said (paraphrased), "Hold it right there. Why do you call Me good? Haven't you heard a thing I've said? There is none good but One—that is, God. Now either I am God, or I am not good because I am a false teacher." And so He hung this man on the horns of a dilemma. Jesus is either God, or He is not good. He is not merely a "good man." He is either who He claimed to be, or He is a deceiver or a lunatic. Liar, lunatic, or Lord of all? Which is He to you?

And so it is with the written Word of God. It is either the Word of God in truth, as it says thousands of times, or it is a very bad book and should indeed be consigned to the flames.

What Does *Inspiration* Mean?

What does the word *inspiration* mean? Norman Geisler and William Nix, authors of *A General Introduction to the Bible*, point out: "The inspiration of the Bible is not to be confused with a poetic inspiration. Inspiration as applied to the Bible refers to the God-given authority of its teachings for the thought and life of the believer."[3]

Benjamin Breckinridge Warfield of Princeton, one of the greatest Greek scholars of all time, explained the divine origins of the Scriptures:

> . . . by a special, supranatural, extraordinary influence of the Holy Ghost, the sacred writers have been guided in their writing in such a way, as while their humanity was not superseded, it was yet so dominated that their words became at the same time the words of God, and thus, in every case and all alike, absolutely infallible.[4]

An equally competent Old Testament scholar and Semitic language expert, Edward J. Young, said:

Inspiration is a superintendence of God the Holy Spirit over the writers of the Scriptures, as a result of which these Scriptures possess Divine authority and trustworthiness and, possessing such Divine authority and trustworthiness, are free from error.[5]

Many people confuse *inspired* with *inspiring*. Some say, "Oh, yes, the Bible is inspired, but so is Shakespeare or Milton or Plato or Socrates or Aristotle or Thomas Paine"—or any other writer that might touch their fancy. So it seems that almost anyone who was anyone was inspired. What they really mean is that many of these writers are "inspiring," and with that I have no quarrel. But to say they have been "inspired" by God to write the infallible will of the Almighty would be a tragic exaggeration.

Perhaps the situation would be less confusing if the word *inspiration* in some Bible versions had been translated differently. The King James translation of 2 Timothy 3:16 does not help: "All Scripture is given by inspiration of God." The actual Greek word *theopneustos* means "God-breathed"; the Scriptures are breathed out by God. This is more expiration than inspiration. That is why the English Standard Version renders this, "All Scripture is breathed out by God" (2 Timothy 3:16).

INSPIRATION IS VERBAL

I myself believe that the Bible is the inspired Word of God. Just what does that encompass? It encompasses not merely ideas, as some have thought, because ideas without words cannot be expressed. In many cases in the New Testament, Old Testament texts are quoted, and the whole thrust of the argument rests upon a single word—in one case, even upon a single letter. For example, Paul said, "Now the promises were made to Abraham and to his offspring. It does not say, 'And to offsprings,' referring to many, but referring to one, 'And to your offspring,' who is Christ" (Galatians 3:16). Therefore, if the words were not inspired, then Christ, who spent much time discussing the words of the Old Testament, was wasting His time. So we believe that this inspiration is verbal.

INSPIRATION IS PLENARY

Furthermore, I believe that the Bible is plenarily inspired, which means that it extends, as one Scottish man said, "from kiver to kiver," from the front to the back, from Genesis to Revelation. It includes the entire Bible. It is plenary as opposed to partial.

We say that all of the Bible is inspired. This is what is known as plenary inspiration. The neo-orthodox and others of a more liberal mind will say that the Bible is not the Word of God, but rather it contains the Word of God; that all of the Scripture is not inspired—just some parts of it. Of course, they have never been able to explain to anyone how we are to know which part is inspired and which is not.

Does the Scripture teach that the entire Bible is inspired? Listen again to what the New Testament declares: "All Scripture is breathed out by God" (2 Timothy 3:16). Not some of it, not part of it, but *all* of it. God has inspired it all, and so we believe in plenary inspiration.

Again some have said, "Well, the inspiration applies only to the ideas. God has given people various ideas, and they have clothed them in their own words." What does the Bible say? Does it say, "God spoke all these *ideas*, saying . . ." (Exodus 20:1)? Those of you at all familiar with Scripture will realize that doesn't ring true. "God spoke all these *words*, saying . . ." In fact Jesus said, "one jot or one tittle shall in no wise pass from the law, till all be fulfilled"(Matthew 5:18, KJV). A jot is the smallest letter in the Hebrew alphabet, and a tittle is simply a curlicue on the end of various letters. So, not even a word or a letter or even a tiny part of a letter will pass away. God's inspiration deals with the most minute details.

If the Bible is plenarily and verbally inspired, then it is infallible; it cannot fail. In it we are told the Scriptures cannot be broken (John 10:35). They are the infallible Word of God, and no effort of men will ever in any way destroy them. Many skeptics have tried to destroy the Word of God, and they have failed over and over.

If the Bible is infallible, it is also inerrant—without error (particularly in the original manuscripts). Many times I hear people say, "Oh, the Bible is filled with errors or contradictions." I find the response is always the same whenever I simply say, "Oh, that's very fascinating. I've studied it for fifty years. Would you mind showing me where the errors are?"

Some people back away and are even fearful of touching the book. Some take the Bible in their hands and are perplexed, dumbfounded—they haven't the faintest idea where to look. They are simply like dumb parrots, repeating what they have been told or what they have read from some other skeptic.

That the Bible is the inspired Word of God has been the belief of the church down through the centuries.

About A.D. 90 Clement of Rome, one of the earliest of the apostolic fathers (those who followed immediately after the apostles), said, "The Scriptures are the true words of the Holy Spirit."

In the next century, in A.D. 155, Tertullian, the great church father, was born. He said, "The Scriptures are the writings of God."

Origen, another apostolic father, born in A.D. 185, stated, "There is not one jot or one tittle written in Scripture which, for those who know how to use the power of the Scriptures does not affect its proper work."

Augustine, born in A.D. 354, without question the greatest mind of the first thousand years of this era, said, "I have learned to pay them [the books of the Scripture] such honor and respect as to believe most firmly that not one of their authors has erred in writing anything at all."

Indeed, this has been the view of the church down through the centuries. This view is not based upon mere blind faith or prejudice but is based upon solid evidence. This view is not blind faith but is based upon many infallible proofs.

THE AUTOGRAPHA

Being verbally and plenarily inspired, the Bible therefore has the characteristic of infallibility; it cannot fail in what it says, and therefore it is inerrant and without error. This all applies, however, to what are called the *autographa*, or the original autographs or manuscripts written by Matthew or Mark or Isaiah or Jeremiah or Paul.

The infallible inspiration does not go to every person who ever decided to translate a portion of the Scripture. I have translated portions of the Scripture from both Hebrew and Greek into English. I am not inspired, but the original writings were. Furthermore, God preserved them in a most providential way so that far beyond any other book of antiquity, we know precisely what the Bible said in its original writings.

What evidence is there for this? First of all, in Deuteronomy 18:22 God tells us how we may know if a prophet is sent from Him: "when a prophet speaks in the name of the LORD, if the word does not come to pass or come true, that is a word that the LORD has not spoken; the prophet has spoken it presumptuously. You need not be afraid of him."

God alone knows the future, which "turns on many slippery and very tricky ball-bearings," as one theologian said.[6] God alone can prophesy the future.

The Scriptures are unique in that in the Old Testament alone, over 2,000 prophecies have already come to pass. Nothing vaguely resembles this in any other book in the world. Twenty-six other volumes that claim to be divine Scriptures, or are claimed to be by their followers (since many of these volumes make no such claim themselves), have no specific predictive prophecies.

There are 333 predictive prophecies that deal with the coming of the Messiah alone. Unparalleled in all of the writings of the world, there is no other individual in the history of mankind whose entire life has been detailed prophetically, predictively, by over 300 definite, specific prophecies concerning His life.[7]

The other 1,700 or so prophecies of the Old Testament deal mostly with the cities and nations that were contiguous with—or in close proximity to—the land of Israel. Their future destinies are outlined for us in those prophecies.

Consider three other main points providing evidence that the Scripture is the Word of God.

THE CREATION OF SCRIPTURE

First of all, let us consider the creation of the Scripture—its miraculous birth. Like the living Word of God, Jesus Christ, the written Word of God had a supernatural or miraculous birth. It is unique; no other book has ever been brought into existence in the same way. Most books are written by a single author. Sometimes two or more authors collaborate, but in virtually all cases these are people who live within a single generation.

The Bible, however, was written over a period of about 1,600 years, encompassing fifty-five generations, written by people living on different continents in numerous different countries, speaking different languages, and from different backgrounds—from kings to shepherds, from fishermen to physicians, from herdsmen to publicans to Pharisees. These writings are in different literary genres, such as law, history, poetry, prophecy, biography, apocalypse, and epistles. Sixty-six different books, an entire library, make up a single volume—the Holy Bible—with one single theme: the divine redemption of man by the gracious Triune God.

A thousand different colored strands are woven by the Holy Spirit into a single harmonious and beautiful tapestry. Its message is the same in every book: the generation, degeneration, and regeneration of the human race. The theme is the redemption of man and his paradise lost and paradise regained.

A central figure is found throughout these Scriptures, either in prophecy, prediction, or in reality (in the New Testament). That figure is the Second Person of the Triune Godhead: Jesus Christ, the divine God-man, Redeemer of the lost.

Amazingly, these books do not contradict each other. They are not in confusion but rather tell a single story woven in a most magnificent way throughout all sixty-six volumes of this book. Compare that, if you would, to what we have in the collection of philosophy that the average student might read in college.

If you were to put together any 1,600-year period in the writings of philosophers, you would not find a single theme, a harmony of all of the parts. Instead you would find veritable chaos—one of confusion and contradiction, a cacophony of discordant voices all crying aloud and trying to drown out the past.

For example, Plato writes his magnificent philosophy. Then lo and behold, his own student, Aristotle, turns the whole thing on its head and gives us a philosophy that is virtually diametrically opposite to that which he was taught by his teacher. So we have nothing but confusion and a contradiction of turbulent and tumultuous conflicting voices.

However, in the Bible, always and everywhere there sounds the same harmonious theme of the divine Son of God, from the protevangelium ("first gospel") of Genesis 3:15, where we are told that the seed of the woman will bruise or crush the head of the serpent, until the last verses of Revelation, where Jesus says, "'Surely I am coming soon.' Amen. Come, Lord Jesus!" (22:20). It is the same theme, the same central character, the same great Deliverer of mankind, Jesus Christ, from beginning to end, set forth in all of the books of the Bible. It is the theme of redemption, and a marvelous harmony speaks to the fact that the origin of this book is God.

Though the writers of the various books speak in different languages, write with different styles, have quite diverse degrees of education and sophistication in their writing, use different vocabularies, use different manners of writing in producing their work, the fact is that there is a single mind that speaks through the whole, bringing out with full use of the divergent characteristics of the writers a single and matchless theme. It is the very Word of God.

Author Jim Thomas makes an interesting analogy on this point:

When you think how difficult it is for just ten people to order pizza together—it's one of the hardest things in the world. You get together with a group of family members or friends and you try to order a pizza. Some people want just cheese only. Some people want veggies. Some people want meat pizza. It's almost impossible to order pizza with ten people.

Here are 40 people from all different walks of life, peasants, kings, philosophers, poets, doctors, all different walks of life, all writing in way that suggests a unity that is just nothing short of miraculous. They're all pointing in the same direction. They're telling the story of creation, the fall, redemption, and the consummation that God has planned when He wraps up all of human history.[8]

THE PRESERVATION OF SCRIPTURE

The Bible was not only miraculously born or created, but it has been providentially preserved down through the centuries. Josephus, a first-century turncoat Jewish general (who switched sides and joined the Romans), gave us some wonderful insights into his day and his people. He said, concerning the Old Testament books:

> No one has dared to add anything to them, take anything from them, or to alter anything. All Jews [at least in his day] regard them as the teaching of God, and abide by them, and would gladly die for them.[9]

This kind of concern for the Scripture led to a care that was, of course, superintended by God. It brought the Scriptures down to us in a state of preservation unlike any other writing of antiquity; none come anywhere vaguely close. The Scriptures have been preserved by an incredible providence and preservation of God, in spite of the fact that, unlike any other book that has ever existed, they have been attacked, dynamited, exploded, and overturned more frequently than all other books combined.

Its preservation is like the Irishman's wall. The Irishman built his wall four feet high but five feet wide, so that if someone turned it over, it would be taller than it was at first. So it is with the Word of God. Down through the centuries skeptics have risen up and unloosed their largest artillery against the Word of God. They have turned it over, exploded it, gotten rid of it (they thought), and yet still it stands taller than ever.

One of the most brilliant minds of the last few centuries was, no doubt, that of Voltaire, the acerbic French critic who wrote an entire encyclopedia against Christianity and the Bible. He boasted that though it took twelve apostles to create the New Testament, one philosopher could destroy it— namely, himself. He said that within 100 years, virtually no one would be reading the Bible, but it would be buried and forgotten. However, when Voltaire died, his home in Geneva was purchased by the Geneva Bible Society. Millions of copies of the Bible were turned out on Voltaire's own printing press.[10]

One manuscript of the Bible sold some years ago for millions of dollars. Yet the writings of Voltaire, which virtually nobody reads, can be obtained for a few dollars in many used-book stores. How marvelously God has maintained His Word. And how great is the continuing demand for the Word of God. In 1881, when a revision of the New Testament was completed, it was telegraphed from New York to Chicago (118,000 words)—the longest telegram in history—so it could be published in its entirety in a Chicago newspaper twenty-four hours before it could reach there by train and steam engine.

The late Madalyn Murray O'Hair, America's most famous atheist, had set out to destroy the Bible. She used her own son to try to accomplish that, and now her son is a preacher of the gospel. It is interesting that when, for the first time, the Moscow Book Fair allowed American publishers to show their wares some years ago, one of the publishers offered thousands of New Testaments to the Russian people. They so clogged the aisles of the book fair that traffic was brought to a complete deadlock—a gridlock. The police finally said that they could give the Bibles away for an hour. They then had to close for two hours to let the crowd disperse, and then open for an hour and close for two more. The demand was absolutely overwhelming.

Down the same aisle of the book fair at the American Atheist Society booth, Madalyn Murray O'Hair, their redoubtable president or chairwoman, was displaying her organization's wares. Virtually no one gave her a second glance as she watched people clamor for the Bible—the book she hated so much. Why should they bother to pick up her materials? They had already suffered under the oppression of an atheistic government for seventy years, thank you very much.

THE POWER OF SCRIPTURE

Not only has the Word been miraculously born and providentially preserved, but it shows a miraculous power to change lives and to influence people. It appeals to every conceivable kind of person. Jesus Christ is the universal person who appeals to both men and women equally, to the aged and to the young; so also is it with the Word of God. Thomas Coleridge said:

> In the Bible there is more that finds me than I have experienced in all other books put together: the words of the Bible find me at greater depths of my being; and whatever finds me brings with it an irresistible evidence of its having proceeded from the Holy Spirit.[11]

The author Heinrich Heine exclaimed:

What a book! [How] vast and wide as the world. Rooted in the abysses of creation, and towering up beyond the blue secrets of heaven. Sunrise and sunset, birth and death, promise and fulfillment, the whole drama of humanity are all in this book![12]

And so it appeals to and meets the needs of every kind of human being:
- from the king on his throne to the cobbler in his cottage;
- from the headhunter in New Guinea to the harpooner in Iceland;
- from the illiterate to the most literate;
- from Shakespeare and John Milton to Isaac Newton and Michael Faraday.

And to millions upon millions of others. It has appealed to the deepest needs of many hearts and has transformed the most inveterate and hardened skeptics.

For example, General Lew Wallace set out to write a book that he hoped would destroy the deity of Christ and present the Bible as a fraud. But when he made his historical investigations, he found himself converted by the power of the Son of God. So instead he wrote a book—a book *extolling* the deity of Jesus Christ. You know it well—*Ben-Hur: A Tale of the Christ*.

Or consider the lawyer Frank Morison, who set out to disprove Jesus' resurrection and to prove that the biblical accounts of it were fraudulent. This lawyer's mind, which probed so deeply into the evidence, discovered that the Bible is true. The first chapter of his book is entitled, "The Book That Refused to Be Written." The book that was to demolish Jesus' resurrection turned out to be a book that defended it more ably than most have done.

Henry Stanley said that in the 1880s, when he entered the interior of Africa, he was the most swaggering atheist in the world. In the depths of the jungles of central Africa he came upon David Livingstone—a man so mild, so meek, and yet so firm and so definite in his purpose and desire to proclaim the gospel. Stanley lived in that man's tent for months and listened to Livingstone read from his little Bible day by day. As a result, the most swaggering atheist in the world was transformed by the gospel of Jesus Christ and was brought to the Savior.

CONCLUSION

E. A. Rowell once described himself as the atheist of atheists. He wrote a profound essay on what changed him from unbelief to faith in Christ. With his moving words, we close this chapter:

My parents and other immediate relatives were proud of their unbelief. I was nourished on the vaunting skeptics of the ages.

But I observed the futile amazement with which every skeptic from Celsus to H. G. Wells stood around the cradle of the Christ. I wondered why this helpless Babe was thrust into the world at a time when Roman greed, Jewish hate, and Greek subtlety would combine to crush Him. And yet this most powerful, devastating combination ever known in history served only to advance the cause of the Infant who was born in a stable—the purest human being in the world born in the filthiest place in the world.

No unbeliever could tell me why His words are as charged with power today as they were nineteen hundred years ago. Nor could scoffers explain how those pierced hands pulled human monsters with gnarled souls out of a hell of iniquity and overnight transformed them into steadfast, glorious heroes who died in torturing flames, that others might know the love and mighty power of the Christ who had given peace to their souls.

No agnostic could make clear why seemingly immortal empires pass into oblivion, while the glory and power of the murdered Galilean are gathering beauty and momentum with every attack and every age.

Nor could any scoffer explain, as Jesus Himself so daringly foretold, why by telephone, airplane, and radio, by rail, horse, and foot, His words are piercing the densest forest, scaling the highest mountains, crossing the deepest seas and the widest deserts, making converts in every nation, kindred, tongue, and people on earth.

No doubter could tell me how this isolated Jew could utter words at once so simple that a child could understand them and so deep that the greatest thinkers cannot plumb their shining depths. . . .

But I learned that the paradox was plain and the mystery solved when I accepted Him for what He claimed to be—the Son of God, come from heaven a Saviour of men, but above all, my own Saviour. I learned to thrill at the angel's words: "Behold, . . . unto you is born this day . . . a Saviour, which is Christ the Lord."

By its providential preservation through the years against all attacks, by its unparalleled power to transform hundreds of millions of lives, by the way it reveals the deepest secrets of the human heart and opens up the secrets of eternal life and reveals the only way of human salvation, the Bible, not only by its thousands of fulfilled prophecies, but in these ways as well, manifests itself, and evidences itself to be the very inspired Word of the Living God.[13]

PART VI

THE SPHERE
OF THE
FAMILY

Introduction to Christianizing the Sphere of the Family

Over the years of my ministry, I have noticed a repeated pattern in terms of the people who seek me out for counseling, especially when it comes to family matters. I find single people coming to me who wish so much that they were married. And I find married people coming to me who wish so much that they were single—or at least that they were no longer married to their particular spouse.

This reminds me of the old rhyme:

> *As a rule, a man's a fool.*
> *When it's hot, he wants it cool.*
> *When it's cool, he wants it hot—*
> *always wanting what is not.*

There is a great need to Christianize the family. This is more true in our day, it seems, than in previous eras. We want to now explore a Christian world-and-life view of the family. We will consider its implications for marriage, parenting, and also singleness. God created marriage as the first human institution, and He created the family as the building block of society.

21

A CHRISTIAN VIEW OF THE FAMILY

Therefore a man shall leave his father and his mother and hold fast to his wife, and they shall become one flesh.

GENESIS 2:24

A number of years after the Pilgrims landed on American shores in 1620, the population had grown considerably and reached 70,000 souls. A large community, given the forty-five or so who survived the first winter.

How many divorces did they have that year? According to modern standards it would be something like 35,000. They didn't have 3,500. They didn't even have thirty-five, or fifteen, or five, or two, or one. They had zero. Zip. Zilch. *No divorce.* The next year: again, no divorce. The following year: one divorce. The next year: zero. The next year: zero. It went on like that for some time. One divorce every three years out of 70,000 people and growing.

The Pilgrims and their spiritual cousins, the Puritans, applied a Christian worldview to all of life, including the family. They had much stronger families because of it. In the next few chapters we want to explore a Christian view of the family. First, in this and the next chapter, we will gain an overview of the issue—including the vital importance of marriage itself, because the husband-wife relationship is the bedrock of the family. Next we will look at what the Bible says about the father in the home and what the Bible says about the mother in the home. We will also look at what the Bible says about the single life. If millions more Christians applied a biblical view in the area of family life, we would revolutionize our culture.

THE DETERIORATION OF MARRIAGE

We saw earlier how the descendants of the Pilgrims at one point experienced one divorce out of a population of 70,000. That was in the seventeenth century. More than a hundred years later, and a whole stream of different settlers later, the state of marriage began to deteriorate. By 1812 there was one divorce out of every 110 marriages. By 1961 that had come down to one divorce for every 3.7 marriages. In recent years the number of divorces has been almost half the number of new marriages. We have rolled up the worst record of marital failure in the history of the world.

The Futurist magazine says that at present trends, which seem to be continuing, the normal consequence of getting married—in fact, the expected consequence—will be that each marriage will end in divorce. Probably "'til death do us part" will be eliminated from the marriage vow and will be replaced with "until divorce do us part." In fact, some have suggested a contract to be renewed at their wish every year. Something needs to be done about this. Only the church can do it. Let me say that again. Something needs to be done, and only the church can do it. When all else fails, says the maxim, read the instructions. Now you would suppose that any country having rolled up the disastrous record of marital failures that we have would be eager to read the instructions. Certainly all else has failed.

But not so. Not only are they not eager to read the instructions—they are affronted at them. They don't want to hear them. I suppose that is because many people think they know what the instructions say. The problem is, the overwhelming majority of Americans in the church (and out) have completely misunderstood the instructions. Therefore, I would like to try to say a word about those instructions in this chapter.

Please note: We are not saying that 50 percent of marriages end in divorce. Pollster Lou Harris has shown that to be a fallacy. Where that statistic came from in the first place was that in a particular year the number of divorces in that year was half the number of new marriages, not half of all marriages. Furthermore, those who get divorced and remarried repeatedly gum up the statistics. They skew the results.[1]

Let's put it this way: If you get married, it isn't as if you only have a 50-50 chance for your marriage to survive. If you do the right things—for example, save your sexuality for when you get married, pray together when married, go to church together, etc.—you greatly reduce the chances of getting divorced. For example, sex educator Pam Stenzel says that if individuals enter into a marriage as virgins, they only have a 2 percent chance of getting divorced. People talk today about the high percentage of Christians getting divorced. But look at the low percentage of *obedient* Christians getting divorced. If you follow God's ways, you will save your virginity for your spouse, and you will greatly increase your chances of staying together as a couple.

The family is extremely important. It is the building block of society. Why are we in such trouble as a society? Because of the breakdown of the family.

If we have a truly Christian worldview, that will have a strong and positive impact on the renewal of the American family. The old slogan is so true: As the family goes, so goes society. Whatever hurts the family hurts society. The family is the number one department of health and human services in the nation. Therefore, government should do everything in its power to protect any familial authority. Government should get out of the way and let the family do its job—with rare exceptions, such as cases of genuine child abuse. It is important for us in modern America to get back to the tried and true biblical principles of family relationships—including honoring our parents and recognizing the unique role of mothers and fathers.

CHRIST COMES FIRST

One of the first principles of the family that people should keep in mind is that Christ comes first. Your relationship to Jesus is more important than your relationships with your father or mother, with your brother(s) and sister(s), with your spouse, or with your children. Christ comes first.

Jesus said, "Whoever loves father or mother more than me is not worthy of me, and whoever loves son or daughter more than me is not worthy of me" (Matthew 10:37).

In Luke, the same idea is taught with more forcefulness and in hyperbole—i.e., deliberate exaggeration: "If anyone comes to me and does not hate his own father and mother and wife and children and brothers and sisters, yes, and even his own life, he cannot be my disciple" (Luke 14:26).

One time coauthor Jerry Newcombe was on the road around Valentine's Day. He called a florist to request flowers to be sent to his wife, and he asked for this message to accompany the flowers:

Roses are red,
Violets are blue.
I love you the most,
Except for you know who.

The florist didn't understand this message and was initially reluctant to send it. But Kirsti, Jerry's wife, picked up on it right away.

The bottom line is that a Christian view of the family puts the family in its proper God-given context. The family is not an idol to worship. It must never replace our love for God the Father, God the Son, or God the Holy Spirit.

That being said, who can we love on earth more than our earthly family? No one.

That being said, when Christ is the center of the family, things go much better.

Many Christians today have a defective and sub-Christian view of the family. Even if they give lip service to high ideals for the family, in reality they treat their families in ways that are not worthy of the gospel. Some husbands are kinder to their dogs than they are to their wives. Some mothers treat their cat nicer than they do their children.

A BAD WITNESS FOR THE WORLD

When divorce happens in the church, it is the church's business. Every time a family in the church gets a divorce, the testimony of the church is weakened. How are we going to say to the world, "God has the answer to the problems of marriage and divorce" if divorce is common in our ranks? People then say, "Oh really? Well, the statistics show that you're right behind the world when it comes to divorce."

We have been inundated with the whole world-and-life view of modern feminist, rebellious, humanist America. And we are doing little better than they. The church has lost a great deal of its effectiveness and its influence for good in the society because of the breakdown of families within the church. However, remember what we said above about virgins getting married. Statistically, they have a much lower rate of divorce.

Let me also say that there are biblical grounds for divorce—namely, adultery (Matthew 5:32) and also the irremediable desertion of a believer by an unbeliever (1 Corinthians 7:15). Those are the only two allowable grounds for divorce in Scripture. I didn't write the Bible; I can't add a third or a fourth ground to it. I might be tempted to do so, but I can't.

That is why it is imperative that the church exercise discipline over its members—for example, those who divorce for nonbiblical reasons or those whose sin (adultery or desertion) presents biblical grounds for divorce. What's at stake in such cases is the honor of Jesus Christ and the glory of His gospel. Now, many people rebel against that. And we're very good at rebelling against things, aren't we? We are a rebel race at heart. We started out by rebelling against God.

Yes, it is the church's business and the country's business. Edward Gibbon, the great historian on the rise and fall of Rome, tells us that it was the breakdown in families that led to the collapse of Rome. Yes, it is the country's business, and it is God's business. I wish that everyone who decides to enter a divorce court and who gets a lawyer would remember the statement God has given to us in Malachi 2:16: "'I hate divorce,' says the LORD God of Israel" (NIV). Think about that.

IS LOVE THE BASIS OF MARRIAGE?

Before we discuss the matter of love in the home, let me say one thing that I think is very important. Contrary to much popular understanding of the subject, love is not the basis for marriage, though apparently most people in America suppose that it is. Unfortunately, what most people call love, the feelings of love, is not what the Bible means by love. When the Bible talks about love, it refers to acts of kindness and forbearance. The feeling of love, the Hollywood style of love, romantic love, comes and goes, and it provides a very poor foundation for marriage. The recent record of failures in marriage would certainly indicate this.

A COMMITMENT AND A COVENANT

The basis for marriage is commitment. It is a commitment of one man to one woman/one woman to one man, for life. It is based upon a solemn vow: "For better, for worse; in sickness and in health; 'til death do us part." It is a commitment that regardless of what comes our way, we are going to work it out. We are committed to the fact, as Christians, that divorce is not a viable option. Unfortunately, that concept has broken down in our society. It is very important whether a person sees divorce as a possible option when getting married or as no option at all. If it is seen as no option at all, that will make a vast difference in the relationship.

I heard a story about a minister who was celebrating his fiftieth wedding anniversary. Somebody asked, "Reverend, in all of those fifty years, did you ever think about divorce?"

He thought for a moment and said, "No."

The person inquiring exclaimed, "You never one time thought about divorce?"

He replied, "Divorce, never; murder, yes."

Someone pointed out that the story is no longer funny—not in this day of notorious cases where husbands have been put on trial for murdering their wives.

I trust that story is apocryphal. For 99.99 percent of people, murder is not considered to be an option for settling marital problems. I would hope that it would not be a viable option for anyone. God help us if it should become one. Suicide is sometimes seen as another possible solution in the midst of marital problems. However, for a Christian, that also is not a viable option. If the thought should ever cross one's mind, it must be immediately rejected as not a possibility or solution.

But the foundation of marriage is based upon a commitment before God of one man and one woman for life. It is a covenant—a triangle: God, man, woman. Just as the Mayflower Compact was a covenant between God and the signers, Holy Matrimony too is a covenant. When marriage is only an agreement between two people, they can agree to whatever they want, but a church wedding is so much more. There is a third party involved—God Himself. Therefore, to break a marriage covenant is not only an affront to the spouse, family, relatives, church, and country, but it is an affront to the covenant-keeping God. Does that mean that divorce is an unforgivable sin? No. But surely too many Christians today cavalierly disregard their marital vows.

Preparation for Eternity

Did you ever consider the fact that marriage is a preparation for eternity? It is a school of sanctification. Some of you wonder why your spouse rubs you the wrong way so much. Did you ever stop to think that maybe it is because you have so many rough edges that need to be rubbed off? Many a person has found all sorts of undesirable characteristics that have run into the grindstone of marriage and have been ground off. God is quite willing that we get rid of them in a less painful way. Unfortunately, many of us are not willing.

Marriage is a school where we learn forgiveness, forbearance, love, and the development of relationships, which is the most important thing. As our relationship to Christ is like our relationship to our spouse, so we need to learn the meaning of that relationship, that commitment, that love, and that trust, which is so very important.

A Commitment or a Money-Back Guarantee?

Some people seem to look upon marriage as an experiment, a probation, a temporary arrangement, a ninety-day, money-back guarantee—"'til the divorce court doth us part," "'til the midlife crisis doth us part." No! It is a God-ordained, permanent relationship. I believe most of the problems that exist in marriage start right here, because people look upon marriage as some sort of probationary experiment. If it works out, "Fine." If not, "Well, that's too bad. We tried." But because they do not look on it as an irrevocable, indissoluble, and permanent union, they never are really able to maintain what Christ says exists in that union.

THE FALLACY OF ROMANTICIST LOVE

Believe it or not, I think we might learn something here from an institution that is probably about as foreign to our way of thinking and as alien to the modern American mind-set as anything I can imagine. Yet I think there is something we can learn from it. I am speaking about the institution of arranged marriages—something we would look upon as ludicrous—our parents picking our wives or our husbands for us. Why, the average "modern Milly" would find such an idea to be totally contrary to everything she has learned in modern romances. May I remind you that the great majority of all of the marriages that have ever been performed in this world have been arranged by parents. Second, may I remind you that in almost any society of that sort, they have a vastly superior record of success to ours.

So, lest we break our arms patting ourselves on our backs for our superior view on the approach to marriage, I think we should understand that the statements in the preceding paragraph are indeed the case. I doubt, however, that anyone reading this book would be able to so disassociate himself from the mind-set in which he has grown up that he would be able to accept it. However, I think we can learn something from it.

I think of a young lady from India who was to be married to a young man whom she had never seen. In many cases they never see each other until the wedding ceremony. She received a letter from him in which he was trying to begin a relationship prior to the marriage—getting acquainted and so on. She refused to open the letter and sent it back, saying that she believed love should be developed after marriage and not before.

Now, that is alien to our thinking. Why? Is not the sagest advice that we can give to any young person contemplating marriage to ask, "Do you love him?" or "Do you love her?" Well, if so, then that is all that is needed. But . . .

In explaining her view, the young woman said, "We have no choice in the selection of our mother or of our father or of our brothers or of our sisters or of our grandfathers or grandmothers, and yet we learn to live with them and to love them, though we had no choice in their selection. So can it be with our husband or our wife."

You see, these people have learned something that we often have forgotten or have been deceived about: Namely, love is not some romantic sort of exotic bird that comes flapping down with its wings and sets our hearts aflutter and then disappears just as mysteriously. Rather, love, as 1 Corinthians 13 tells us, is a way of treating other people. No emotion is mentioned in that whole chapter, but there is instruction about how to deal with people. "Love is patient and kind; love does not envy or boast; it is not arrogant or rude. It does not insist on its own way" (vv. 4-5).

People such as the woman quoted above have learned that is what love is, and when people treat other people the right way, that feeling we call love will develop. We may have that feeling in great abundance before we are married. And if we treat our spouse in a contrary manner, we will find, before long, that the mysterious bird has flapped his wings and flown away. We say, "Alas, what can we do? There is nothing left but the divorce court, because, you see, I don't love him anymore." "I don't love her anymore. It's not there any longer. It is gone. It's dead." That is all a bunch of baloney. We have been fed a lie, and we have believed it, and we have based our whole society on the romanticist concept of love. And in so doing we have rejected the biblical teaching about the subject.

I remember when I was about sixteen, they were singing, "Will I ever find the girl on my mind? The one who is my ideal. . . . Or will I pass her by and never even know that she is my ideal?" I thought that was just great. I used to joke all the time that if I ever found the girl who was my ideal, she most certainly would keep going when she heard me sing. I want to tell you that sixty years later, I think that is all a bunch of hogwash. It is a romanticist delusion. We are told that if we can just find that one soul mate, then we will experience the pitter-patter of our heart, the flip-flapping of the wings of the bird of paradise, and we will sail off into the sunset. That is, until one or the other does not treat his spouse as 1 Corinthians 13 says, and then all of a sudden the bird falls like a dead owl, and we wonder what happened. We have been led down a primrose path.

Marriage is not based so much upon love (and this may startle some of you) as it is on commitment—the commitment to believe that marriage is a permanent, indissoluble relationship between two who have become one. Until we have that commitment, we do not have the fertile ground in which the seeds of love can take hold.

Why have there been so many divorces in our time, even among many professing Christians? Because of two devastating causes: 1) the view that marriage is based solely on the feeling of love; and 2) no-fault divorce laws that have been adopted nationwide and have vastly increased the number of divorces in our time. A third lie has also been devastating: "Marriage is just between the two of us." No, it is not.

Marriage is a holy relationship. It came from God, it was ordained by God, and it will not succeed unless God is in it. It was instituted by God and chosen by Christ to represent that relationship between Himself and the Church. We must realize that without God at work in our marriage, it is not going to succeed. We must realize the importance of the basics. Many people's marriages have failed because they have simply forgotten the basics of having God in it, of praying together, of reading God's Word together, of having Christ be very real in their home or working together to further God's kingdom. "What therefore God has joined together, let not man separate" (Matthew 19:6).

Jesus said that Moses, because of the hardness of their hearts, allowed the Israelites to put away their wives (Matthew 19:8). Sometimes we forget what causes divorce. What are the causes? Psychological problems? Incompatibility? The wrong genes? What is the problem? The Bible makes this very clear. The reason for divorce is very simply sin. I don't mean that your husband is necessarily a murderer or a bank robber, or even necessarily that he is an adulterer. All sorts of other sins can destroy a marriage. There is the sin of selfishness, the sin of anger and unresolved hostility, the sin of lovelessness, the sin of a lack of appreciation, the sin of unkindness, the sin of seeking our own instead of our partner's well-being. All of these sins drive people apart. Only Christ, by His shed blood, can get rid of sin and bring people together again.

CONCLUSION

One time a new employee had just come aboard at a ministry, and it did not take long before he realized there was a person there whose "gift" seemed to be making people miserable. Many people think that ministries have only saints, and they get disappointed when they find self-proclaimed Christians who treat others worse than the heathen do. He asked a long-time employee what on earth that person was doing in a Christian ministry. The answer came quickly: "Oh, he is here for the purification of the saints." God puts difficult people in our lives so we can learn patience and trust in God. We do well to remember what C. S. Lewis said about difficult Christians in our paths. He said in effect, think how much worse she would be if she weren't a Christian.

Sometimes we forget that God's highest purpose for us in this world is not for us to be happy. Before we can be happy, we must be holy. God's first purpose for us in this world is that we might be holy so we will be happy, here and hereafter, once we are holy. There is never any true happiness without holiness.

Therefore, God ordained that in marriage we will have a lot of rough edges worn off. Sometimes when people get married, they have an incredible number of rough edges, and they begin to grind on each other. It hurts, and they squeal, and they yell, and they do not even realize that in the providence of God, He is working on their lives. They have had all of those rough edges before, but there has never been another millstone close enough to grind them off. So over the years the edges are getting worn off, and they get smoother; God is at work. But too easily we want to flee from that situation—take all of our rough edges and run. However, God says, "No. Stay here." He is at work in our lives. I am sure there are some rough edges in your life right now, and God is using your spouse to rub them down, and it hurts. I would urge you to submit to the process, to let God do His work.

A good marriage is the best way to go through life. To share the burdens and to multiply the joy, to comfort and encourage each other and to help each other live for God and rear godly children—there is no higher calling and no better way to live. God has ordained marriage because it's great, and it brings happiness and contentment to those involved.

22

CHRISTIAN MARRIAGE

... speaking the truth in love, we are to grow up in every way into him who is the head, into Christ.

EPHESIANS 4:15

✠

Some years ago a man got his picture in almost every newspaper in the country by doing a remarkable thing. He walked all the way across the North American continent on foot—from the Atlantic to the Pacific. Now that's quite a trek in anybody's book. When he got to California, reporters met him and questioned him about his travels. They asked him if he ever felt that he wouldn't make it, if he ever felt like he was going to have to give up, if he ever thought that he was defeated. He replied, "Yes, many times." When asked what it was that almost defeated him, he said, "Well, you may be surprised. It wasn't the rushing and roaring traffic of your big cities or the screeching of brakes and the honking of horns. It wasn't even the interminable prairie of the Midwest that seemed to stretch on and on forever. Nor was it the blazing and burning sun over the hot Western desert. It wasn't even the snowcapped mountains and icy gorges of the Rocky Mountains. What almost defeated me over and over again was the sand in my shoes."

I believe this is also true in many marriages in our land. It is the unheralded, seldom-discussed sand in the shoes that really underlies many of the more spectacular reasons for marital failure that we read about in the newspapers or are included in divorce decrees. When I refer to sand in the shoes, I am speaking of the abrasive sand of criticism, which I think is probably one of the most ubiquitous causes of problems in marriage. Having counseled with many people over the years, I have found this to be almost a problem to some degree in virtually every marriage.

Since marriage is the foundation of the home and the most important relationship in the home, we want to devote a whole chapter on some of the biblical teaching on marriage—the Christian worldview on marriage.

A KINGDOM-BUILDING UNIT

A Christian marriage is a kingdom-building unit. Do you remember what the Pilgrims said in the Mayflower Compact when they explained the purpose of their voyage? It was "for the glory of God and the advancement of the Christian faith."[1] That is exactly what the purpose should be for each and every Christian marriage. It shouldn't be for our happiness—although that is certainly a natural by-product of a Christ-centered marriage. But as in everything, it's not about us—it's about Him. So a Christian marriage is about Christ.

I married because I believed that together my wife and I could do more for the kingdom of God than either of us could do alone. God put us together as a team for His glory and purposes. A Christian marriage is a team. It is not just two people living in the same house, each with his or her own agenda. When you get married, it's no longer I, but we. The Bible says, "the two shall become one flesh" (Matthew 19:5, NIV). This not only refers to sex but to oneness in purpose, oneness in existence. "What therefore what God has joined together, let not man separate" (Matthew 19:6).

God equips each couple with gifts and ministry potential as a unit that neither of them could do alone. When children are born into such a family, they become part of the ministry and the kingdom-building efforts. In a Christian family, children often bring countless young people into the home— some to visit and some to stay. The children know that a truly Christian home is the Lord's and that it is to be used for His purposes. Our children should be partners in ministry, and as they leave home to start their own lives, they will look for spouses who can partner with them in kingdom-building.

THE IMPORTANCE OF BEGINNING WELL

It is vital in a marriage to begin well. "Well begun is half done" is an old saying. That is true in the preparation of marriage—with premarital counseling, prayer, thought, and the study of God's Word. We need to begin our marriage well each day. Therefore, I am more and more convinced that the first sixty seconds, or less, of a day greatly determine how any type of relationship during that day is going to progress. Furthermore, I am sure it is very seldom that the relationship progresses any higher than it begins. Therefore, it is very important to begin each day of our married life rightly. We are put together to serve each other. God wants to show His love to your spouse through you. Being mindful that marriage is a ministry helps give us an eternal perspective in our marriage.

MARRIAGE SAVERS

One effective measure to help the struggling American family is "marriage savers," which is the brainchild of columnist Mike McManus, author of *Marriage Savers* (Zondervan, 1993). He points out that 75 percent of weddings take place in church. Therefore, churches could help lower the divorce rate. How? As a starter, by mandating a very simple, common-sense policy: requiring couples to undergo a few sessions of premarital counseling. A lot of couples who get married should not have gotten married, but they never sat down and talked about things in advance. Requiring a minimum of premarital counseling can help prevent bad marriages in the first place. In some communities, McManus has managed to persuade a quorum of churches to agree not to conduct any weddings without the minimal requirement of three premarital counseling sessions. This is not too heavy a burden on couples, and it helps prevent bad marriages.

Suppose, for example, that many churches in a community have made this joint agreement, and suppose a couple approaches the Methodist church for a wedding and is told of the requirement. Suppose they find this too stringent, so they go to the Baptist church, where they face the same requirement. It's the same with the local Presbyterian church, and on down the line. By sticking with this minimal, common-sense approach, these churches are effectively preventing new bad marriages and new divorces.

McManus has managed to convince churches in Modesto, California, and Peoria, Illinois, among other communities, to adopt this approach. Within a short time of implementing this, the divorce rate in those communities went down. By insisting on a Christian approach to marriage, the church of Jesus Christ can have an enormous impact on family life in America.

Even if a couple has not begun well, through the power of Jesus Christ there is hope for working through conflicts.

It is usually true that husbands and wives are apart from each other more in a waking day than they are together, but there are times of meeting and greeting, and we need to begin those well. For example, this is important when a husband comes home from work. Let me hasten to say that I am not setting myself up as a paragon of virtue here. But I have attempted to do these things, and I have found they work. I haven't been consistent in doing them, but I can still recommend them.

I would like to give five suggestions using the acrostic PRIDE:

- Prayer
- Remembrance
- Ideal
- Demonstration
- Enthusiasm

First, before you meet with your spouse, you ought to prepare yourself by *prayer*. For example, pray before your spouse comes home, before you get out of your car, or when you are driving home. In that prayer there should be forgiveness, so that you do not drag the bones of an old fight or argument into the new relationship. May His grace and mercy be fresh that day for you as you learn to forgive and forget those things that are past. Ask the Spirit of God to fill you with love that you might be the husband or wife you ought to be as you come into that meeting.

Second, *remembrance*. By that I mean the remembrance of the good times in your life. After all, husbands, you must have had some reason to marry your spouse. Wives, there must have been something about your husband you liked. Unfortunately, we tend to fixate upon the negative and forget the things that were positive. I would urge you to remember the good times. Remember when you were dating and you hadn't seen him/her for a week or two? Let that thought go through your mind as you prepare to meet your spouse.

Third, the *ideal*. Grasp again the vision of the ideal of what a marriage relationship ought to be. Any kind of meeting of individuals, whether it is for two minutes or two hours, can be very cold and hostile and negative, or it can be lukewarm, which is where most people are. Too often a lukewarm relationship falls so far short of the warm and loving relationship that God wants us to have between spouses. So, remember that ideal of what God would have us to be. Think about the times when you have been away for weeks and then have come back together.

One word of caution about the ideal. Many marriages today have taken God out of the equation, and that puts the marital partner in an impossible situation. All our needs for intimacy, belonging, and unconditional love are placed on the spouse to fulfill. But we are finite human beings, and only God can fulfill all our needs. We must have our relationship with Him in order. The only true prince coming on a white horse to make all things right is Jesus Christ. No earthly man can be that, and no earthly wife can be the perfect princess who tames the beast and turns frogs into princes. We must not put onto our spouse the role of savior and redeemer. Only Christ will love us perfectly, and only when we get to heaven will we truly belong, and only there will we know perfect intimacy. Many modern marriages have fallen apart because the ideal was so high that no human could ever measure up.

Fourth, *demonstration*. It has been said that it takes four hugs a day to keep a person from getting neurotic. You may wonder, "What should I do if I am single? Hug myself?" Well, possibly there are some friends who are enthusiastic enough to greet you that way. Certainly it is vital in the marriage relationship to hug one another. Unfortunately, it is true that there is a great deal of touching when people are dating and far less of it after they are married.

We show love in different ways. Touching is one way. Words of encouragement and praise are another. Acts of service show love. Gift-giving and surprises are another way some people show their appreciation for each other. All these demonstrations are usually present in courtship. It is important that we continue to demonstrate our love. Try it one day when you don't feel very loving toward your spouse, and watch how showing love can bring the feelings back.

As numerous marriage counselors have pointed out, touching and hugging cause the feelings of what is called romantic love. What happens is that people get married and stop touching to a large extent. Then they wonder what happened to that feeling of romantic love. Keeping the spark alive is so important when you greet each other in the morning, when you go off to work, when you come home again, and when you go to bed. These are four wonderful opportunities to end neurosis in your home.

Lastly, *enthusiasm*. Unfortunately, many times we greet each other with a very low level of enthusiasm. The corners of the mouth are turned down. The kids have been cutting up. It's been a bad day at the office. Things have not gone well. And all this is brought into the relationship. Then we wonder why the thermostat seems like it is turned down so low. We need to try to build each other up with enthusiasm. That can make such a difference in a relationship.

Years ago in college I had a good friend whom I remember as always having a big smile on his face and extending a warm greeting to everyone he met. It was a real pleasure to meet him. Occasionally we meet people like that. There are others whom we meet who show no enthusiasm—there is no smile, and we really don't want to be around them. They may sometimes wonder why it is that people avoid them. I would urge such people to be more like my college friend who had such a winsome personality. I will never forget that in the first few moments of meeting, he so lifted my spirits—and not only mine, but everyone else's as well.

"Well begun is half done." Marriage is not just a relationship that goes on without interruption all of your life. There are brief periods of time that you spend together. I would urge you to try to craft these in such a way that they will yield the kind of overall marriage you would like to have.

MAKING HIS OR HER DAY

For another aspect of marriage, there is a phrase from a totally different context: "Go ahead. Make my day." Our relationship with our spouse should be an attempt to make their day. As one counselor said, "When we were dating, we had a date." That was the attempt to make the other person's day; that was why he brought a corsage or flowers or candy or whatever, to do something to make the day special. It is amazing how that thought can get totally lost after years of marriage and is seldom considered at all. How many times do you think during the day, *What can I do today to make my spouse's day?* How many times do you think about how to make it special, to put some sparkle or fizz into it, to show your love?

I heard about one mother who had eight children. She told each bride (her own daughters and her future daughters-in-law): "Remember that every dinner is a date." All eight children seem to be happily married.

What does your spouse really enjoy? I suppose with many couples the husband likes something that the wife doesn't like at all. She expresses her disapprobation whenever the occasion arises, and vice versa. And some wives enjoy things the husband cannot understand at all. May I suggest something? Why don't you try to learn to like those things your spouse likes? You may never really become overzealous about them, but trying will make a tremendous impact on your spouse. You might even come to like it. More than that, your spouse will come to see that you really desire to please him or her.

How many times we see couples putting each other down rather than lifting each other up. They do this by finding fault, by criticizing, and by making fun of one another. Would that God would grant us the ability to never do that again, but rather to learn to lift one another up. As one person said, "When you have disagreements, don't get historical." You know what I mean. "You always . . ." And if we are not being historical, perhaps we are sounding prophetic: "You're never going to amount to anything." Most of us are neither historians nor prophets. But we are all called to minister to the needs of another in the moment. I would urge you to remember that.

IS THERE LOVE IN YOUR HOME?

May I say to you that life is very short. The family is going to be gone before long. Even the career is going to be over before you know it. But God has placed you here to develop a relationship. What kind of relationship is being developed between you and your spouse? Is there really love in your home? I often think that when wedding vows are made and the couple is joined together, the wife is placing most of her earthly hopes for happiness in the hands of a single young man, and this young man is placing most of his hopes for happiness in the hands of this young woman. Husbands, your wife has placed her hope of happiness in your hands. Wives, your husband has placed his in yours. How well have you handled that trust? How well have you succeeded in being a husband who loves his wife or a wife who loves her husband? Would your spouse say that my wife/husband has indeed made this world a little bit of heaven?

Husbands, love your wives. Wives, love your husbands.

WHERE SELDOM IS HEARD . . .

Many professing Christians live sub-Christianly, particularly in reference to their families, by not controlling their tongues. The Bible says, "Death and life are in the power of the tongue, and those who love it will eat its fruits" (Proverbs 18:21). How pleasant it is to live in a home "where seldom is heard a discouraging word." Oh, give me that home.

James tells us: "no human being can tame the tongue. It is a restless evil, full of deadly poison. With it we bless our Lord and Father, and with it we curse people who are made in the likeness of God. From the same mouth comes blessing and cursing. My brothers, these things ought not to be so" (James 3:8-10).

It seems that virtually all writers in this field are agreed that perhaps the most important factor in developing a happy home is the matter of communication. Dr. Jay Adams in an excellent book on the subject (*Christian Living in the Home*) says, "Communication comes first."[2] He even has a chapter by that title—"Communication Comes First." It was the first thing in this universe, wasn't it? We read that in the beginning, God spoke, and it was done (Genesis 1:3ff.). We find that Christ is described as the Eternal *Logos* or the Word that became flesh (John 1:1, 14). It is interesting to note that of all the creatures on this planet, only man has been given the power to speak. It is obvious that this, then, is vitally important to our relationship in our home.

In fact, any sort of interpersonal relationship is going to depend upon communication, whether it be between nations, neighbors, parents and children, or husbands and wives. Communication is vital. In fact, I think it is probably much more important than most of us realize.

After examining the results of many years of marital counseling, a marriage counselor discovered that the major complaint of women is that their husbands do not communicate with them or listen to them. This was *the* major source of marital problems. Communication comes first.

It is interesting to note in Paul's epistle to the Ephesians that he deals at some length with the relationships between husbands and wives, parents and children, and masters and servants—interpersonal relationships. However, before he gets to this, he has a rather thorough discussion about the matter of communication as being primary and foundational for any such relationship. He deals in chapter 5 with husbands and wives, and you might note in the fourth chapter of Ephesians that he says we are to speak the truth in love (v. 15). This is the basic foundation upon which interpersonal relationships are to be formed at any level between any rational sentient beings. I want to tell you, that's not always easy to do. It's easy to speak the truth perhaps. Some people pride themselves upon the fact that they always speak the truth. They tell it as it is. They call a spade a spade. I have noticed over the years in talking with people who make a statement like that, it's always other people's spade they're talking about; and they may speak the truth, but they are as loving as a bucket full of hydrochloric acid. Maybe you have known such people. Perhaps it is your unpleasant circumstance to be married to one. We must speak the truth *in love*.

Other people try to be loving, but they don't speak the truth. They feel that would be hurting someone, and therefore they would not tell the truth about how they feel about some situation. We are to speak the truth in love, and any deep personal relationship must be based upon complete honesty toward one another. Probably one of the main reasons why there are not only problems in marriages, but husbands and wives progress to a certain level of relationship but never grow deeper and more intimate is because so much of the iceberg is underwater. So much is never said because it might hurt the other person.

In our time there is a great emphasis in psychological circles on what is known as ventilation. Ventilation simply means that you just let it all hang out. You say whatever you feel. We have a lot of encounter groups and support groups and various other therapy groups that get together and just let it all hang out. If they are filled with wrath and indignation and they're mad at someone across the table, they just give them a tongue-lashing and excoriate them.

Is that biblical? It's certainly popular, but I don't think it's biblical. The Bible says that we are supposed to speak the truth in love, and Paul goes on to say that what we say should be said for edifying, for building people up. Furthermore, we are not to be merely concerned about how our talk makes us feel but are to have concern for how it makes other people feel. We are not to speak the truth in unrighteous anger. We are to speak the truth in love. We often go to one extreme or the other. It seems that we either don't speak the truth at all, or if we do, we ventilate all of our hostile feelings upon another person.

God has another way of our dealing with these emotions as we bring them to Jesus Christ. "Speaking the truth in love," Paul says in Ephesians 4. We are told that we have heard the truth as it is in Jesus, and "Therefore, having put away falsehood, let each one of you speak the truth with his neighbor, for we are members of one another. Be angry and do not sin; do not let the sun go down on your anger" (vv. 25-26). Because we are one, we are therefore to speak the truth one to another.

If every married couple learned to never let the sun go down on their anger, we would cut the divorce rate drastically. If we could clear up all hurts and anger before the day is over and never carry over one day's problem to the next, we would live so much better. When Paul gives this admonition, he says the reason for not going to bed angry is so we don't give the devil a foothold (v. 27). If we hang on to anger, it develops into bitterness. But if we clear the air and forgive each other each day, bitterness cannot take root, and we will be spared much grief. You might have to stay up really late, but decide that you will never again go to bed angry.

Also, we are told to let no corrupt communication proceed out of our mouth, but only that which is edifying, ministering grace unto the hearers. Further, we are told that "sexual immorality and all impurity or covetousness must not even be named among you" (Ephesians 5:3), and he lays out guidelines for the content of our speech. Further, he says it's a shame even to speak of those things that are done by the heathen in secret (v. 12). Rather, we are told what our speech should be about: "addressing one another in psalms and hymns and spiritual songs, singing and making melody to the Lord with all your heart, giving thanks always and for everything to God the Father in the name of our Lord Jesus Christ" (vv. 19-20).

The number one form of communication is speaking. The Bible has a lot to say about talking and when to speak and when to be silent—what not to say and what to say. We read a good bit in James about the sins of the tongue, which is a small rudder that can steer a great ship. We see that the little rudder of the tongue has steered many a marriage onto the reefs of destruction because of the sins of the tongue.

The Bible forbids many kinds of sins of the tongue. For example, it forbids *cursing and profanity*, which certainly minister unwholesome, pernicious, and harmful attitudes in any home. It is interesting to note that profanity is the only sin, the only breach of the Decalogue, for which there is no temptation. There is no temptation to take God's name in vain. With all other sins, there can be premeditation, but with profanity, one can just blurt it out, without previous thought. You would not take your mother's name and use it as a curse word. This is an indication of the total depravity of mankind. In the Old Testament it was punished by death.

The Bible also frequently speaks about the sins of *bitterness* and *wrath*. *Complaining* takes the place of thanksgiving. *Anger* replaces joy. *Criticizing and fault-finding* are probably two of the most damaging sins of the tongue in homes. Psychologists have found that children who are continually criticized rarely turn out to be emotionally healthy when they grow up. For some people, criticism and fault-finding have become a way of life. They even consider it a virtue. They don't realize that the Bible continually commands us to judge not, so that we will not be judged. Yet, how many people have ruined their marriages by this type of behavior.

If you examine the conversation that goes on in many homes between people, you very frequently find *backbiting*. This deals with some absent party, someone who is not there, and usually the commentary is not flattering. Are you a backbiter? The Bible says God is angry with a backbiter (Roman 1:30). Someone wrote that backbiting is to another person what a knife is to the back. So obviously this is a very serious sin.

CONCLUSION

One day a couple on the mission field went to see a counselor. After discussing all the problems they have had, the wife blurted out, "I didn't love this man when I married him, and I have never loved him since." It was just like opening a dam. Everything suddenly came out: all of the problems, all of the deep feelings that were there, but they had been unable to deal with. This family that had failed on the mission field, their marriage now dissolving, returned home. By the grace of God and through Christ-centered counseling, they ended up with a new relationship; they were eventually back on the field, serving and glorifying Christ. Would to God that more of our Christian couples today would work out their conflicts and find peace and joy in Christ the way this couple did. If more and more Christian couples patterned their marriages on the Word of God, including what it has to say about taming the tongue, there would be far less divorce among our people.

Remember that love covers a multitude of sins. By self-sacrificing love, Christlike love, we can work out our differences and learn to like and enjoy each other. By giving all, we gain all.

23

CHRISTIAN PARENTING

Train up a child in the way he should go; even when he is old he will not depart from it.

PROVERBS 22:6

☩

Three hundred years ago there lived two men. One of them was Jonathan Edwards. You have no doubt heard of him. He was the minister mostly responsible for the Great Awakening in this country, a great Calvinistic preacher, the one who preached that famous sermon "Sinners in the Hands of an Angry God." He was also the most original and outstanding philosopher America ever produced. Some view him as among the best theologians in church history.

At the same time there lived a man by the name of Max Juke, a derelict. He was a vagabond, a ne'er-do-well. Sociologists have fixed upon these two families and have examined them carefully, and what they discovered is fascinating. In the past 300 years Jonathan Edwards, Puritan clergyman, produced from his marriage with Sarah 265 college graduates, twelve college presidents, sixty-five university professors, sixty physicians, 100 clergymen, seventy-five army officers, eighty prominent authors, 100 lawyers, thirty judges, eighty public officials, three Congressmen, two U.S. Senators, and one Vice President of the United States.[1]

On the other hand, Max Juke, derelict, vagabond, and an ungodly man, married an equally ungodly woman, and these two ne'er-do-wells have given to this country 300 who died in infancy, 310 professional paupers, 440 crippled by disease, fifty prostitutes, sixty thieves, seven murderers, and fifty-three assorted criminals of other varieties. Yes, the success and godliness of our marriages is something in which society has a very vital interest.

The purpose of this chapter is to explore some biblical principles related

to child-rearing. The Bible is the owner's manual to how we approach life. It
has many profitable words to say related to parenting.

HOW TO REAR GODLY CHILDREN INTO GODLY ADULTS

It is a worthy goal to rear children to be godly so that they become godly
adults. Alas, many Christian young people—just like many Christian adults—
do not have a Christian worldview. They essentially have a humanistic view
cloaked as a spiritual one. That is not going to cut it. This is part of the reason modern Christianity is in such a disconnect.

We are to teach our children the Holy Scriptures. Read the Bible to them.
Tell them the Bible stories when they are very, very young. Help them to mem-
orize the Bible—to hide it in their heart. Of course, that means we do that
with them. "I have stored up your word in my heart, that I might not sin
against you" (Psalm 119:11).

Set before them a godly example. I can tell you one thing: If you are not
a godly man or woman, you may have hidden that from your boss and your
friends; but if you are a hypocrite, your kids know it right off. They see
through you like a pane of glass, and everything you do will be to no avail if
your children believe you are a fake. Set before them a godly example as you
live out your Christian faith. Include them in activities such as serving the
poor and visiting shut-ins. Ask God, as a family, what you should be involved
in, and brighten the world with your children.

Teach them how to give—to live as generous people, sharing with others, everything from toys to candy. If they learn early to give to others, they
will become generous adults. Teach them how to tithe so they will become
faithful stewards of Christ as they grow up. Usually it is much easier to give
and to tithe when you learn how as a child.

I think of a man who came to Dr. Peter Marshall, former chaplain of the
U.S. Senate, and said to him, "Dr. Marshall, I have a problem. I used to tithe
regularly some years ago, but . . . but now, you see, God has blessed me to
the place that I am earning 500 thousand dollars a year, and I obviously can't
afford to give about fifty thousand dollars."

Dr. Marshall said, "I can certainly see your problem. Let's pray about it.
'Heavenly Father, I pray that you would reduce this man's salary back to the
place that he can afford to tithe.'"

The man said, "No, no, Doctor, don't pray that prayer. I'll tithe."

We need to ground our children in the gospel of Jesus Christ. We need
to teach them how to share their faith. That will strengthen them greatly

in their own faith and understanding and commitment to Jesus Christ. We need to take them to Sunday school—no, to *bring* them to Sunday school. I personally was sent to Sunday school. My parents didn't take me. When I was about fourteen and old enough to put up a loud enough squawk, they allowed me not to go. They were not in a very solid position to oppose that because they weren't going either. So *bring* your children to Sunday school.

We need to enroll our children in a Christian school if possible. Some people don't have access to such a school. Some teach their children at home. In fact, the homeschool movement is growing tremendously in quantity and in quality. It is absolutely vital that our children receive a spiritual education and understanding. If Christian schooling is not an option, teach them the Christian worldview at home.

Before our children can be led to Christ, they first have to be drawn to us. Therefore, it is vitally important to show love to your children. Never be afraid to show your love. That involves things like hugging them when they are very little, and as they get older as well. How many times did you hug your child this week? Psychologists now know that physical touch produces a bonding with a young child. If that is lacking, there are dire consequences in a child's life. They do not develop their emotions fully, and they don't empathize with others the way they should. Many serial killers had been children with whom nobody ever bonded. They have no feeling of sympathy or empathy for anyone, and that is why they find it so easy to kill. Tell your children how much you love them, and tell them you are proud of them, and show them by touching and hugging them.

Spend time with your children. I heard about a judge who was receiving an award for his great oratorical skills and elocution. His son did not seem to be thrilled at the occasion. A friend of the father asked the son, "You don't seem to be very happy. Don't you appreciate your father's eloquence?"

He said, "All I remember about his 'eloquence' was, 'Get lost, kid. I'm busy.'"

It is interesting and sad that he never forgot that. Children never do. They will remember things like that all of their lives. Many runaways have been heard to say, "I can never do anything right. My parents always told me about everything I did wrong."

If you want people to blossom and bloom, whether it's in business, friendship, work, or at home, you don't encourage that by finding fault. You do it by noticing the good they do.

Spend time with your children. How important that is.

DON'T PROVOKE YOUR CHILDREN

One of the scriptural admonitions for parents is addressed specifically to fathers. The apostle Paul writes that fathers are not to enrage their children: "Fathers, do not provoke your children to anger, but bring them up in the discipline and instruction of the Lord" (Ephesians 6:4).

This principle applies not only to fathers but to mothers as well. Paul speaks to the fathers not because of some oriental depreciation of women, but because the woman is included in this because the husband is head of the wife (as the previous chapter, Ephesians 5:23, points out). Though the father is to direct the religious training of the children, the wife is to join in enthusiastically, since she, in most cases, spends far more time with them than he does.

In this admonition we see the responsibility of parents both negatively and positively. Negatively, we are not to "provoke your children to anger." The word "provoke" (*parorgizo* in Greek) means "to chafe, to work up to a passion, to exasperate." We provoke our children to anger by such things as chastening them unjustly, harshly, with hastiness of temper, with undue severity, or with a vast multiplicity of commandments. The reason for this command is given in its repetition found in Colossians 3:21, where Paul says the same thing and adds, "lest they become discouraged."

THE FATHER AS HEAD OF THE HOUSEHOLD

It's not politically correct to say it, but biblically the father is the head of the household. Sometimes men have abused their authority as the head of the household and so have contributed to a misunderstanding of the issue. But the Bible says this:

> Wives, submit to your own husbands, as to the Lord. For the husband is the head of the wife even as Christ is the head of the church, his body, and is himself its Savior. Now as the church submits to Christ, so also wives should submit in everything to their husbands. Husbands, love your wives, as Christ loved the church and gave himself up for her. . . .
>
> Children, obey your parents in the Lord, for this is right. . . . Fathers, do not provoke your children to anger, but bring them up in the discipline and instruction of the Lord. (Ephesians 5:22-25, 6:1, 4)

The first issue to consider is that of authority. Men read that they are the head of the wife, but they do not go on and read that they are her head even as Christ is the head of the church and the Savior of the body for good. That is the purpose of headship—to keep the body functioning. The head keeps the hand from burning itself and the foot from stepping on a nail. Gentlemen, you are the head of the body for the wife.

It is amazing how frequently when a person is given a little bit of authority, he struts around like some sort of little Caesar or Napoleon, exercising his despotic tyranny on all of those who, unhappily, come beneath his rule. That is a very sad thing. There is a great need for restraint in the exercising of authority. When a person has a lot of power, even a good person, he needs to exercise a great deal of restraint.

Jesus Christ has infinite power and all authority, and yet how lovingly He exercises that authority by sweet reasoning, by serving, and by love. Gentlemen, we should learn a lesson from that.

Second, the man reads the Scripture, and he discovers that he is the head of the wife and that the wife is subject under him, and he therefore arrives at what seems to him to be an ineluctable conclusion—namely, that his will is sovereign in that marriage, and what he says goes. But this is a poor reading of the text. Some men have even twisted this idea to allow them to beat their wives. This is completely contrary to the overall message of the passage, which includes the point that husbands are to love their wives as Christ loved the church. If the husband is to be willing to lay down his life for the sake of his wife, he will not be trying to beat her into submission, either physically or verbally.

The children are under the authority of the parents in the divine order, the wife is under the authority of the husband, and the husband is under the authority of Christ. So it is Christ's will that is sovereign in our homes, and it is that will, gentlemen, that we are to seek out and to seek to bring to pass in our homes.

Third, we must consider the mistake husbands make when they read they are to love their wives—when they confuse personal relations with physical things. How many foolish husbands or fathers have supposed that by the provision of things, he has loved his wife or his children. Many a silly man has awakened to discover that his wife despises him, and his children can't stand the sight of him. He is perplexed, and he says in righteous indignation, "Why? Haven't I provided them everything in the world?" Perhaps so, except what people need most, which is loving, personal relationships.

It is tragic that one of the greatest causes for marital failure, in fact for failure of any kind in life, is the silly confusion that seems to exist in the minds of so many people between persons and things. They never seem to learn that they are to love people and use things—to use things to help build our relationship with people. Yet the overwhelming majority of people in this world love things and use and manipulate people to get them. This is an utter perversion of the divine order for our lives. Do you do that? You do it, gentlemen, if you suppose that by giving your wife things, you have loved her.

THE CROWN OF A GODLY MOTHER

In 1990, when the first George Bush was President, his wife was invited to give the commencement address at Wellesley College. Hundreds of angry coeds protested. They were outraged that a woman who had never done anything but rear a family (nothing significant at all about this woman) would be invited to speak at Wellesley, where in those sacred halls of higher learning, for a generation or more, women have been told that rearing a family and staying at home is an abominable thing to do. She was, nevertheless, allowed to come and speak. At the end of her speech she said something, I think, that needs repeating. She said:

> At the end of your life, you will never regret not having passed one more test, not winning one more verdict or not closing one more deal. You will regret time not spent with a husband, a friend, a child, or a parent.[2]

I think that note needs to be rung again and again. Ultimately in life, the things that really count are the relationships we have—first with God, and then with our spouse, our parents, our children, and our friends.

THE POWERFUL IMPACT OF MOTHERS

Many outstanding men in this world would disagree with feminists' evaluation of mothers. They are men of no little accomplishment themselves.

Thomas Edison wrote: "I did not have my mother long, but she cast over me an influence that has lasted all my life. The good effects of her early training I can never lose. I was always a careless boy, and with a mother of different mental caliber, I should have turned out badly, but her firmness and her goodness were potent powers to keep me in the right path. My mother was the making of me."[3] Where would we be today without that mother? We would be in the dark and still lighting candles!

Charles Spurgeon, perhaps the greatest preacher who ever lived, said, "I cannot tell how much I owe to the solemn words and prayers of my mother."[4]

Dwight L. Moody, the great evangelist of a century ago, said, "All that I have ever accomplished in life, I owe to my mother."[5]

We even have a statue to a mother in this country. We know it in another context. It is called the Statue of Liberty. Frederic Auguste Bartholdi, who sculpted it, used for his ideal model his own mother. For him, it was a statue of Mom.

One of the great mothers of our country was Abigail Smith. She was a minister's daughter and the only woman besides Barbara Bush to become the wife of one President (John Adams) and the mother of another (John Quincy Adams). Both owed a lot to that faithful mother.

Dr. G. Campbell Morgan, one of the greatest preachers of this century, and his wife reared four sons, all of whom became ministers of the gospel of some note. At a family reunion a friend asked one of the sons, "Which Morgan is the greatest preacher?"

The son looked at his father, who replied, "Mother." No doubt her preaching to those children had a great deal to do with the way they turned out.[6]

Susannah Wesley is famous as the mother of nineteen children. She did it all on a pastor's salary. Busy? Well, she wasn't too busy to take one full hour each week to give spiritual instruction to each of her children. Two of her sons, John and Charles, turned the tide of England's spiritual life around when it was at its lowest ebb.

These and millions more attest to the impact that women, and mothers in particular, have had upon their children.

FALLOUT FROM THE FEMINIST MOVEMENT

We live in a time when many mothers have been deceived. As Mary Pride, a former feminist, once said, "Today's women are the victims of the second biggest con game in history." (The first, she said, was when the serpent persuaded Eve that she needed to upgrade her lifestyle and "be like God.") "Now the courts rip away our legal protection via 'no-fault' divorce, nonexistent alimony and joint custody. 'Womens' magazines have followed *Playboy* and *Hustler*, degrading us to the level of prostitutes as they glamorize uncommitted sex."[7]

Yes, there has been quite a deception. What has the feminist movement accomplished for most women who have followed it? It's led them down the path of easy no-fault divorce, where they discover there is no alimony, and now they have a couple of kids they have to take care of somehow. And we've created an entire new class of poor in the process. Large sections of the poor in America are mothers without husbands and with children. They are frenzied, trying to get ready to go to work each morning and usually not to a well-paying job. They were told about all of the glamorous things that lay ahead for them; so they take their children off to day care and then rush to work, always wondering what's happening to their children. Finally they get home again to fix dinner and clean the house. Maybe they have a date once in a rare moon, and they go out with a man who has ditched his former wife and is doing very, very well. He's making the same money he was making before, and he doesn't have all of his previous expenditures. He doesn't have a home to keep up, a wife to take care of, children to feed and put braces on their teeth, and all of the rest. His spendable income has increased dramatically, while hers has gone dramatically down. As Mary Pride says, the feminine movement did not free women—it freed men. You have been conned, ladies, as more than one woman has thought when her date let her out at the door with his 45,000-dollar sports car and she walked to her apartment—up three floors. Who has really been freed?

The other results of the feminist movement have perhaps been even worse. David Gelernter, a Yale computer professor, wrote an article for *Commentary* magazine, entitled "Why Mothers Should Stay at Home." He points out that American children are not doing well; they are having problems with drugs, suicide, and violence. He says of the "Motherhood revolution": "Although nobody wants to admit it, casualties are mounting from one of the great social revolutions of the age." "Practically all the indicators of youth health and behavior," notes the education expert William Damon in his recent book *Greater Expectations*, "have declined year by year for well over a generation."[8]

Thank you, feminists. You didn't tell us what this was going to do to our children, and that indeed is tragic. Many decades ago the proportion of married women age twenty-four to thirty-five, the child-bearing years, in the labor force was 16 percent. In the 1960s it rose to 32 percent. Then it went up to 39 percent in 1970. By 1975 that figure had risen to 48 percent. By 1980 it was up to 59 percent, and 65 percent by 1985. It may have tapered off a bit in the last two decades, but you still have millions and millions of mothers working outside the home, many of whom would prefer to be at home rearing their children. The unfair tax code, which in effect penalizes the stay-at-home mom, has forced millions of mothers out the door who would rather focus on their children.

THE IMPACT ON CIVILIZATION

False ideas like feminism have destroyed nations in the past. In 1947 historian Carle Zimmerman of Harvard University wrote about the "Last State of

Disintegration" of the cultures of Greece and Rome before they fell. I want you to notice something: This was written more than fifty years ago, before most of the various pathologies that now plague America had even developed in the 1960s or the 1970s. Back in 1947, historian Zimmerman wrote about what happened in Greece and Rome at least 1,500 or more years earlier. Notice: we think we are so modern. But this is what was happening almost 2,000 years ago.

- Marriage lost its sacredness and was frequently broken by divorce.
- The traditional meaning of marriage was lost. Alternative forms of marriage arose.
- The feminist movements abounded.
- There was increased public disrespect for parents, parenthood, and authority in general.
- There was an increase in juvenile delinquency, promiscuity, and rebellion.
- There was a refusal of people with traditional marriages to accept family responsibilities and have children.
- There was an increasing desire for and an acceptance of adultery.
- Finally, there was a tolerance for and a spread of sexual perversions of all kinds—especially homosexuality.[9]

That was about 2,000 years ago. Yes, we're very modern, aren't we? What we have learned is how to destroy a culture and an empire, and this is the way twenty-six former empires fell. I think it is time that we quit listening to the modern gurus who tell us that God's way is wrong and here is the modern, up-to-date, scientific approach that is going to lead us to a new paradise. In each case they have led us into all kinds of problems.

Motherhood is as noble a profession as there possibly could be, and God designed you, ladies, for a great and glorious and wonderful life. It certainly has its problems, but it has its rewards as well.

Christian parenting is a high calling for the mother and a high calling for the father.

CONCLUSION

I close with my paraphrase of a story by Michael Carmody[10] that has touched my heart because it underscores our need to commit ourselves to our families, second only in priority to our commitment to the Lord.

It is a story about a very busy man in a modern world. His name was John Carmody. John said, "It is strange the things you remember in times like this. It isn't the great majestic plans you had for your business and your family, the designs you were going to bring to pass, but it is the simple things, the little things, that seemed so unimportant at the time."

John Carmody was standing in the living room, staring out the window as the rain was pouring down. He was trying to focus his mind on those great plans he had for his business—the new plant, the new machinery. The strange thing was that he couldn't even remember what they were. They were just a fog swirling around in the corner of his mind.

One little thing was all he could think about now. It didn't seem important at the time it occurred. A couple of weeks ago he had come home very excited. Tomorrow was the big board meeting. He was going to make a presentation about the new plant they were going to build, about the new machinery they were going to get, about the computerization of their business, and about the bottom line. Oh, it was big business, and it was important for his plans—his career and his family.

He sat down in his favorite chair, put his briefcase in his lap, took out his presentation, and began to go over it so it would be absolutely perfect. He hadn't gotten through more than two lines when he heard a little voice say, "Look, Daddy, look, Daddy, it's a new book. Isn't it pretty, Daddy?"

And there stood little Margie.

"Oh, yes, a new book. Humph. Well, that's fine, Margie. Now run along, honey. Daddy has a lot of work to do."

"Daddy, Daddy, could you read me a story out of the book? Just one little story, Daddy?"

"Now, now, Margie, Daddy's busy. Daddy's very busy. Why don't you go talk to your mother? Maybe she could read you a story."

"Mommy's much busier in the kitchen than you are, Daddy. She said that you'd probably read me a story."

"Can't you see, Margie, that Daddy's busy right now? I have important work to do, honey. Later. I'll do it later."

"Isn't it a lovely picture, Daddy? Look at the lovely picture."

"Um? Huh? Yes, honey, it's a lovely picture, but not now, honey. Later. I'll do it later, sweetie."

Little Margie stood there like a quiet, obedient little girl as Daddy went over the inventory, the new factory, and the new mechanized works he was going to bring in, the computerization and the bottom line. It was all so very exciting. He hardly even noticed the little finger that was tapping on his hand, and the little voice that said, "Daddy, later, Daddy, later, when you have time, would you read just one little story? Would you read it to yourself, Daddy, only . . . only read it out loud . . . loud enough that . . . that I could hear it? Daddy, would you do that? Huh?"

"Oh, sure, Margie, I will be glad to do that, but later, honey. Now run along, sweetheart. Daddy's busy."

Now John Carmody couldn't remember any of those business plans. He hadn't been to the office today, and he couldn't even recall what those plans were. Instead he reached down and picked up Margie's lovely little book. It wasn't new anymore; it was creased right down the cover, and it had a big smudge of dirt on it. He began to look through the pages, trying to find that lovely little picture. As he began to read the story, his lips moved stiffly.

He did not see his wife standing in the doorway. In fact, he mercifully forgot the horror, the anguish, the anger caused by that wretch who had careened drunkenly around the corner and was now in jail for manslaughter. His wife was standing there, pulling on white gloves in stark contrast to her crisp black dress, and she said, with a carefully modulated tone, "It's time to go."

Time to go to see Margie one last time. John Carmody didn't hear those words either, because he was reading softly to himself. Softly, yet out loud . . . loud enough perhaps . . . "Once upon a time there was a little girl who lived in the Black Forest in a woodcutter's hut. She was so fair that the birds stopped their singing when they looked at her. Then there came a day when . . ." Reading out loud softly, yet perhaps loud enough that Margie might be able to hear. Maybe.

24

THE SINGLE LIFE: HEAVEN OR HELL?

Then the LORD *God said, "It is not good that the man should be alone; I will make him a helper fit for him."*
GENESIS 2:18

✛

A silent epidemic is sweeping the nation. It hasn't been highlighted on the evening news or chronicled in the daily papers; there are no legislatures passing laws about it and no demonstrators holding protests concerning it. But it is there and spreading, nevertheless. It is the disease of loneliness. Thus says Louise Bernikow in *Alone in America: The Search for Companionship*. She traversed this nation from Boston to Los Angeles, from Seattle to Houston. She interviewed thousands of people and concluded that she had discovered what she called "'the desert of loneliness,' a barren social wasteland filled with many people who merely exist."[1]

Furthermore, it is spreading, because loneliness begets loneliness. People tend to shy away from lonely people. It doesn't necessarily involve only the single people in this country either. Married people can be just as lonely as singles. Lying in bed with your back turned to your partner can be very, very lonely. In fact, the famed Christian psychiatrist Dr. Paul Tournier said that loneliness is the malady of our times. He writes:

> Every doctor knows what the terrible loneliness of modern man is . . . the spirit of our times tends toward isolation—isolation and mistrust. . . . The whole philosophy of our age produces in modern men an independent, possessive, and vengeful spirit that sets them against one another. It is supposed to lead them to happiness; the result is the accumulation of suffering in discord and loneliness.[2]

A Los Angeles psychiatrist said that mankind's biggest problem is simply loneliness.[3] You never read that in the newspapers. We hear about population explosions. We hear about ecological disasters. We hear about nuclear threats of annihilation. But how many times have you ever heard that man's biggest problem is loneliness? Not often, if ever, I am sure. In fact, the time in which we live has been called The Age of Loneliness.

HEAVEN OR HELL?

"The Single Life: Heaven or Hell?" That is my subject. It seems to me as I look back over a good many years of counseling, as I mentioned earlier, that about half the people I have talked to have been singles who were miserable and wanted to be married. The other half were married people who were miserable and wanted to be single. The grass always seems to be greener on the other side of the altar. What is the truth?

We certainly get a picture of marriage and the single life from the media in our culture, a picture that has drastically changed in the last few decades. Forty years ago many series on television portrayed a positive view of marriage: *Father Knows Best, Leave it to Beaver, Ozzie and Harriet,* and many others. When singles were portrayed in the movies or television, usually there was an idealistic view of romantic love, and the girl was generally being pursued to the altar.

Today it is very, very different. We practically never see a picture of a healthy family on television or in the movies. If there are pictures involving families, usually there are just bits and pieces. But if there is an entire family—one with a mother, father, and children—it is almost inevitably depicted as dysfunctional, grossly distorted, and unhappy.

Today if singles are portrayed, they are not pursuing anybody to the altar. If anything, they are running in the opposite direction. They are generally promiscuous, sex-crazed people. They meet the girl one moment, and the next moment they hop into bed.

MARRIAGE—PRESENTED AS A FAILURE

So we have a picture of marriages as complete failures, and the single life as swinging, fun, and promiscuous—a very different picture from forty years ago.

This has had an impact upon the families and singles in our society. Hollywood, as always, would deny that. They say, "We simply hold up a mirror to society and reflect what is going on." Hogwash. The truth of the matter is, they hold up a mirror to one part of society—their part—and generally it is the most degenerate and most debauched part they can find. They hold that mirror up and turn the spotlight on it long enough until—what do you know? Society begins to look more and more like that picture. Generally they hold that mirror up to the most seamy side of society, to the gutter, to the sewer, to the toilet. From the way some people talk, you would think they were brought up in a bathroom because they use toilet language constantly.

It just so happens that not everybody in this country is like that. I, for one, don't talk that way, and I have a very strong suspicion that you don't either. Why don't they hold up a mirror to that part of society? They say virtue is not interesting, vice is. They have their own agenda, and the result has been very sad. That is not to put all of the blame on Hollywood. But we also must not allow Hollywood to shrug off their responsibility. If what is on the tube does not affect the way people act, why do they spend hundreds of billions of dollars in advertising? They know they are going to affect the way people act. They know they can persuade people to buy the advertised products, and they know they can, and will, affect people's moral views and choices.

Unfortunately, in the church I think singles have often been given less attention in our great emphasis upon marriage and the family (which is, of course, vitally important). But there are many single people in our society today. Let me make it clear that almost everything I preach from the pulpit is applicable to both married and single people. Think about it. The gospel applies to both. *Everyone* needs to grow in the grace and knowledge of the Lord, learn more about the Scriptures, and learn more about how to walk with Christ. Even if I am writing or speaking particularly of marriage, most singles hope to be married someday. This will help them, perhaps, not to make a shipwreck of their marriage in the future.

THEIR OWN PARTICULAR PROBLEMS

Singles do have their own problems, which we need to address. Many of them are, indeed, very frustrated and sometimes even desperate. For example, author Ray Mossholder reveals a letter that a lady of thirty-two wrote to him. She said:

> Dear Ray,
>
> I'm going to be very honest with you. I'm in a panic. All of my close friends are married. I'm not. I'm a thirty-two-year-old secretary and have wanted to be married since I was seventeen. I have read the Yale-Harvard study on singles and know my chances for marriage seem less than the chances I'll be eaten by a

giraffe. What am I to do with the rest of my life? How am I ever going to enjoy growing old alone? Since all the guys in my age-range are taken now, shall I marry a Cub Scout or some old man or just die a lonely old maid?

Over the Hill at Thirty-two

Any ladies feel like saying amen to that? It has been said that figures don't lie, but liars do figure. Not only that, researchers make mistakes as well. Some have documented the downright fraudulent aspects of the *Kinsey Report* that were pawned off on the American public as scientific and correct. We know now they were anything but. Now researchers—even the ones involved in the famous Yale-Harvard study on singles—admit they made mistakes. Indeed they did.

Let us look at some of the statistics in our country today. Two in five adults are single—40 percent. Of that 40 percent, 56 percent of all single adults in America have never been married. How about ladies in that critical range of twenty-five to thirty-four, for whom the panic attack is coming on fast? Do they have any more chance of getting married than they do of being "eaten by a giraffe," as our thirty-two-year-old secretary said? Here are the facts. In America, among roughly 2.9 million never-married women in this country, between the ages of twenty-five and thirty-four, there are almost five million never-married men. Simply stated, for every three never-married women in America between twenty-five and thirty-four, there are five never-married men.

Why, ladies, you just died and went to heaven. Some of you are saying, "Where are they?" They are around somewhere; so you have a far better chance of marrying than of being met by a hungry giraffe. At age forty a woman who has never been married has nearly a one in four chance of being married (25 percent). If you are a forty-year-old man, the chances of your getting married are one in three (33 percent). In fact, the U.S. Census Bureau estimates that nine out of ten Americans will eventually marry. So your plight is not nearly as desperate as you think. Take heart, dear one. The Lord has not forsaken you, and you need not fear marauding giraffes.

MEDIA STEREOTYPES

Singles have been stereotyped by the media as promiscuous, bed-hopping sex fiends, though that is not the case with Christian singles. Many singles in our churches are living godly lives in spite of the temptations they face.

It is interesting, I think, that in Paul's writings to the Corinthians he refers not to married women and to singles, but rather to married women and virgins—for virtually all unmarried women in Israel were virgins. Today the rate of promiscuity in America is many times higher than in Japan, an almost completely heathen nation. How is it that they are able to control themselves and many American young people are not?

I also speak from experience. I was a non-Christian single, and then I was a Christian single for several years. I know the difference, and I know what God can do. I read of a lady in her sixties who has been a Christian most of her life. She can testify to the fact that though she has been single all of her life, God has been faithful, in spite of temptations, to enable her to live a continent life, being faithful to the Lord. She knows that God enables people to keep His commands.

Singles are sometimes stereotyped as not being mature, for if they were mature, they would be married, it is said. I'll grant that some singles are immature. But some married people were immature and ran off and got married precisely because they were immature and probably lived to rue the day.

There are also singles who are very mature. If you are going to try to stereotype singles as being immature, you have a problem. Consider Jesus. Jesus never even had a date. He never went steady. He never kissed a girl (in the sense by which we know that). He never was engaged. He never got married. He never had any children. He never had any grandchildren. Yet the whole world proclaims that He was the most mature, well-balanced, wise person who ever lived and had very positive relationships with people of both sexes. He is a model both for married people and for single people.

MARRIED COUPLES IN THE NEW TESTAMENT

One speaker to singles said that he asks groups of singles to shout out the names of married couples in the New Testament who were serving God. I did that at my church, in a contemporary service. Someone said Aquila and Priscilla, there was a long lull, then somebody came up with Joseph and Mary . . . and that was about it.

Then I asked them to shout out the names of single persons in the New Testament who were serving the Lord, and we came up with a whole list of them: Jesus, Paul, John the Baptist, John the Apostle, Titus, Timothy, Mark, Epaphroditus, Apollos, Phoebe (the deaconess of Cenchrea), Mary Magdalene, and many others. So many mature people were serving the Lord in that day. Scripture says that if a person is single, he or she has a unique opportunity to serve God.

By the way, do various passages contradict themselves? We all know that the Bible teaches it is not good for a man to be alone (Genesis 2:18). They are supposed to have a wife. Right? Wrong. The Bible never says that. "But isn't that what Genesis says?" No, it doesn't. What it says is, "Then the LORD God said, 'It is not good that the man should be alone,'" referring to Adam. I checked my Hebrew Bible, and it does have the definite article there as well. It is "the man"—Adam. "It is not good that he be alone." No truer statement has ever been said than that. If he had been alone, you and I wouldn't be here.

DIFFERENT CIRCUMSTANCES

But Paul says, "To the unmarried and the widows I say that it is good for them to remain single as I am" (1 Corinthians 7:8). Now, do these passages contradict each other? No. God was dealing with a specific circumstance of Adam. Paul also was facing specific circumstances. The persecution against Christians was just beginning to heat up, and it was going to usher in several hundred years of massive persecution, during which many Christians who were married saw their wives or husbands tortured and killed and saw their children tortured to get them to renounce and recant their faith. It was a very, very difficult time.

As a general practice, the Bible tells us that marriage is to "be held in honor among all, and let the marriage bed be undefiled" (Hebrews 13:4a). The general principle is that marriage is good and is a very important institution upon which not only the church but the nation is based. But God calls some people to singleness. In fact in 1 Corinthians 7:7 Paul says that singleness is a gift from God. Some have the gift of singleness; some have the gift of being married. Each person has his own gift. The whole monastic movement came out of the idea that Christians could serve God better if they were single.

THANK GOD FOR SINGLENESS

So I would encourage all who are single to do a number of things. One, I would encourage you to thank God and praise Him for the gift of being single. That will change your whole perspective. Some of you have been blaming Him for your singleness.

SERVING GOD

Second, I would encourage you to use your singleness as a special opportunity to serve God. You have opportunities that married people don't have, as Paul says in 1 Corinthians 7: The person who is single can give himself devotedly to the Lord; his attention is not divided. He desires to please the Lord.

The married man also wants to please the Lord, but he must also be involved with the things of this world—how he can please and care for his wife, pay for his mortgage, bring home the bacon, save for the college education of the kids, and all of the rest—things that the single person is not burdened with. So the single person has a peculiar opportunity to serve God. I would challenge you if you are unmarried to dedicate yourself, to consecrate yourself to using your singleness as a time of service to God.

Evelyn Ramsey, a physician and linguist, says: "I realize now there would have been no way I could have read the books I've read, written the words I've written, gone to the places I've gone, studied the courses I have studied, learned the languages I have learned, maintained the schedule I have maintained, mended the people I have mended—if I had been encumbered by a husband and family." She is a missionary, doctor, and linguist to the people of Papua, New Guinea, and she rejoices in the particular opportunities that have been hers in her lifetime of serving the Lord.

DEVELOPING YOUR SPECIAL GIFTS

Third, I would urge you also to develop your own particular gifts and skills and your interpersonal relationships. I have no doubt that just as there are immature married people, there are immature singles, and in the case of a single, that immaturity may very well hinder his or her getting married. I know some single people who I think would make very poor marriage partners because they are immature. It is obvious in their attempts at interpersonal relationships. They have never learned how to relate to other people. Let me say this: If you can't relate to other people as a single, you are going to have a disaster in your marriage because then you can't botch your interpersonal relationship and just walk away like a single can. You are stuck, and if you are a Christian, you are stuck for life. So you had better begin to learn how to deal with other people, to relate to other people, to develop your own character and your own interpersonal skills. That is vitally important. Maybe this is one of the things God wants you to do.

I thank God for Christian singles who are mature and are serving the Lord in wonderful ways. Single men are serving God in ways that a married person couldn't begin to. They have the time to dedicate to the service of the Lord. Single women are serving God in wonderful ways, and I thank the Lord for that. But some singles are wandering around in a fog. They have never matured or developed their own skills. If you are one of them, I would urge you to give yourself to doing that very thing.

I would urge you also not to seek to get married, not to seek a spouse. Rather, I would urge you to seek the Lord and serve Him, because that is what God wants you to do with your gift of singleness. Maybe because you haven't learned that lesson, God has not given you a spouse. But if you will do that, you will put yourself in the place where you are most likely going to meet a godly and dedicated Christian who would make a godly husband or wife for you.

TRUSTING THE LORD COMPLETELY

Finally, I would urge you to trust the Lord for His will for your life in this matter and to praise Him for whatever that may be. Whatever God commands you, He will enable you to do. If you trust Him and seek Him, He will take care of the matter of your singleness.

It occurred to me recently that when I was single, I was single, but I never ever thought about myself in that way. I was who I was. I was Jim Kennedy. I was a Christian at one point, later in my single life, and I lived as a single for a number of years.

I would urge you to identify yourself not as a single or as a married but as a believer in Jesus Christ who is completely dedicated and consecrated to Him, who doesn't have one foot in the church and one foot in the world, but whose heart is fixed with a single eye upon Christ. I would urge you to serve Him and leave the outcome to the Lord, instead of bemoaning your singleness or your married state and making a pitiful exhibition of yourself, thereby contributing to the false stereotypes.

God will bless your life. Whatever plan He has for you, He will make it a blessing to you. May God, indeed, make you, either as a single person or as a married person, one who is consecrated to Him and who is trusting Him for all things.

CONCLUSION

General William Booth, who founded the Salvation Army, had come to the end of his life. He was an old man, a great patriarch, a great spiritual statesman. Before he died he wanted to send a last communique to all of the officers in the Salvation Army. That telegram contained only one word, one word that he wanted to leave with all of those people. It was this: "Others."

Are you bored? Remember, *others*.

May this be my motto. May I live for others. May I live like Christ. You can make more friends in two months by showing an interest in others than you can in twenty years trying to make people interested in you.

CONCLUSION
WHERE THERE IS NO VISION

Where there is no vision, the people perish.
PROVERBS 29:18, KJV

⊕

As a gentleman was walking down the street, he passed a large construction project where numbers of men were laying bricks. He said to one of them, "What are you doing?"

He said, "I'm laying bricks, stupid. What does it look like I'm doing?"

He asked another man, "What are you doing?"

He replied, "I am making a wall."

He asked a third man, "What are you doing?"

He said, "I am building a magnificent cathedral to the glory of God."

What is the difference between just laying bricks and building a cathedral to the glory of God? It is *vision*—something that is essential if anything great is to be accomplished.

A BIBLICALLY-INFORMED VIEW OF THE WORLD

If we are to have a truly Christian world-and-life view, we need to have a biblically-informed view of the world. That's what this book has been all about. Many Christians today need to have a vision—one informed by the Bible. We need a biblical perspective on:

• our origins. Do we have a noble origin and a noble destiny, or are we just accidental twigs?

• how we view human life. If we are just accidental twigs, then who cares if Stalin kills tens of millions of human beings, provided he's helping evolution along?

- how we educate our children.
- what principles we apply to government and the economy.
- how Christians live, individually and corporately.
- how we live in our families. Or even more basic: what is a family?

In short, Christians need to drop the compartmentalized view of Christianity that has gripped so many in our culture today. We need to recognize that this is our Father's world, He is its Lord, and we need to redeem as much of it as we can while there is yet time.

Some will object to the idea that He is indeed Lord of all or that any part of our culture or nation can be redeemed. They will say that prophecy demands that the world will get worse and worse until the end. Of course, this could also be self-fulfilling prophecy. Virtually every generation since Christ's first advent thought they would be the ones to experience His second coming. We don't know when Jesus Christ will return. But we must stop treating involvement in this world as if we are just polishing the brass on a sinking *Titanic*. We are to do more than that. He Himself told us to "occupy" until He comes (Luke 19:13, KJV).

Today it would seem that many evangelicals have abandoned their role as salt and light in society because they are sure Christ is coming back in their lifetime. They are convinced that ours is the generation that will see the return of Jesus. Listen to what David Moore, pastor of the popular Southwest Community Church and author of *Five Lies of the Century*, says about the Second Coming and our nation's future if the present trends continue. During one of the Reclaiming America for Christ conferences, we interviewed him for *The Coral Ridge Hour*. When asked, "Can we reclaim America for Christ?" he replied:

> I certainly hope so. The reason that I invest some of my time and energy in this arena is because I believe it's a winnable battle, and I wouldn't give a chunk of my life to something that's over. I'm always concerned about the pastors who will preach with the spirit of, "Well, you know, we're the last faithful twelve, and it's over, and we've given away the country. And we just have to wait for Jesus to come and rescue us." Well, He's going to return, and He will rescue us in His time. But what if it's a hundred years [from now]? What if it's 500 years? What kind of world do I want my children in? What kind of world do I want my grandchildren raised in? And if I don't get involved to tell the truth and be involved and to impact politics and use the little sphere of influence that I have for something that's wholesome, my grandkids may wonder why I gave away the farm.[1]

VISION

Again, the Bible says, "Where there is no vision, the people perish." Vision is absolutely essential if any great undertaking is to come to pass. Vision is essential if we are to have a purpose; purpose grows out of vision. Do you have a great vision as to what your life is endeavoring to accomplish? Do you have a purpose in mind, a purpose in heart that comes from such a vision?

• a vision that grasps your soul with fingers of steel and will not let you go.

• a vision that focuses your mind just as a magnifying glass focuses the rays of the sun.

• a vision that inflames your heart with a blue-white flame.

• a vision that gives purpose and meaning and direction to all that you do in life.

Or do you live your life simply because every morning you just seem to wake up again, and here you are, and you will try to get through one more day? How important spiritual vision is. "Where there is no vision, the people perish." Though they may not die physically, they become part of the walking dead who have no vision or purpose for life.

People must wonder sometimes what the church is all about. What are they trying to do? What are they up to?

Years ago when the church I pastor was in a smaller location, we did not have large narthexes—the people had to line up outside in the hot sun, and sometimes the line would extend for a block. Someone driving by in a car was overheard saying, "They must be giving away something free in there." Actually, he wasn't far wrong; that *is* what we were doing. In the name of Christ, we were giving away the gift of eternal life.

About fifty years ago I was called to start our church, which began as a mission to a largely unpopulated area. I came with vision. I mentioned it to a handful of people sitting in a hot elementary school cafetorium (that's a cross between a cafeteria and an auditorium). I said, "We can change the world." I must confess I am sure they all probably thought I was mad, but that vision persists down through all these years.

I think it is vital that each one of us have some idea of what God's vision for our life is. We are not free merely to choose our own; we are Christians. We are bought with a price. We have a Master and a Lord whom we serve. What is His vision for us? What would He have us become in this life? Vision gives significance, value, and meaning to our very existence. The vision God has given to us in His overall vision or revelation of the Scripture is very clear: We are to reach the world for Christ.

I would add two explanatory notes to that. We are not merely to reach the world for Christ, but we are to transform it by the power of His gospel and His Holy Spirit. Secondly, we are to transform not only individuals, but also the societies in which we live. For example, if we are to be successful in the work Christ has given us in this country, we will not only bring men and women to Christ:

• We will change the very institutions of the nation, so that millions of babies will not be slaughtered before they see the light of day.

• We will see to it that pornography and prostitution and every manner of vileness will not be flaunted before the eyes of our young people in this nation.

• We will strive toward having the worst evils removed.

And by doing this, Christ will be glorified in the land. After all, He is Lord of all, and He is the one who should receive the glory for what goes on in this world. That is my goal. That is the goal of my church. I hope that it is your goal.

KINGDOM OF SELF

Perhaps the most discouraging thing I have faced along the way has not been the onslaught of the world, it has not been the vicious articles that have been written, and it has not been the atheists whom I have debated. The most discouraging and surprising thing to me was to find out that even some who are Christians do not share these goals. I guess I was very naive to suppose that everyone who came to know the Lord Jesus Christ would be vitally concerned to make Him known to others as far as they could possibly reach.

However, I have discovered that is not the case, and there are many people who could care less what happens to the world. They don't care about lost people in India or China or Africa. They don't care about the many millions of babies who have been killed. They don't care about the great social ills that have plagued our country. They don't care about any of these things. All they want is something for themselves—to make them feel good, to make them be able to function a little better. That has come as a big surprise to me.

I said I was naive, and surely I was. I should have known that selfishness does not cease automatically when one comes to Christ or joins the church. That is probably the church of Jesus Christ's greatest problem throughout the world. Everywhere we see that the work of Christ is stymied by human selfishness.

Selfishness is the very essence of sin. If the outer husks of sin were stripped off, we would finally get down to the kernel, which is selfishness. That is where people live their lives. All they do, they do for the kingdom of self—for themselves. What they can gather, what they can enjoy—that is the kingdom they are interested in. "My wife and I, our daughter Sue, and my son John—us four, no more. The rest of the world can literally go to hell." I thought that perhaps when people came to know Christ, it would automatically be different. After all, Christ

- is the altogether selfless one;
- laid aside the glory of heaven;
- came out from His Father's palace and into this world of woe;
- went about doing good;
- cared not about building anything for Himself but ceaselessly sought

to bring others to know the Father and to receive eternal life.

I thought that spirit would be dominant in the church. I was wrong. That is not necessarily the case.

Take Up His Cross

May I say that the very essence of being like Christ is to be crucified with Him; it is to lay down our lives for His sake. It is to take up His cross and follow Him. As long as we are living self-centered lives, we are antitheses of what Christians ought to be.

I am reminded of Edith (not her real name), a very self-centered lady. Someone commented that Edith was like a small country bounded on the north, south, east, and west by Edith. She was her whole world. Everything revolved around her, and she was not interested in anything else.

What really dominates and motivates our lives? Do we have the selfless spirit of Christ, or is the essence of sin—selfishness—still coiled like a poisonous serpent deep in our souls? It may have been baptized and confirmed; it may have taken upon itself the name of Christian. Whether in the church or out of the church, it is the same ugly and heinous thing. It is that which is hated by God. It is the essence of our rebellion against the Almighty.

Whether we think of Lucifer, who said, "I will be like God and will sit on the top of the mountain," or of Eve, who took the fatal fruit of the forbidden tree and said in effect, "It looks good to me, and I think it will taste good. It will make me feel good, and I don't care about anything else," it is the same basic sin. However, you dress it up or whatever you call it, selfishness is absolutely antithetical to the spirit of Christ. Jesus calls us to lay down our lives and take up our cross, and that is the end of selfishness.

The French have a disease they say is pandemic in the world. It is called *la maladie du moi*, "the malady of the self"; it is me-sickness. The me generation has not ended; it still goes on. Charles Kingsley once wrote: "If you wish to be miserable, think about yourself, what you want, what you need, what you like—you can be as wretched as you choose."[2]

God knows that in dying to self we learn to live. There is no other way. That lesson is so important that God carved it into the very topography of the Holy Land, in the Sea of Galilee and the Dead Sea. Someone put it to poetry:

> *I looked upon a sea and lo 'twas dead,*
> *Although by Hermon's snow and Jordan fed.*
> *How came a fate so dire? The tale soon told—*
> *All that it got it kept and fast did hold.*
> *All tributary streams found here their grave*
> *Because that sea received but never gave.*
> *O sea that's dead, teach me to know and feel*
> *That selfish grasp my doom shall seal.*
> *And help me, Lord, myself, my best to give*
> *That I may others bless, and like Thee live.*

OUR VISION

Christ is the altogether lovely one. It should be the great passion and zeal, the consuming vision of our hearts, that Jesus Christ be known throughout all of the earth, and that everywhere He might be trusted and loved and served. That is the vision of the church I pastor, and, I hope, of yours as well. That is the vision and the purpose and the goal of my heart. I hope it is of yours also. I hope that vision will grasp your soul and never let it go. I hope you will give whatever strength or power or wealth or influence or ability you have to see that Christ's name is known in every clime, in every nation throughout all of this earth—that His name might be exalted upon this world that He has made, that men and women and children around the globe will bow to this wonderful Lord.

I hope you will be loyal to that vision and will never let it go. This is the reason for our existence—that we might glorify Him; that we might know Him and make Him known; that we might enjoy Him forevermore. What a glorious vision that is. What a wondrous task Christ has given to us.

If your life would have meaning, if your life would have significance and purpose and reason for its existence, then take hold of that vision, become a part of that dream, lay hold on that purpose, and God will give you an intensity and a zeal that will make your life meaningful and will cause you to tingle right down to your toes.

"Where there is no vision, the people perish." May God grant to all of us the vision that people throughout the entire world may not perish because they have heard through our efforts, through our faithfulness, the glad tidings of eternal life from the King of kings, the Lord of all.

Soli Deo gloria.

NOTES

INTRODUCTION

1. Charles Colson and Nancy Pearcey, *How Now Shall We Live?* (Wheaton, IL: Tyndale House, 1999), 20.
2. Robert B. Reich, "The Last Word: Bush's God," *The American Prospect*, June 17, 2004.
3. For example, Paul Johnson, the great historian, says the twentieth-century state has "proved itself the great killer of all time." *Modern Times* (New York: Harper and Row, 1983), 729.
4. Quoted in Gary DeMar, *Thinking Straight in a Crooked World* (Powder Springs, GA: American Vision, 2001), 19.
5. Colson and Pearcey, *How Now Shall We Live?*, 17.
6. Ibid., 14.
7. John J. Dunphy, "Religion for a New Age," *The Humanist*, January/February 1983, 26.
8. See Gary DeMar, *Thinking Straight in a Crooked World*.
9. H. G. Wells, quoted in ibid., 50-51.
10. Gary DeMar, *War of the Worldviews* (Powder Springs, GA: American Vision, 1994), 19.
11. Jean Paul Sartre, quoted in ibid.
12. DeMar, ibid., 31.
13. Albert Camus, in ibid., 20.
14. Samuel Beckett, quoted in Richard Coe, *Samuel Beckett* (New York: Grove Press, 1964), 18, quoted in ibid., 18.
15. H. J. Blackham, quoted in DeMar, *War of the Worldviews*, 17.
16. Bertrand Russell, *Why I Am Not a Christian* (New York: Clarion, Simon and Schuster, 1957), 107.
17. Abraham Kuyper, *You Can Do Greater Things Than Christ*, trans. Jan H. Boer (Jos, Nigeria: Institute of Church and Society, 1991), 74. This comes from the first volume of Kuyper's book, which was first published as *Pro Rege, of Het Koningschap van Christus* in 1911.

CHAPTER 1: THE ROOT OF THE PROBLEM

1. John Lenczowski, "The Treason of the Intellectuals: Higher Education, the Culture War and the Threat to U.S. National Security," *Policy Counsel* (Fall 1996), 45.
2. Ernest Gordon, et al., "Is Baer Right?" *Christianity Today*, February 17, 1984, 18.
3. Fyodor Dostoevsky, *The Brothers Karamazov*, trans. Andrew H. MacAndrew (Toronto: Bantam Books, 1970), Book XI, Chapter 8, 760.
4. Justice William Brennan, for the majority, U.S. Supreme Court, *Stone v. Graham*, 1980.
5. Elizabeth Mehren, "Humans a Mere Afterthought, Evolutionist Says," *The Cleveland Plain Dealer*, December 17, 1989.
6. Fred Hoyle, *The Big Bang in Astronomy*, 527, quoted in Henry M. Morris, *Evolution in Turmoil: An Updated Sequel to the Troubled Waters of Evolution* (San Diego, CA: Creation-Life Publishers, 1982), 29.
7. Adolf Hitler, *Mein Kampf* (Boston: Houghton Mifflin, 1971), 288, 290, quoted in *The Christian News* (New Haven, MO), October 23, 1989, 11.
8. Adolf Hitler, *Mein Kampf*, trans. James Murphy, Chapter XI, "Race and People," http://gutenerg.net.au/ebooks02/0200601.txt.
9. Stephane Courtois, Nicolas Werth, Jean-Louis Panne, Andrzej Paczkowski, Karel Bartosek, and Jean-Louis Margolin, *The Black Book of Communism*, trans. Jonathan Murphy and Mark Kramer (Cambridge, Mass: Harvard University Press, 1999), 4.

10. Anton Pannekoek, *Marxism and Darwinism,* trans. Nathan Weiser (Chicago: Charles H. Kerr & Company, 1909/1912); www.marxists.org/archive/pannekoe/works/1912-dar.htm.

11. Ian Taylor, *In the Minds of Men: Darwin and the New World Order* (Toronto: TFE Publishing, 1984), 411.

12. Arthur Keith, *Evolution and Ethics* (New York: G. P. Putnam's Sons, 1947), 15.

13. Paul Lemoine, *Encyclopedie Francaise,* 1950s, Vol. 5, quoted at www.talkorigins.org/faqs/ce/3/part12.html.

14. Jean Rostand, *Age Nouveau* (a French periodical), February 1959, 12, quoted in ibid.

CHAPTER 2: "THIS IS MY AMOEBA'S WORLD"

1. Arthur Guiterman, "Ode to the Amoeba," reproduced at www.anagrammy.com/literary/rg/poems-rg11.html.

2. Clarence Darrow, quoted in Norman L. Geisler (in collaboration with A. F. Brooke II and Mark J. Keough), *The Creator in the Courtroom: "Scopes II"* (Milford, MI: Mott Media, 1982), 11.

3. This is found in a footnote of the U.S. Supreme Court decision of *Torcaso v. Watkins,* 1961.

4. H. S. Lipson, "A Physicist Looks at Evolution," *Physics Bulletin* (Vol. 31, 1980).

5. Charles Darwin, *On the Origin of the Species,* 1859, in William J. Federer, ed., *Library of Classics,* 2002, a CD-ROM.

6. Quoted in Henry Morris, *Men of God—Men of Science* (San Diego: Master Books, 1984), 35.

7. Ibid., 89.

8. Rene Vallery-Radot, *The Life of Pasteur,* trans. R. L. Devonshire (Garden City, NY: Doubleday, Page and Company, 1923), 462.

9. Quoted in *Heroes of History,* Vol. 4 (West Frankfort, IL: Caleb Publishers, 1992), 36.

10. Ibid., 34.

11. Morris, *Men of God—Men of Science,* 34-35.

12. Ian Taylor, *In the Minds of Men: Darwin and the New World Order* (Toronto: TFE Publishing, 1984), 49.

13. H. W. Buxton, *Memoirs of the Life and Labours of the Charles Babbage ESQ. F.R.S.,* Vol. 13 (Cambridge, MA and Los Angeles: The MIT Press & Thomas Publishers, 1988), 316.

14. Morris, *Men of God—Men of Science,* 56.

15. Taylor, *In the Minds of Men,* 160-161.

16. Ibid., 350.

17. Frances Leigh Williams, *Matthew Fontaine Maury, Scientist of the Sea* (New Brunswick, NJ: Rutgers University Press, 1963), 340.

18. James M. Houston, ed., *The Mind on Fire: An Anthology of the Writings of Blaise Pascal* (Portland: Multnomah, 1989), 147.

19. Will and Ariel Durant, *The Age of Voltaire; The Story of Civilization,* Vol. 9 (New York: Simon & Schuster, 1965), 561.

20. Stephen Jay Gould, *Dinosaur in a Haystack: Reflections in Natural History* (New York: Harmony Books, 1995), 422.

21. For this list of Christian scientists, we are indebted to Henry Morris, *The Biblical Basis for Modern Science* (Grand Rapids: Baker, 1984), 463-465.

22. "Iconoclast of the Century: Charles Darwin (1809-1882)," *Time* magazine, December 31, 1999, quoted in Lee Strobel, *The Case for a Creator* (Grand Rapids, MI: Zondervan, 2004), 24.

CHAPTER 3: THE COLLAPSE OF EVOLUTION

1. *Webster's Collegiate Dictionary,* Fifth Edition (Springfield, Mass.: G. & C. Merriam, 1941), 753.

2. Charles Darwin, Introduction, *On the Origin of the Species,* 1859, in William J. Federer, ed., *Library of Classics* (St. Louis: Amerisearch Inc., 2002), a CD-ROM.

3. Transcript of an interview with Jonathan Wells on location in Seattle, WA (Ft. Lauderdale, FL: Coral Ridge Ministries-TV, March 2004).

4. Ibid.

5. Ibid.

6. Ibid.

7. Darwin, *On the Origin of the Species,* Chapter VI, under the subheading "Modes of Transition," CD-ROM.

8. Michael Denton, *Evolution: A Theory in Crisis* (Chevy Chase, MD: Adler and Adler, 1986), 162, quoted in Strobel, *The Case for a Creator,* 56.

9. Stephen Jay Gould, quoted in "Evolution of Evolution," *The Bible-Science Newsletter,* July 1981, 5.

10. Stephen Jay Gould, "Evolution's Erratic Pace," *Natural History,* May 1977.

11. Ibid.

12. Transcript of an interview with Stephen Meyer on location in Seattle, Washington (Ft. Lauderdale, FL: Coral Ridge Ministries-TV, 2004).

13. Interview with Wells, Coral Ridge Ministries-TV.

14. Jonathan Wells, *Icons of Evolution: Science or Myth? Why Much of What We Teach About Evolution Is Wrong* (Washington, D.C.: Regnery Publishing, 2000), 82-83.

15. Interview with Wells, Coral Ridge Ministries-TV.

16. Stephen Jay Gould in a response to Michael Behe (*New York Times,* August 13, 1999), in *Natural History* magazine, March 2000. Quoted in Wells, *Icons of Evolution,* 108.

17. Gould, quoted in ibid., 109.

18. Interview with Wells, Coral Ridge Ministries-TV.

19. Ibid.

20. Interview with Meyer, Coral Ridge Ministries-TV.

21. Interview with Wells, Coral Ridge Ministries-TV.

22. Ibid.

23. Stephen Jay Gould, February 15, 1980, quoted in "Evolution of Evolution," 6.

24. Interview with Michael Behe, on location in Bethlehem, PA (Ft. Lauderdale, FL: Coral Ridge Ministries-TV, 1998).

25. Ibid.

26. Interview with Meyer, Coral Ridge Ministries-TV.

27. All quotes from Richard Lumsden come from an interview and segment on Dr. Lumsden's testimony (Ft. Lauderdale, FL: Coral Ridge Ministries-TV, September 1996).

CHAPTER 4: A NOBLE ORIGIN, A NOBLE DESTINY

1. Transcript from an interview with Jonathan Wells on location in Seattle, Washington (Ft. Lauderdale, FL: Coral Ridge Ministries-TV, March 2004).

2. L. H. Matthews, "Introduction," Charles Darwin, *Origin of Species* (London: J.M. Dent and Sons, Ltd., 1971), x-xi, quoted in Luther D. Sunderland, *Darwin's Enigma: Fossils and Other Problems* (San Diego, CA: Master Books, 1984), 30-31.

3. Bertrand Russell, quoted in Oliver R. Blosser, "Why Creation Is Superior to Evolution in the Education of Children," *CEA Update* (Pine River, WI: Creation Education Association), January/February 1990.

4. Ernst Mayr, "Evolution," *Scientific American* (Vol. 239, September 1978), 47.

5. Rene Dubos, quoted in ibid.

6. Julien Offray de la Mettrie, quoted in Erwin W. Lutzer, *Exploding the Myths That Could Destroy America* (Chicago: Moody Press, 1986), 52.

7. Bertrand Russell, *Why I Am Not a Christian* (New York: Clarion, Simon and Schuster, 1957), 107.

8. Oliver Wendell Holmes, quoted in Lutzer, *Exploding the Myths,* 55.

9. Lutzer, *Exploding the Myths That Could Destroy America,* 42.

10. George Orwell, *1984,* quoted in John Whitehead, *The End of Man* (Wheaton, IL: Crossway Books, 1986), 201.

11. Hal Higdon, *The Crime of the Century: The Leopold and Loeb Case* (New York: G. P Putnam's Sons, 1975), 20.

12. Wolf Larson, quoted in ibid., 29.

13. Quoted in John Whitehead, *The Second American Revolution* (Elgin, IL: David C. Cook, 1982), 52.

14. Zig Ziglar, *See You at the Top* (Gretna, LA: Pelican, 1977), 57.

15. B.F. Skinner, quoted in ibid., 135.

16. Francis Schaeffer, *Back to Freedom and Dignity* (Downers Grove, IL: InterVarsity Press, 1972), p. 23, quoted in ibid., 144.

17. W. O. Saunders, quoted in Earle Albert Rowell, *Prophecy Speaks: Dissolving Doubts* (Hagerstown, MD: Review and Herald Publishing Association, 1933), 112-113.

18. Technically, it states: "All hope abandon, ye who enter here." Dante, *Inferno*, Canto III, Line 9, quoted in John Bartlett, *Familiar Quotations*, 1020. In another translation, it states: "No room for hope, when you enter this place."

19. Robert Ingersoll, quoted in Rowell, *Prophecy Speaks: Dissolving Doubts*, 112-113.

CHAPTER 5: THE BIBLE AND LIFE

1. Mother Teresa, "Whatsoever You Do . . ." Speech to the National Prayer Breakfast, Washington, DC, February 3, 1994, www.priestsforlife.org/brochures/mtspeech.html.

2. www.inthefaith.com/archives/001330.php.

3. Warren Throckmorton, "I Had An Abortion," August 15, 2004. www.townhall.com/columnists/GuestColumns/Throckmorton20040815.shtml.

4. Helga Kuhse, cited in Rita Marker, *Deadly Compassion: The Death of Ann Humphry and the Truth About Euthanasia* (New York: William Morrow, 1993), 94.

5. www.punkvoter.com/guest/guest_detail.php?GuestColumnID=17.

6. Cal Thomas, *Uncommon Sense* (Brentwood, TN: Wolgemuth & Hyatt, 1990), 5.

7. William J. Brennan, *The Abortion Holocaust* (St. Louis: Landmark Press, 1983), 123.

8. Byron White, dissent in *Roe v. Wade,* U.S. Supreme Court, January 22, 1973.

9. Transcript of an interview with Michael Farris on location in Washington, DC (Ft. Lauderdale, FL: Coral Ridge Ministries-TV, 1996).

10. Norma McCorvey with Gary Thomas, *Won by Love* (Nashville: Thomas Nelson, 1997).

11. Transcript of an interview with U.S. Representative Charles Canady on location in Washington, DC (Ft. Lauderdale, FL: Coral Ridge Ministries-TV, 1996).

12. Transcript of an interview with Brenda Shafer on location in Las Vegas, Nevada (Ft. Lauderdale, FL: Coral Ridge Ministries-TV, 2000).

13. Ibid.

14. Transcript of an interview with U.S. Representative Thomas Coburn, M.D., on location in Washington, DC (Ft. Lauderdale, FL: Coral Ridge Ministries-TV, 1996).

15. Transcript of an interview with U.S. Representative Bart Stupak on location in Washington, DC (Ft. Lauderdale, FL: Coral Ridge Ministries-TV, 1996).

16. Interview with Shafer, Coral Ridge Ministries-TV.

17. Ibid.

18. Ibid.

19. Ibid.

20. Ibid.

21. Ibid.

CHAPTER 6: LESSONS FROM THE NAZIS REGARDING HUMAN LIFE

1. Adolf Hitler, quoted in Tom Dowley, gen. ed., *A Lion Handbook: The History of Christianity* (Oxford, England: Lion, 1977, rev. 1990), 589-590.

2. Heinrich Himmler, quoted in ibid., 600.

3. William L. Shirer, *The Rise and Fall of the Third Reich* (New York: Simon and Schuster, 1960), 240.

4. Adolf Hitler, quoted in Armin Robinson, ed., *The Ten Commandments: Ten Short Novels*

of Hitler's War Against the Moral Code, with a Preface by Herman Rauschning (New York: Simon and Schuster, 1943), xi.

5. Bertrand Russell, *Why I Am Not a Christian* (New York: Clarion, Simon and Schuster, 1957), 193.

6. C. Everett Koop, quoted in Ronald Reagan, *Abortion and the Conscience of the Nation* (Nashville: Thomas Nelson, 1984), 61-63.

7. Leo Alexander, quoted in ibid., 64.

8. Koop, quoted in ibid., 70.

9. Malcolm Muggeridge, quoted in ibid., 83.

10. Ibid., 86 (emphasis his).

11. Ibid., 88-89.

12. William J. Brennan in D. James Kennedy, "Who Lives? Who Dies? Who Cares?" *The Coral Ridge Hour* (Ft. Lauderdale, FL: Coral Ridge Ministries-TV, 1995).

13. William Brennan, *Dehumanizing the Vulnerable: When Word Games Take Lives* (Chicago: Loyola University Press, 1995).

14. William J. Brennan, *The Abortion Holocaust: Today's Final Solution* (St. Louis: Landmark Press, 1983).

15. William Brennan, "Who Lives? Who Dies? Who Cares?"

16. Ibid.

17. Ibid.

18. Ibid.

19. Hugh Gallagher, quoted in ibid.

20. Ibid.

21. Brennan, in ibid.

22. Brennan, *Dehumanizing the Vulnerable*, 70 (emphasis his).

23. Adolf Hitler, quoted in ibid., 6.

24. German Supreme Court, quoted in ibid., 7.

Chapter 7: Cloning and the Stem-Cell Research Debate

1. Transcript from an interview with Wesley J. Smith (Ft. Lauderdale, FL: Coral Ridge Ministries-TV), 2002.

2. Transcript from an interview with Alexander Morgan Capron on location in greater Los Angeles (Ft. Lauderdale, FL: Coral Ridge Ministries-TV), 2002.

3. Ibid.

4. Transcript from an interview with Scott Rae on location in greater Los Angeles (Ft. Lauderdale, FL: Coral Ridge Ministries-TV), 2002.

5. Ibid.

6. Interview with Capron, Coral Ridge Ministries-TV.

7. Transcript of an interview with Robert Evans (Ft. Lauderdale, FL: Coral Ridge Ministries-TV), 2002.

8. Interview with Capron, Coral Ridge Ministries-TV.

9. Interview with Evans, Coral Ridge Ministries-TV.

10. Interview with Smith, Coral Ridge Ministries-TV.

11. Tony Perkins, Family Research Council press release, Washington, DC, July 15, 2004.

12. Claudia Kalb and Debra Rosenberg, "Stem Cell Division," *Newsweek*, October 25, 2004, 46.

13. Interview with Capron, Coral Ridge Ministries-TV.

14. Ibid.

15. Transcript of an interview with David Prentice (Ft. Lauderdale, FL: Coral Ridge Ministries-TV, 2002).

16. Transcript of an interview with Jim Branham (Ft. Lauderdale, FL: Coral Ridge Ministries-TV, 2002).

17. Ibid.

18. Transcript of an interview with Marc Hedrick (Ft. Lauderdale, FL: Coral Ridge Ministries-TV, 2002).
19. Ibid.
20. Ibid.
21. Interview with Smith, Coral Ridge Ministries-TV.
22. Ibid.
23. Interview with Hedrick, Coral Ridge Ministries-TV.

CHAPTER 8: SUICIDE IS NOT A VIABLE OPTION

1. Charles Krauthammer, "The Netherlands Experience," *Human Events*, November 9, 1991.
2. Francis Schaeffer and C. Everett Koop, *Whatever Happened to the Human Race?* (Old Tappan, NJ: Revell, 1978), pp. 89-90, quoted in Joyce Ann Schofield, "Care of the Older Person: The Ethical Challenge to American Medicine," *Issues in Law & Medicine*, Vol. 4, No. 1, Summer 1988, 55-56.
3. Krauthammer, "The Netherlands Experience."
4. Leon Kass, quoted in ibid., 18.
5. Charles Hodge, *Systematic Theology*, 3 vols., (Grand Rapids, MI: Eerdmans, 1952), 3:367.
6. *Time* magazine, March 19, 1990, 70.

CHAPTER 9: A CHRISTIAN VIEW OF POLITICS

1. George Washington, quoted in http://ilovefreedom.com/quotations/George_Washington.htm.
2. Catherine Drinker Bowen, *Miracle at Philadelphia: The Story of the Constitutional Convention May to September 1787* (Boston: An Atlantic Monthly Press Book, a division of Little, Brown and Company, 1966/1986), 61.
3. Abraham Kuyper, quoted on http://en.thinkexist.com/keyword/square_inch/.
4. Ben Franklin, speech on June 28, 1787, before the Constitutional Convention. See David Gibbs and Jerry Newcombe, *One Nation Under God* (Seminole, FL: Christian Law Association, 2002) for the speech.

CHAPTER 10: CHRISTIAN STATESMANSHIP

1. Speech to the Delaware chiefs, May 12, 1779, in George Washington, *Writings* (New York: Library Classics of the United States, 1997), 351.
2. Martin Luther King, Jr., *The Wisdom of Martin Luther King in His Own Words*, edited by the staff of Bill Adler Books (New York: Lancer Books, 1968), 106.
3. Abraham Kuyper, "Calvinism and Politics," The Stone Lectures, 78; www.kuyper.org/stone/lecture3.html.
4. James Madison, *Federalist #51*, quoted in John Eidsmoe, *Christianity and the Constitution* (Grand Rapids, MI: Baker, 1987), 102.
5. Karl Marx, *The Communist Manifesto*, trans. Samuel Moore (Chicago: Henry Regnery Company, 1948, 1969), 56-57.
6. For example, Stalin killed between 40,000,000 and 60,000,000 people. Mao killed about 72,000,000 people. See D. James Kennedy and Jerry Newcombe, *What If Jesus Had Never Been Born?* (Nashville: Thomas Nelson, 1994), 234-237.
7. Frederica Mathewes-Green, "The Genoveses Find God," *National Review*, February 24, 1997, 56.
8. Paul Johnson, *Modern Times* (New York: Harper and Row, 1983), 729.

CHAPTER 11: A NATION BUILT ON CHRISTIAN PRINCIPLES

1. *Church of the Holy Trinity v. the United States*. No. 143, Supreme Court of the United States 143 U.S. 457, 36 L.Ed. 226, 12 S.Ct. 511, February 29, 1892.
2. Ibid.
3. *Time* magazine, January 30, 1995.
4. *Church of the Holy Trinity v. the United States*.

5. John Eidsmoe, *Columbus & Cortez: Conquerors for Christ* (Green Forest, AR: New Leaf Press, 1992), 90.
6. *Church of the Holy Trinity v. the United States.*
7. Quoted in David J. Brewer, *The United States: A Christian Nation* (Smyrna, GA: American Vision, 1905/1996), 15.
8. The Charter of Maryland, 1632. See www.yale.edu/lawweb/avalon/states/ma01.htm.
9. Brewer, *The United States*, 16.
10. Ibid.
11. *Church of the Holy Trinity v. the United States.*
12. *The World Almanac and Book of Facts 2001* (New York: World Almanac, 2001), 457.
13. *Church of the Holy Trinity v. the United States.*
14. Ibid.
15. Ibid.
16. Ibid.
17. Ibid.
18. Fyodor Dostoevsky, *The Brothers Karamazov*, trans. Andrew H. MacAndrew (Toronto: Bantam Books, 1970), Book II, Chapter 6, 80.
19. This statement echoes a sentence from the Northwest Ordinance, which we shall explore in the first chapter in the Education section of this book.
20. Dostoevsky, *The Brothers Karamazov*, 80.
21. Ibid.
22. Ibid.
23. Ibid.
24. Ibid.
25. George Bancroft, *History of the United States of America, from the Discovery of the Continent*, 6 vols. (New York: D. Appleton and Company, 1859/1890), 1:294.
26. Ibid.
27. Norine Dickson Campbell, *Patrick Henry: Patriot and Statesman* (Old Greenwich, CT: Devin Adair, 1969/1975), 99-100.
28. Bancroft, *History of the United States of America*, 1:295.
29. John F. Kennedy, Inaugural Address, January 20, 1961, quoted in Caroline Thomas Harnsberger, ed., *Treasury of Presidential Quotations* (Chicago: Follett, 1964), 20.

CHAPTER 12: THE BIBLE AND THE ECONOMY

1. *The Cheapskate Monthly* (P.O. Box 2135, Paramount, CA 90723) is a newsletter published to encourage financial confidence and responsible spending.
2. Mary Hunt, *The Financially Confident Woman* (Nashville: Broadman & Holman, 1996), 19.
3. Barbara Dafoe Whitehead, "Dan Quayle Was Right," *The Atlantic*, Vol. 271, No. 4, April 1993, cover story.
4. The year of this particular statistic, which comes from the Food and Nutrition Service, U.S. Department of Agriculture, is 1999. *The World Almanac and Book of Facts 2001* (Mahwah, NJ: World Almanac Books, 2001), 155.
5. These statistics apply to Fiscal 2000. Financial Management Service, U.S. Dept. of the Treasury, cited in ibid., 127-128.
6. Dr. Frank Wright, former Director of the D. James Kennedy Center for Christian Statesmanship and current Director of the National Religious Broadcasters (the NRB), who earned his Ph.D. in economics, points out that not all of what we could call "social spending" is transfer payments. He writes, "A workable definition of transfer payments would be: money given by the government to its citizens. Examples would include Social Security, unemployment compensation, welfare, and disability payments. The determining factor would seem to be direct payments made to individuals. Broad-based public health expenditures, trust fund payments, and administrative expenses might be examples of the

true costs of a welfare state, but they would likely not be counted as transfer payments." Source: E-mail to Jerry Newcombe, January 3, 2003.

7. Cheryl Wetzstein, "Welfare Study Shows Ideas Changing," *The Washington Times, National Weekly Edition,* November 25-December 1, 2002, 14.

8. The exact source of this quote is unknown. An exhaustive search through the writings of Alexis de Tocqueville, one of those to whom this is commonly attributed, yields no results. Sometimes this quote is attributed to Alexander Tytler, who later became Lord Alexander Fraser Woodhouselee, in his book *The Decline and Fall of the Athenian Republic.* One Internet source lists the quote this way: "A democracy can not exist as a permanent form of government. It can only exist until the voters discover that they can vote themselves largesse from the Public Treasury . . . with the result that a democracy always collapses over loose fiscal policy"; www.freedonia.org/spectre.html.

9. Transcript from a Coral Ridge Ministries TV interview with Star Parker, February 27, 1998.

10. Quoted in a George Grant book review of Star Parker and Lorenzo Benet, *Pimps, Whores, and Welfare Brats,* World Magazine, March 15, 1997, 24.

PART IV: THE SPHERE OF THE SCHOOL

1. Dr. James Dobson and Gary L. Bauer, *Children at Risk: The Battle for the Hearts and Minds of Our Kids* (Dallas: Word, 1990), 35.

CHAPTER 13: A TEACHING RELIGION

1. Michael Weisskopf, *Washington Post,* February 1, 1993 (emphasis ours).

2. Andy Rooney, remarks at Tufts University, November 18, 2004; www.tuftsdaily.com/vnews/display.vART/2004/11/19/419d9928aafe0.

3. John Eidsmoe, *Christianity and the Constitution: The Faith of Our Founding Fathers* (Grand Rapids, MI: Baker, 1987), 22.

4. Loraine Boettner, *The Reformed Doctrine of Predestination* (Philadelphia: Presbyterian and Reformed, 1975), 396.

5. Here is the alphabet as presented in the *New England Primer,* first published in 1692. Please note that some letters and spellings are different from modern English.

A In ADAM'S Fall
  We sinned all.

B Heaven to find;
  The Bible Mind.

C Christ crucify'd
  For sinners dy'd.

D The Deluge drown'd
  The Earth around.

E ELIJAH hid
  By Ravens fed.

F The judgment made
  FELIX afraid.

G As runs the Glass,
  Our Life doth pass.

H My Book and Heart
  Must never part.

J JOB feels the Rod,—
  Yet blesses GOD.

K Proud Korah's troop
  Was swallowed up.

L LOT fled to Zoar,
  Saw fiery shower on Sodom pour.

M MOSES was he who Israel's Host
  Led thro' the Sea.

N NOAH did view
  The old world & new.

O Young OBADIAS, DAVID, JOSIAS,
  All were pious.

P PETER deny'd
  His Lord and cry'd.

Q Queen ESTHER sues
  And saves the Jews.

R Young pious RUTH,
  Left all for Truth.

S Young SAM'L dear,
  The Lord did fear.

T Young TIMOTHY
  Learnt sin to fly.

V VASHTI for Pride
  Was set aside.

W WHALES in the Sea,
  God's Voice obey.

X XERXES did die,
  And so must I.

Y While youth do chear
  Death may be near.

Z ZACCHEUS he did climb the Tree
  Our Lord to see.

6. *The New-England Primer* Boston: Edward Draper's Printing-Office, 1690/1777; reprinted by David Barton, Aledo, TX: WallBuilders, 1991.

7. William J. Federer, *America's God and Country* (St. Louis: Amerisearch, 2000), 161.

8. Quoted in Lynn Buzzard and Samuel Ericsson, *The Battle for Religious Liberty* (Elgin, IL: David C. Cook, 1982), 81.

9. Harvard University, 1636, Old South Leaflets. Benjamin Pierce, *A History of Harvard University* (Cambridge, MA: Brown, Shattuck, and Company, 1833).

10. Cotton Mather, *The Great Works of Christ in America: Magnalia Christi Americana*, 2 vols. (Edinburgh: The Banner of Truth Trust, 1702/1853/1979), 2:33.

11. Statutes of the College of William and Mary, quoted on http://personal.pitnet.net/ primarysources.

12. George Bancroft, *History of the United States of America, from the Discovery of the Continent*, 6 vols. (New York: D. Appleton and Company, 1859/1890), 1:361.

13. Yale, Elihu, entry in *World Book Encyclopedia* (Chicago: World Book, 1997), 21:551.

14. Timothy Dwight, in *The Annals of America*, 20 vols. (Chicago: Encyclopedia Britannica, 1968, 1977), 4:33-39.

15. Ibid.

16. Ibid.

17. Ibid.

CHAPTER 14: WHO STOLE THE TRUTH?

1. D. James Kennedy, *Truths That Transform* (Ft. Lauderdale, FL: Coral Ridge Ministries, 2004).

2. Nancy Pearcey, *Total Truth* (Wheaton, IL: Crossway Books, 2004).

3. Alan Keyes, in D. James Kennedy, *What If America Were A Christian Nation Again?* (Ft. Lauderdale, FL: Coral Ridge Ministries-TV, 2003), video.

4. Ibid.

5. Barry Lynn, quoted in ibid.

6. Alan Keyes, quoted in ibid.

7. Pat Buchanan, quoted in D. James Kennedy, *The First Amendment on Trial* (Ft. Lauderdale, FL: Coral Ridge Ministries, 2004).

8. Michael Farris, quoted in Kennedy, *What If America Were A Christian Nation Again?*

9. Hugo Quinonez, quoted in ibid.

10. Neil Postman and Charles Weingartner, *Education as a Subversive Activity* (New York: Dell, 1969); www.wordiq.com/definition/Inquiry_education.

11. Robert Audi, gen. ed., *The Cambridge Dictionary of Philosophy* (Cambridge, England: Cambridge University Press, 1995), 446.

12. Ibid.

13. Sir James Jeans, *The Mysterious Universe* (New York: Macmillan, 1930, 136.

14. Reginald Heber, "Holy, Holy, Holy! Lord God Almighty," 1826, Donald P. Hustad, ed., *Hymns for the Living Church* (Carol Stream, IL: Hope Publishing Company, 1974), #1.

CHAPTER 15: THE HUMANISTS AND EDUCATION

1. John Eidsmoe, *Columbus and Cortez: Conquerors for Christ* (Green Forest, AR: New Leaf Press, 1992), 70. Note that in later centuries the Janissaries included Muslim warriors and were an elite military power to be reckoned with.

2. *The Works of Orestes Brownson*, 1828, quoted in Dennis L. Cuddy, "A Chronicle of Education with Quotable Quotes," *The Florida Forum*, May 1993, 2.

3. Paul Blanshard, *The Humanist*, March-April 1976, quoted in D. L. Cuddy, "How American Education Was Misdirected," *Lincoln Review*, Summer 1985, Vol. 6, No. 1, 47.

4. *McGuffey's Reader*, 1854, quoted in Tal Brooke, "The Battle for America," *Movieguide*, January 28, 1992, 2.

5. "Washington's Farewell Address," reproduced in *Compton's Pictured Encyclopedia and FactIndex*, Vol. 15 (Chicago: F.E. Compton, 1965), 26.

6. Ibid.
7. Thomas Sowell, *Inside American Education: The Decline, the Deception, the Dogmas* (New York: The Free Press, a division of Macmillan, 1993), 3.
8. Ann Landers, "1911 School Test Keeps Ann Humble," *Miami Herald,* April 30, 1987.
9. Cuddy, "A Chronology of Education with Quotable Quotes," 1908, 4-5.
10. See Gary Habermas, *Ancient Evidence for the Life of Jesus: Historical Records of His Death and Resurrection* (Nashville: Thomas Nelson, 1984) or Josh McDowell, *Evidence That Demands a Verdict* (Nashville: Thomas Nelson, 1999).
11. Martin Luther, quoted in *The Rebirth of America* (Philadelphia: Arthur S. DeMoss Foundation, 1986), 127.
12. Ibid.

CHAPTER 16: VIOLENCE IN THE SCHOOLYARD

1. Wayne Steger, in D. James Kennedy, *Violence in the Schoolyard* (Ft. Lauderdale, FL: Coral Ridge Ministries, 1999), video.
2. George Grant, in ibid., video.
3. Linda Graham, quoted in ibid.
4. www.schoolsecurity.org/trends/school_violence03-04.html.
5. Wayne Steger, in Kennedy, *Violence in the Schoolyard*, viedo.
6. Misty Bernall, in ibid., video.
7. Ibid., video.
8. Steger, in ibid.
9. Joe Lieberman, in ibid.
10. George Gallup, Jr., in ibid.
11. In "The Bible in Schools," Rush wrote that in light of the Bible's diminishing role as a textbook, "I lament that we waste so much time and money in punishing crimes, and take so little pains to prevent them" by teaching the Bible. Benjamin Rush, *The Bible in Schools* (American Tract Society, c. 1830, 1994).
12. William J. Murray, in Kennedy, *Violence in the Schoolyard*, video.
13. David Barton, *To Pray or Not to Pray: A Statistical Look at What Happened When Religious Principles Were Separated from Public Affairs* (Aledo, TX: WallBuilders, 1988).
14. Ibid., 120.
15. George Washington wrote: "Let it simply be asked—Where is the security for property, for reputation, for life, if the sense of religious obligation desert the oaths, which are the instruments of investigation in courts of justice? And let us with caution indulge the supposition that morality can be maintained without religion." George Washington, "Farewell Address," 1796, *Annals of America* (Chicago: Encyclopedia Britannica, 1976), 3:612.
16. David Barton, in Kennedy, *Violence in the Schoolyard*, video.
17. Gwen Hadley, in ibid.
18. William Brennan, for the majority, *Stone v. Graham,* U.S. Supreme Court, 1980.
19. Grant, in Kennedy, *Violence in the Schoolyard*, video.
20. Steger, in ibid.
21. www.nationalreview.com/thecorner/04_04_18_corner-archive.asp.
22. Gallup in Kennedy, *Violence in the Schoolyard*, video.
23. Ibid.
24. Darryl Scott, in ibid.
25. Ibid.
26. Steger, in ibid.

CHAPTER 17: THE BIBLE AND THE SOUL

1. Karl Menninger, *What Ever Became of Sin?* (New York: Hawthorn Books, 1973), 14.
2. Ibid.
3. Ibid.

4. Meg Greenfield, condensed from *Newsweek*, July 28, 1986, "Why Nothing Is 'Wrong' Anymore," *Readers Digest*, November 1986, 224.
5. Ibid.
6. Chuck Colson, "The Danger of Being Normal," *Signs of the Times*, January 1988.
7. William Saroyan, quoted in Charles W. Colson, *Loving God* (Grand Rapids, MI: Zondervan, 1983), 96-97.
8. George Owen, quoted in Frank S. Mead, *The Encyclopedia of Religious Quotations* (Old Tappan, NJ: Fleming H. Revell, 1965), 308.

CHAPTER 18: THE OLD LAMPLIGHTER

1. Harry Lauder, quoted in G. B. F. Hallock, *Five Thousand Best Modern Illustrations* (New York: George H. Doran Company, 1927), 256.
2. http://home.mn.rr.com/efchrist/March%2031%20Notes.htm.
3. John Wesley, quoted in Walter B. Knight, *Knight's Illustrations for Today* (Chicago: Moody Press, 1970), 274.
4. Charles C. Luther, 1877, "Must I Go, and Empty-handed?" ed. Donald P. Hustad, *Hymns for the Living Church* (Carol Stream, IL: Hope Publishing Company, 1974), #478.

CHAPTER 19: WILL THE CHURCH FORGET?

1. Donald E. Wildmon, "300,000 Silent Pulpits," *Citizen's Bar Association Bulletin*, Vol. 3, No. 12.
2. *Liberty* magazine, September/October 1984.
3. Extensive examples of the church making major reforms in history can be found in D. James Kennedy and Jerry Newcombe, *What If Jesus Had Never Been Born?* (Nashville: Thomas Nelson, 1994).
4. Ibid., 84.
5. Jonas Clark, quoted in Franklin P. Cole, *They Preached Liberty* (Ft. Lauderdale, FL: Coral Ridge Ministries, c. 1985), 112 (emphasis his).
6. "NAF Study Reveals Shakespeare in Decline," *Inside Academia* (Washington, D.C.: National Alumni Forum), Fall 1996, Vol. II, No. 1, 1.
7. Jonathan Yardley, "For English Departments, a Major Change," *Washington Post*, December 30, 1996, D2.
8. Robert H. Bork, *Slouching Toward Gomorrah* (New York: Regan Books, HarperCollins, 1996), 54.
9. William Butler Yeats, "The Second Coming," quoted in ibid., vii.
10. Ron Reno, "Guess Who Stopped the Gambling Juggernaut?" *Citizen*, 1999, 2. See www.family.org/cforum/citizenmag/features/a0008685.cfm.
11. "Alabama Rejects Governor's Plan for a Lottery," Associated Press, October 13, 1999.
12. Reno, "Guess Who Stopped the Gambling Juggernaut?," 1.
13. Tom Grey remark on "Easy Money," Frontline; http://www.pbs.org/wgbh/pages/frontline/shows/gamble/interviews/grey.html.
14. Donald E. Wildmon, "That's What Christians Do Now," AFA, December 11, 2000; http://www.afa.net/church/twcdn.asp.

CHAPTER 20: THE FIGHT FOR GOD'S WORD

1. Here are some details about the Jesus Seminar. The critical point to understand about them is that there was no *new* evidence in the Scripture that drove them to their conclusions; it was rather their own liberal approach that led them even to undertake the project in the first place. The Jesus Seminar is best understood as worn-out, liberal theologians who have turned to a publicist instead of the truth—the Jesus of Scripture. The late Dr. James Montgomery Boice of Tenth Presbyterian Church in Philadelphia pointed out that the Jesus Seminar is "really an example of liberal ministers and professors coming out of the closet. All they're really doing is in *public* what they do in a more private way in the classroom and in their own studies." Dr. Boice points out the obvious: "Imagine a group of scholars, now, two thousand years from the time that Jesus lived and whose words were written down

by eyewitnesses, a group of scholars *two thousand years later* voting in a meeting on what Jesus really said and what He didn't. That is laughable."

"It just seems like the more preposterous you can be," observes Knox Seminary professor and best-selling author R. C. Sproul, "the more radical you can be, the easier it is to get a degree or to get a hearing in certain academic circles."

Liberal and *unbelieving* are synonymous when it comes to theology. So the Jesus Seminar is essentially unbelieving scholars sharing their unbelief. When they ask a question like, "Did Jesus make this statement or not?" and then vote on that anonymously, as the Jesus Seminar did, what they're voting on is simply their own prejudices. There is nothing in the historic record, nothing in the biblical manuscripts, that supports what they say. And while manuscripts may differ in places when it comes to spelling or words, they are in complete agreement in *every* point of theology.

So if there are any things in question, they are all listed in the critical apparatus of the Greek New Testament. But the people of the Jesus Seminar weren't dealing with the *manuscript* evidence; they were dealing with, frankly, their own feelings, and with extra-biblical writings (primarily, the second-century document, the Gospel of Thomas—which the early church decidedly rejected as Gnostic heresy).

Material in the Gospels where manuscripts differ in spelling or in words deals with maybe 1 or 2 percent of the text; the New Testament documents are very reliable. Instead, what the Jesus Seminar has done is to get rid of 82 percent of the text. Textually, they stand on quicksand.

An important book rebuts the Jesus Seminar from an evangelical perspective: *Jesus Under Fire: Modern Scholarship Reinvents the Historical Jesus*, eds. Michael J. Wilkins and J. P. Moreland (Grand Rapids, MI: Zondervan, 1996). Among those who have written essays for this book is Dr. Gary Habermas, author and coauthor of numerous books on the historicity of Jesus Christ. In the chapter entitled "Where Do We Start Studying Jesus?," pp. 43-44, Denver Seminary professor Craig Blomberg has this to say about the group:

> The Jesus Seminar and its friends do not reflect any consensus of scholars except for those on the "radical fringe" of the field. Its methodology is seriously flawed and its conclusions unnecessarily skeptical. . . . The conservative nature of oral tradition in ancient Judaism, particularly among disciples who revered their rabbis' words, makes it highly likely that Jesus' teaching would have been carefully preserved, even given a certain flexibility in the specific wording with which it was reported . . . there is a huge volume of scholarship to support the picture of Christ that Matthew, Mark, Luke, and John portray.

2. C. S. Lewis, *Mere Christianity* (New York: Collier Books, Macmillan, 1952, 1984), 56.

3. Norman L. Geisler and William E. Nix, *A General Introduction to the Bible* (Chicago: Moody Press, 1986), 191.

4. B. B. Warfield, *The Inspiration and Authority of the Bible* (Philadelphia: Presbyterian and Reformed, 1964), 160.

5. Edward J. Young, *Thy Word Is Truth* (Grand Rapids, MI: Eerdmans, 1957), 27.

6. Remarks in a class by William Childs Robinson, Columbia Theological Seminary, Decatur, Georgia.

7. For more details on this, see D. James Kennedy and Jerry Newcombe, *Christ's Passion: The Power and the Promise* (Ft. Lauderdale: Coral Ridge Ministries, 2004), chapter 2.

8. Transcript of an interview with Jim Thomas on location in New Orleans (Ft. Lauderdale: Coral Ridge Ministries-TV, 2000).

9. Flavius Josephus, quoted in W. Graham Scroggie, *Is the Bible the Word of God?* (Chicago: Moody Press, 1922), 13.

10. James C. Hefley, *What's So Great About the Bible?* (Elgin, IL: David C. Cook, 1969), 53.

11. Thomas Coleridge, quoted in Scroggie, *Is the Bible the Word of God?*, 101.

12. Heinrich Heine, quoted in ibid., 100-101.

13. Earle Albert Rowell, *Prophecy Speaks: Dissolving Doubts* (Washington, D.C.: Review and Herald Publishing Association, 1933), 94-95.

CHAPTER 21: A CHRISTIAN VIEW OF THE FAMILY

1. www.truthorfiction.com/rumors/d/divorce.htm.

CHAPTER 22: CHRISTIAN MARRIAGE

1. The Mayflower Compact, *The Annals of America*, Vol. 1 (Chicago: Encyclopedia Britannica, 1976), 64.
2. Jay E. Adams, *Christian Living in the Home* (Grand Rapids, MI: Baker, 1972), Chapter 3, 25-41.

CHAPTER 23: CHRISTIAN PARENTING

1. Virtually all of these men and women were godly, but tragically, the last person listed, the Vice President, lived a life in rebellion to the Christian beliefs to which he was exposed as a child. Aaron Burr was a terrible man of low character and even killed Alexander Hamilton in a duel. Later Burr would be rightfully accused of treason. Suffice it to say that Burr's problem was that he decidedly went against the Christianity of his famous grandfather. Thankfully, Burr was the exception, not the rule in that family.
2. Barbara Bush, quoted in James Dobson and Gary Bauer, *Children at Risk* (Dallas: Word, 1990), 157.
3. Thomas A. Edison, quoted in Paul Lee Tan, *Encyclopedia of 7700 Illustrations* (Rockville, MD: Assurance Publishers, 1984), 845.
4. Charles Spurgeon, quoted in Walter B. Knight, *Knight's Master Book of New Illustrations* (Grand Rapids, MI: Eerdmans, 1956), 423.
5. Walter B. Knight, *Knight's Master Book of New Illustrations* (Grand Rapids, MI: Eerdmans, 1956), 417.
6. Tan, *Encyclopedia of 7700 Illustrations,* 841.
7. Mary Pride, *The Way Home* (Wheaton, IL: Crossway Books, 1985), 3.
8. David Gelernter, "Why Mothers Should Stay Home," *Commentary*, Vol. 101, No. 2, February 1996.
9. "Broken Families: Hearings Before the Subcommittee on Family and Human Services of the Committee on Labor and Human Resources, United States Senate," Ninety-eighth Congress, First Session, Part 2 (Washington, D.C.: U.S. Government Printing Office, 1984), 139-140.
10. Michael Carmody, "Will You, Daddy?" www.cathye.com/dadwillyoudaddy.htm.

CHAPTER 24: THE SINGLE LIFE: HEAVEN OR HELL?

1. Dan Benson, "Loneliness: The Silent Epidemic," *Potential,* October 1986.   .
2. Paul Tournier, *Escape from Loneliness*, trans. John S. Gilmour (Philadelphia: Westminster Press, 1962), 5, 18, 28.
3. Leonard Zunin, cited in Paul Lee Tan, *Encyclopedia of 7700 Illustrations* (Rockville, MD: Assurance Publishers, 1984), 754.

CONCLUSION: WHERE THERE IS NO VISION

1. Transcript from interview with David Moore (Ft. Lauderdale: Coral Ridge Ministries-TV, March 1998), 17-18.
2. www.beingvirtuouswomen.com/grandmas_attic/oct2002.htm.

INDEX